Passschendaele

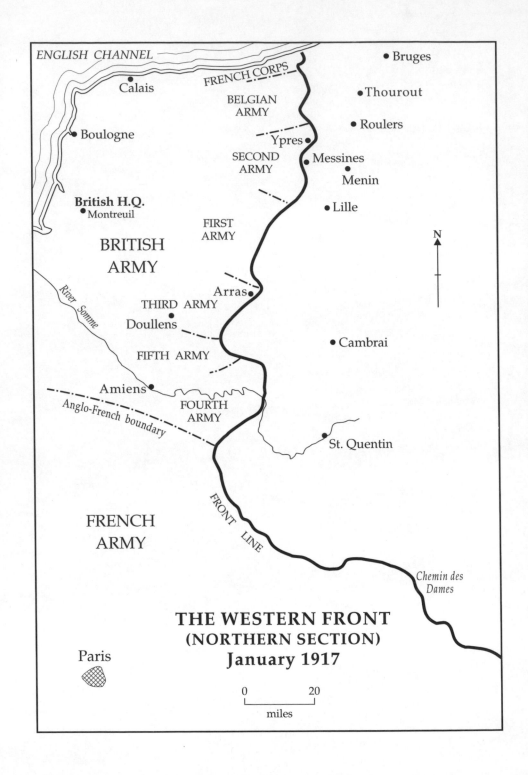

ENGLISH CHANNEL

Bruges

Calais

FRENCH CORPS

Thourout

BELGIAN
ARMY

Roulers

Boulogne

Ypres

Messines

SECOND
ARMY

Menin

British H.Q.
Montreuil

Lille

N

BRITISH
ARMY

FIRST
ARMY

River Somme

Arras

THIRD ARMY

Doullens

Cambrai

FIFTH ARMY

Amiens

Anglo-French boundary

FOURTH
ARMY

St. Quentin

FRONT LINE

FRENCH
ARMY

Chemin des
Dames

**THE WESTERN FRONT
(NORTHERN SECTION)
January 1917**

Paris

0   20

miles

Passchendaele

The Untold Story

Robin Prior and Trevor Wilson

Yale University Press
New Haven and London

Set in Sabon by Best-set Typesetter Ltd, Hong Kong
Printed and bound in Great Britain by Biddles Ltd, Guildford and Kings Lynn

Library of Congress Cataloging-in-Publication Data

Prior, Robin.
    Passchendaele: the untold story / Robin Prior and Trevor Wilson.
    Includes bibliographical references and index.
    ISBN 0–300–06692–9 (alk. paper)
    1. Ypres, 3rd Battle of, Ieper, Belgium, 1917.   I. Wilson, Trevor.
II. Title.
D542. Y72P75   1996
940.4′31–dc20   96–754
                                                                  CIP

A catalogue record for this book is available from the British Library

For Heather
and for Ray and Janet
RP

For Nirej
and for Travis
and for Craig
and for young Lucy
Best of friends
TW

Contents

Illustrations

Plumer's Successes

The Final Battles

Maps

Acknowledgements

The authors wish to thank their colleagues in the History Departments at the Australian Defence Force Academy and the University of Adelaide for support and encouragement during the preparation of this book. They also wish to acknowledge the assistance of the libraries of those institutions, the Bridges library and the Barr Smith library. For preparation of the maps included here, they owe a profound debt to Keith Mitchell of the Cartography Department, Research School, Australian National University. For preparation of the manuscript, they are grateful to the following: Christine Kendrick, Julie McMahon, Marion Pearce, and Elsa Sellick. For meticulous research in a variety of archives, they wish to acknowledge great assistance from Irene Cassidy in England and from Elizabeth Greenhalgh and Helen Boxall in Australia. The research staff at the following institutions have enabled the authors to make use of their rich and varied archives: the Imperial War Museum, London, Australian War Memorial, the Public Record Office, the Liddell Hart Centre at King's College, London, and the Royal Artillery Institution Library, Woolwich. And for kind permission to reproduce the illustrations, the authors would like to thank the Imperial War Museum, London. Finally, the authors are greatly in the debt of Robert Baldock of Yale University Press for his enthusiasm regarding this project, and to the staff of the London branch of Yale University Press for so expeditiously converting the manuscript into a book.

Introduction

There is a dearth of comprehensive accounts of the British army's struggle in Flanders in the second half of 1917. This seems strange. No Great War campaign excites stronger emotions. And no word better encapsulates the horror and apparent futility of Western Front combat than 'Passchendaele'. Yet the literature on this episode is astonishingly thin.

If we ignore some recent pot-boilers on Passchendaele (like the work which referred, early on, to Helmuth von Moltke, the Prussian military master, as 'Schlieffen's predecessors . . . Helmuth and Moltke', and from there went steadily downhill), we must go back to 1958 for an effective account of the Third Ypres campaign. This was Leon Wolff's *In Flanders Field,* a convincing tale at the level of both commanders and combatants (if decidedly slanted against the former and for the latter). But it appeared before the release of the great archive of official documents and individual records.

As a whole, writings about Third Ypres fall into two categories. There are many accounts by participants, graphically relating the experiences of individual fighting men; and a number of these have been skilfully woven together in Lyn Macdonald's 1978 book, *They Called it Passchendaele.* Participant accounts are revealing, but by their nature they are partial. They are little concerned with the shape and course of battles, and scarcely appreciate what commanders were endeavouring to accomplish and sometimes did accomplish.

The other sort of literature is concerned with command, at the military and political level. From an early stage, these writings proved very contentious. The *War Memoirs* of the Prime Minister of the time, David Lloyd George, damned the British commander-in-chief, Sir Douglas Haig, up hill and down dale. This view was endorsed in the writings of the military commentator Sir Basil Liddell Hart (who, in addition to his own books, advised Lloyd George when the latter was writing his memoirs). By way of riposte, ʳthe high command was vigorously defended in Sir James Edmonds's volume of the Official History dealing with the Third Ypres campaign (*Military Operations: France and Belgium 1917*, vol. 2). But this appeared as late as 1948, by which time Edmonds (who had sometimes managed a measure of detachment towards Haig) had become almost as much a partisan as, from an opposite point of view, were Haig's critics.

The controversy has continued, with no abatement in the tones of condemnation and exculpation. John Terraine's *Haig: the Educated Soldier* (1963) was an important work in arguing a case for the commander-in-chief, and so in forcing debate on a matter which had long gone unargued. But, on the issue of Third Ypres, his attempt to exonerate Haig once again involved a considerable level of special pleading. A yet more immoderate work from the opposite position appeared as recently as 1992, in the form of Denis Winter's *Haig's Command*. In an earlier book, *Death's Men* (1978), Winter had shown himself a skilled and sympathetic historian of the common soldier. But his ill-documented, conspiracy-ridden tirade against Haig was of an altogether lesser order. Indeed, it appeared only to reveal that, at least as concerned military command, Great War studies have yet to escape their protracted adolescence.

A curiosity in the literature of Third Ypres is a further work of John Terraine, *The Road to Passchendaele: a Study in Inevitability* (1977). This claims to be an accumulation of original documents from which readers are at liberty to draw their own conclusions about responsibility for, and the merits of, the campaign. But even the subtitle of the book is of doubtful objectivity. And among the supposed original documents quoted at length is to be found the Official History, which (as has been noted) is a tendentious work not at all contemporary with the events it is describing.

Outside the English language, only one contribution of note has been made to the debate over Third Ypres. This comes from Germany, in the form of the memoirs of General Ludendorff. Concerning the Passchendaele offensive, Ludendorff is at pains to stress the terrible losses which the British attacks imposed on his army, and the severe draining of German morale that resulted. Germany's forces on the Western Front, he concludes, faced with dread the prospect of a renewal of Haig's assaults in the following year, and longed themselves to go on the offensive.

These statements have brought much comfort to the defenders of the British high command. They appear to be compelling evidence that Third Ypres had served Britain well. But this view cannot be accepted at face value. Certainly, as a corrective to the facile belief that troops standing on the defensive in the First World War had a relatively easy time of it, Ludendorff's statements merit attention. But his memoirs are by no means a disinterested or impartial document. The German commander had his own, highly personal, reasons for praising Haig's accomplishments at Third Ypres. He wished to demonstrate that, in late 1917 and early 1918 (if not before, when he had apparently taken a different view), great offensives were the appropriate form of action on the Western Front, and hence that he was entirely justified in flinging his own forces against the British line in the west in March 1918 – at the very moment when the winter which had at last forced Haig to call a halt was giving way to spring.

Ludendorff's own resort to the offensive, it needs to be noted, was every bit as open to question as was Haig's. Hence the controversy over the merits and demerits of the Third Ypres operation is not at all settled by Ludendorff's subsequent endorsement of Haig's strategy.

In *Passchendaele: the Untold Story* we seek to provide as comprehensive an account as, thanks to the availability of documents and the perspective allowed by the passage of time, has now become possible. The book is based on a great archive of material not previously consulted, or at least not exploited for a work on this subject. This includes documents held at the Public Record Office, the Imperial War Museum, the Liddell Hart Archive at King's College, London, the National Army Museum, and the Australian War Memorial (whose documentation is by no means confined to the Anzac contribution). So it employs the minutes of the War Cabinet and other political bodies, the personal diaries of high-ranking commanders such as Sir Douglas Haig and Sir Henry Rawlinson, the war diaries of the principal army groups and a great many smaller units, accounts by serving soldiers, and German-language records of key enemy units as well as the German and French official histories.

The book embraces all aspects of the story. It examines the political dimension at a level which has hitherto been absent from accounts of Third Ypres. It deals with the shifting ambitions and stratagems of the high command. It examines the logistics of war and the exercise of command at intermediate levels: what the British army, in the existing state of military weaponry and technology and know-how, and employing such supplies of men and guns as were then available, could hope to achieve and attempted to achieve. And it covers the experience of the men on the ground, in the context of what was being accomplished – whether they realized it or not – and what was never going to be accomplished.

Part I
Setting the Scene

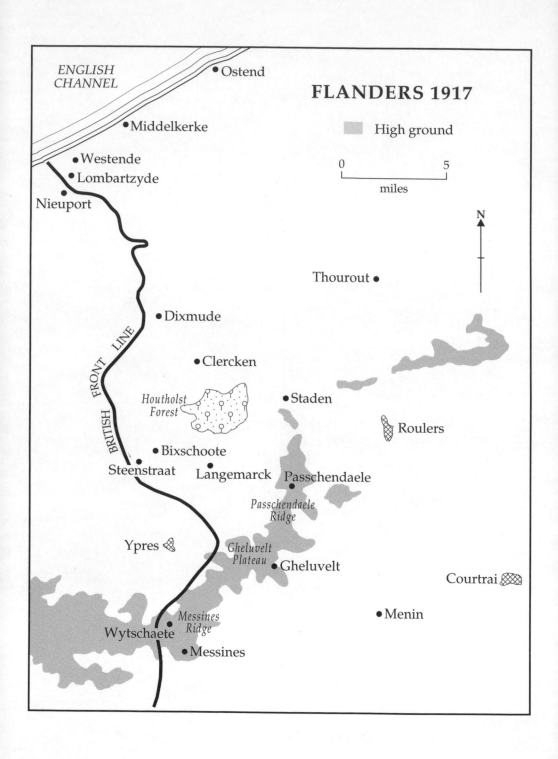

ENGLISH
CHANNEL

• Ostend

FLANDERS 1917

• Middelkerke

High ground

• Westende
• Lombartzyde

0   5

Nieuport •

miles

N

FRONT LINE

Thourout •

• Dixmude

BRITISH

• Clercken

Houtholst
Forest

• Staden

Roulers

• Bixschoote

Steenstraat •

• Langemarck

• Passchendaele

*Passchendaele
Ridge*

Ypres ⬧

*Gheluvelt
Plateau*

• Gheluvelt

Courtrai ⬧

• Menin

*Messines
Ridge*

Wytschaete •

• Messines

1

The Conundrum

I

By the time the Flanders campaign opened on 31 July 1917, battle had been raging in France and Belgium for all of three years. During that time, painful truths had emerged. They concerned the difficulties confronting any attempts to launch a successful offensive – difficulties springing from the particular conjunction of weaponry which dominated the battlefield. Some of these truths Sir Douglas Haig, Britain's commander-in-chief on the Western Front, took trouble to notice. Others he studiously ignored.

II

The manner of delivering a land offensive had changed markedly since the early weeks of the war. The German invasion of Belgium and France in August 1914 had been war in the established manner: that is, in the style the Prussians had employed with devastating success in the period 1864–71. Its premise was the superiority which the force delivering an offensive, if marshalled and directed with appropriate skill, could exert over defending armies. Huge numbers of soldiers were mobilized, packed into railway carriages, and dispatched to the front. At the railhead they detrained and marched into battle. Ahead of them, scouting for the enemy, rode the cavalry.

The successful sweep of the German army through Belgium and northern France in the opening weeks of August 1914 appeared to validate this method of waging war. Certainly, the offensives delivered simultaneously by the French on the southern part of the Western Front came seriously to grief. But this seemed only to show that, as in 1870, one side knew how to execute offensives and the other did not.

On its way from Belgium to Paris in August 1914, the German army did encounter some devoted resistance. At Mons and Guise, stubborn British and French infantry, employing rifles with great skill and such artillery as they could muster, temporarily halted the German advance. But these were delaying actions only. They made it possible for the defenders to sustain an ordered retreat. They did not call in doubt the efficacy of the offensive.

Yet, as all the world suddenly learned, even the mighty German army was not unstoppable. At the Marne, within sight of Paris, its onward rush was abruptly halted and put into reverse. But what happened at the Marne did not appear to show that defence was now getting the upper hand. While the Germans had been bearing down on the French capital, the French command had assembled a whole new army on the outskirts of Paris. The Germans, still fully engaged by the Allied forces they had driven from Belgium, failed to notice this. Their first intimation came when they were struck viciously in the flank by the new French aggregation lying in wait for them. Outmanoeuvred, the German right wing was driven into hasty retreat. The French and British assumed the advance.

The dominance of the offensive, therefore, remained – for the moment – unshaken. But even as highly placed French and British officers were debating about how many (or how few) weeks it would take them to drive the enemy back over the Franco-German border, a different perception of war emerged. The retreating Germans fell back across the river Aisne and took up position on the high ground above. There they dug trenches, sited machine-guns, erected barbed wire, and set in place many artillery pieces. Against these basic defences of early twentieth-century warfare, the French and British forces flung themselves in vain. Moreover the Germans brought down such savage fire on the areas where the Allies were assembling for their attacks that the British and French were also compelled to dig protective trenches. A local stalemate ensued.

Only in retrospect did the significance of these events reveal themselves. The immediate response of each adversary was to regard the Aisne as a temporary halt, and to seek a resumption of the war of movement and advance elsewhere. This could not occur to the south of the Aisne. There deadlock had already taken hold. The great French fortresses lining the Franco-German border had halted the invading Germans but had provided no opportunity for a French counter-advance. However, to the north of the Aisne, stretching all the way to the North Sea, lay open territory with no trench defences. First one side and then the other sought to exploit this situation by moving northwards so as to strike at the exposed flank of the other. But all that resulted was a repetition of events on the Aisne. The side about to be outflanked also moved north, and set about digging trenches. These improvised defences proved sufficient to repel the improvised assaults being thrown against them. So another local stalemate developed, followed by a further move north, a further attempt to turn the flank, and a further local stalemate.

By late 1914 this attempt to exercise a war of movement had carried both sides to the Belgian coast, at Nieuport, where the prospect of getting around the side of the enemy vanished for both combatants. Along the whole length of the Western Front, from the Belgian coast to the Swiss Alps, the forces of Germany confronted the forces of France and Britain. Everywhere along this front, the two sides dug trenches and deepened them and then dug a second set behind the first and put up more protective barbed wire and sited guns and brought in ever larger quantities of artillery.

Yet none of this meant that the combatants were now opting for quiescence, or were intending to seek victory on an altogether different battlefield. Each remained intent on victory, and could not envisage achieving it except by launching attacks. And each acknowledged that this meant attacking in France and Belgium, because there alone could the contending powers of Western Europe bring their forces to bear against each other. So while the adversaries were constructing trenches so as to prevent their own front from being pierced, they were also devising operations intended to breach the enemy's front at selected points. Their intent was to assemble, at what seemed a vulnerable or vital point, such a volume of offensive weaponry and fresh troops as would overwhelm the still-rudimentary trench defences facing them. Thereby they would break out into open country and so restore the war of movement.

In October 1914 the German commander, Falkenhayn, accumulated a huge quantity of heavy guns and shells and eager German youths to fling against the northern part of the Anglo-French line. His object was to overwhelm the British trenches in that tiny part of Belgium not yet in German hands, and thereupon to sweep forward to capture the port of Calais. What he actually accomplished was the First Battle of Ypres, October–November 1914.

III

In some respects, the First Battle of Ypres in 1914 and the Third Battle of Ypres in 1917 had a deal in common. They involved a struggle between mainly British and German forces with the French as minor contributors. And they constituted offensives directed towards discernible geographical objectives, namely ports on the Channel coast.

In other respects the one battle was the direct opposite of the other. First Ypres in 1914 was a German offensive: the last throw for that year of the great strike force which, but a few months earlier, had seemed poised to overrun all of Western Europe. British forces were seeking to do no more than hold the line. Third Ypres in 1917 was the reverse. The Germans had no plans for a major Western Front offensive. It was the British who were trying to make a great forward movement to the coast, in the face of determined German resistance.

Expectations too had altered between 1914 and 1917. When the Germans launched the First Battle of Ypres, it was still fairly easy to believe that trench defences would not prove able to withstand assault by large quantities of firepower and highly motivated troops. By 1917, such expectations had been badly dented.

What had generated doubts about the promise of offensive action was just about everything that had happened on the Western Front since the Germans launched that thrust to Calais in October 1914. With all the advantages they had possessed, in great artillery pieces and heavy shells, in numbers and freshness of troops, and in clarity of objectives, their strike to the coast had failed utterly. The British defenders had been pushed back from one rudimentary set of trenches to another, paying dearly for their stubbornness. Yet they never broke, never retreated in disorder, never allowed their line to be ruptured, and managed to exact a huge toll on the manpower of their adversaries. In the end the German command was forced to call off the offensive with none of its purposes (except the elimination of a large proportion of 'Sir John French's contemptible little army') achieved.

Thus the pattern was established for that succession of gruelling and ill-rewarded Western Front offensives which followed in 1915 and 1916: by the French, with some British aid, on the Chemin des Dames and in the northern sector in the spring and autumn of 1915; by the Germans at Verdun in the first half of 1916; and by the British, with some French assistance, on the Somme in the second half of 1916. All of these offensive operations failed in their purpose. Certainly, none proved a comfortable experience for the side standing on the defensive. Loss of life among the forces under attack was severe, and in at least one instance – Verdun – was probably marginally heavier for the defenders than for their assailants. Yet these operations were bound to be judged by whether they had demonstrably advanced the country delivering the attack towards ultimate victory. And plainly, none had achieved that purpose.

So the French, in their great offensives of 1915, had sought to scale the commanding heights of the Chemin des Dames and Vimy Ridge, and had captured neither, at excessive cost. (The British, in lesser supporting operations, fared so badly that Sir John French, commander-in-chief of the British Expeditionary Force (BEF), was removed from his post. He was replaced by Sir Douglas Haig.) The Germans in early 1916 had chosen both to annihilate the French army and to gobble up the succession of fortresses guarding the major administrative centre of Verdun. By the end of the day – a long day indeed – they had certainly killed a great many Frenchmen. But they had surrendered the lives of an almost equal number of their own troops, and they had managed to retain not a single fortress or yard of ground. The British in mid-1916 set out to rupture the German line on a wide front adjoining the river Somme and then to sweep forward – with the cavalry assuming the lead – into open country. All they managed to do, in over four months of campaigning and at heavier cost to themselves than to their adversaries, was to push back the German front a few miles. Their cavalry, except in a handful of disastrous instances, remained unemployed.

When each of these endeavours was eventually called off, the commanders who initiated them cried success. But the successes to which they laid claim proved to be of a different order from what had been promised. They could not announce that Vimy Ridge or Verdun or (on the Somme) Bapaume had changed hands, as expected, because manifestly this was not true. So they adopted the position that they had inflicted losses of life on their adversaries so heavy as to weaken fundamentally their powers of resistance.

These claims, it may be observed in passing, have not proved of benefit to the commanders' subsequent reputations. Ever since, it has been assumed that First World War commanders (and particularly British commanders) were incapable of designing anything more imaginative than operations of mutual slaughter. That is, they were eager to trade one of their own soldiers' lives for one of their enemy's. This view is encapsulated in an eminently patriotic work from 1942, by the arch-conservative historian Sir Arthur Bryant. His *English Saga (1840–1940)* describes the philosophy which had 'taken firm hold of the British military mind' during the First World War:

> The dominating idea was that as the total population of the Allied Powers was higher than that of their foes, the process of scaling down both fighting populations, man for man, as rapidly as possible must end in the ultimate survival of the larger. The quicker the rate of mutual destruction, the military statisticians argued, the sooner the war would be over.[1]

This, it needs to be said, misrepresents not only what commanders like Haig and Joffre and Falkenhayn initially intended to achieve but what, after the event, they claimed to have achieved. (It may be in line with what they actually accomplished, but that is a different matter.) They set out to capture specific objectives of strategic significance. Having failed to do so, they claimed to have inflicted such heavy casualties on their adversaries (much in excess of what their own forces had sustained) as to have brought the war measurably nearer to conclusion. If their aims and attitudes have since been widely misrepresented, that is because of their failure in 1915 and 1916 to improve on the blighted endeavour of First Ypres, and because of what seemed their determination to persist in doing badly what, on so many earlier occasions, they had done badly already.

IV

Two matters call for elaboration. First, what were the unanticipated circumstances which put paid to mobile warfare, so that by Christmas 1914 the dread prospect of stalemate already confronted the combatants in the west? And second, how did the commanders who launched offensives in 1915 and 1916 hope to eliminate the factors making for stalemate, and why were their efforts in vain?

Fundamental to the onset and persistence of stalemate is the phenomenon of trench warfare. Trench warfare, to state the (sometimes overlooked) obvious, is about standing on the defensive. In times of relative quiescence, the troops on both sides occupying the front line took shelter from each other in trenches. In times of offensive action, by contrast, the side on the attack was obliged to move into the open, struggle across no man's land, and overwhelm the opposing trenches. On the face of it, this was not an impossible task. In many episodes of conflict over the ages, a well-marshalled assault delivered by better-equipped and numerically superior forces had proved able to overwhelm a well-placed defender.

Trench warfare, it needs to be stressed, was no recent invention. The troops who went into battle in 1914, although anticipating a war of movement, nevertheless were equipped with entrenching tools just to be on the safe side. Should mischance find them temporarily outnumbered and outgunned and subject to attack, they might provide themselves with cover by digging a hole. A succession of such holes formed a trench and constituted a coherent line of defence.

Yet in the past, these lines had not usually proved unassailable. An attacking force effectively commanded and possessing an advantage in numbers and firepower stood a good chance of overwhelming (if at cost) an opposing line of trenches. But by 1914 something about warfare had

changed. Offensive action against trench defences had become uncon-
scionably difficult.

What had changed was the weaponry now available to the trench
dweller. Developments in military technology had significantly increased
the depth of the killing-ground which an attacking force had to trans-
gress in order to close with the defenders, and had hugely increased the
volume of fire which the defenders could bring to bear upon that
intermediate area. There had been no corresponding multiplication in
the quantities of fire which the attacking force could bring down upon
the trench occupants. The whole technological equation, therefore,
had moved sharply away from those successful offensive operations
launched by the Prussians between 1864 and 1871.

Industrialization, in sum, was at last being applied to warfare. Some
foreshadowing of this had been evident in episodes of the American
Civil War, the Boer War, the Russo-Japanese and Balkan wars. But in
none of these had two advanced industrialized powers taken up arms
against each other. The First World War, and above all the confronta-
tion between Britain and Germany, constituted the first occasion when
modern technology and mass production found expression on both sides
of the battlefield. The war on the Western Front was its most stark and
intractable manifestation.

What was there about the mass-produced weaponry of 1914 and
beyond which rendered assault upon entrenched forces so costly and
(usually) so unfruitful? It is fairly plain why the occupants of trenches
could, to an extent never hitherto possible, inflict injury upon a force
attacking across open territory (no man's land). The bolt-action, maga-
zine-fed rifle, the machine-gun, breach-loaded artillery employing axial
recoil, and the elongated shell delivering shrapnel bullets and high
explosive in a selected and not random fashion, were, in their range and
volume of fire, potent devices against a force advancing over open
ground. Put bluntly, attacking troops were in greater peril for a longer
time than ever in the past. And when at last those who survived the
crossing of no man's land hoped to close with their adversaries, they
found themselves required to penetrate a formidable barrier provided by
another recent invention: barbed wire.

A defending force, below ground and not required to expose more
than a small part of itself, was in altogether happier circumstances.
Happiness, of course, was entirely relative. Trenches were uncomfortable and often, thanks to rain and semi-buried corpses and other unfor-
tunate aspects, squalid. And life in them, if safer than above ground,
was distinctly precarious. Snipers, expert with a rifle in the hunting
of prey, could pick off trench dwellers who exposed themselves even

momentarily – which men above a certain height were always in danger of doing. Machine-gunners, firing obliquely, could penetrate the security of a trench, as could shrapnel bullets and trench mortars. Attacking troops, if they could get close enough, would deal out death with hand grenades and, ultimately, the bayonet. Above all, the trench was vulnerable to well-directed high-explosive shells. At the moment an attack was about to be launched, large numbers of these would, if available, be directed against defended positions in an attempt to render trench occupants incapable of response while the attacking troops were moving forward.

But the balance of advantage plainly lay with the defenders. An attack could rarely be delivered at speed. As already indicated, the distance over which infantry must advance under fire before closing with the enemy had increased significantly. Equally crucially, the soldier on horseback proved – though commanders were reluctant to notice this – without place in this brand of warfare. The cratered terrain of no man's land denied horses the chance to travel at speed, and at its far end usually lay an impenetrable barrier of barbed wire. Even more decisively, the horse presented a conspicuous and inviting target to rifles and machine-guns and artillery, and was quite incapable of taking cover. So during the attempted crossing of no man's land it was simply swept away. The speed of an attack, therefore, was limited to the rate at which foot soldiers, under fire and proceeding over torn-up ground, could get themselves forward.

The infantry possessed few weapons to aid in this progress. The rifle was of little use to an attacking force. On the run it could not be employed with accuracy, and trench defenders offered few targets. The portable machine-gun did not exist in the opening years of the war. The hand grenade was unreliable, its explosive charge was too feeble to remove barbed wire, and – except when projected by a rifle – it only carried the distance a man could throw it. Its true role, like that of the bayonet, was in trench fighting once the crossing of no man's land had been accomplished.

If the attacking infantry were actually to succeed in getting that far, then weapons other than those available to them must play the principal part in clearing the way: diminishing the number of shells falling in no man's land to tolerable levels, suppressing or eliminating enemy riflemen and machine-gunners, uprooting barbed wire. Notwithstanding the contribution of mortars and indirect machine-gun fire, there was plainly only one significant arm for achieving this purpose – as Falkenhayn acknowledged as early as First Ypres, when he called in the mighty guns designed to demolish Belgian forts for the more modest (but as it proved less manageable) purpose of demolishing sketchy British trenches.

V

On the face of it, artillery seemed ideally equipped to assist attacking infantry in overwhelming opposing trenches. Long-range guns (heavy artillery) appeared capable of putting out of action enemy batteries shelling no man's land from well behind the front. And shorter-range guns (field artillery) could surely neutralize machine-gunners and riflemen sheltering in trenches, as well as uprooting the barbed wire which shielded them.

Yet these were not simple tasks. Barbed wire could be much knocked about and still remain an obstacle. A trench, from front on, presented a decidedly narrow target – only the width required for two men to pass each other, and constructed at zigzag so that even a well-directed shell burst would not travel a great distance. Given the capacity of earth (unlike, say, concrete) to absorb a lot of explosive without being seriously displaced, shells which fell short or overshot by even a small margin usually proved ineffective. As for enemy guns well behind the line, the means of pinpointing their whereabouts were slow to develop and usually dependent on favourable weather conditions, the problems of landing shells on such distant and relatively small objects were severe, and in the time between an enemy battery's being located and fire actually being brought to bear upon it, its position might well have been changed.

So the demolition of the guns and trenches of a force on the defensive required a high degree of accuracy on the part of the attacker's artillery. Yet the artillery piece with which the powers entered the First World War was anything but a precision weapon. Some details will make this plain.

If a gun fired a number of shells in quick succession, under identical conditions of wind and weather, not all of these shells would land in the one place. On the contrary, they would be distributed over a rectangular area of some width and breadth. For example, 100 shells fired by a 60-pounder gun might fall anywhere within an area of 39 yards long by 4.5 yards wide. Given that the targets were as narrow or discrete as trenches and machine-guns and artillery pieces, there was little chance of these being eliminated in great numbers unless the volume of shells falling in the area was truly immense. No combatant nation in 1914 or 1915 (or, as events would reveal, 1916) possessed the guns or the missiles required to devastate a substantial defended area.

Artillerymen in the opening years of the war struggled to overcome this problem: that is, to acquire the degree of precision which would enable them to knock out distinct obstacles without employing shells in unlimited (and unavailable) quantities. One method was the employment of a Forward Observation Officer (FOO). This individual occupied an elevated position (such as a church tower or a dugout on the forward slope of a hill) just behind or even in advance of his front line. From there he could observe enemy positions and the fall of shots fired by his battery from well to his rear. By telephone, he would provide the battery with his estimate of the margin by which the shell had fallen short or long or to the side of the target, and the gunners would correct the range and keep on firing until they got it right. Getting it right, it should be noticed, did not mean hitting the target with each shell fired thereafter; simply landing the shell within the gun's zone of fire and trusting that some would score a hit.

The FOO played an important (and perilous) role, but two things detracted from his usefulness. In adverse weather, which might range from rain and low cloud to fine conditions generating dust, the precise shell-burst from a particular gun might be difficult to detect. Secondly, the limit of vision of the FOO meant that he could not survey distant targets – which applied to a large proportion of the enemy's artillery.

A new instrument lay to hand to help overcome at least the last of these difficulties. The balloon, and even more the aeroplane, could observe targets well behind the enemy front. An aerial observer equipped with a radio could spot the fall of shell and direct guns on to distant targets. If equipped with a camera, he could photograph enemy positions and the location of enemy guns well behind the front. This visual information could then be transferred to maps, so that artillery-men could take a bearing from their own position to enemy guns and undertake 'shooting from the map'.

These methods came into play from early in 1915, but their effectiveness was limited by several factors. The lightness and fragility of the First World War aircraft meant that they could not operate in bad weather. Moreover, in the early phases of the war the number of aircraft – not to say pilots – available was severely limited, and the number capable of carrying not just a pilot but an observer and heavy photographic equipment was very small indeed. Then, as flyers grew in number and aeroplanes became capable of lifting heavier loads (so increasing their effectiveness as artillery observers), the war witnessed the emergence of the fighter aircraft. Equipped with a forward-firing machine-gun, the fighting plane was intended for just one purpose: to drive the observer craft of the opposing power out of the sky.

The limitations on the usefulness of aerial photography did not cease with the difficulties of actually securing the photographs. The enemy might relocate his guns after the photographic mission had been completed. And as for the photographs themselves, when transposed to maps they could produce errors of up to 150 yards in the location of a gun. Such errors might be the result of the angle of the camera *vis-à-vis* the object being photographed, or even the fact that a curved surface (the earth) was being reproduced on a flat surface (a photograph).

Factors other than identification of the whereabouts of the target might tell against the accuracy of artillery fire. Changes in wind speed and atmospheric conditions could drastically alter the trajectory of a shell, so that ranging activities by the guns on one day might have no application when an attack was being delivered on the next. A following wind would cause a shell to travel further than it would on a day when no wind, or an adverse wind, was blowing. Hot weather (by thinning the atmosphere) would cause shells to travel further than in cooler weather. A further difficulty was the slight variations likely to be found among different batches of shells ostensibly of the same dimension. Small differences in weight or length would result in significant variations in flight.

The saga of difficulties confronting artillerymen did not cease there. The steady use of a gun during a bombardment could alter the trajectory of the successive shells it was firing, and not always in the one direction. Constant wear of the guns might cause the shells to wobble as they left the barrel and so fall short. But wear could have a contrary effect: the barrel might overheat and turn upwards, thereby increasing the distance travelled by the shell.

It took the British army some time to recognize these problems, let alone find solutions to them. By 1915 atmospheric conditions were known to affect accuracy, but the need for continual adjustment had yet to take hold among the practitioners of gunnery. (The learning process was hampered by the antipathy shown to all things scientific by many senior artillery officers.) As for the problems engendered by shell variations, wear on guns, and the limitations on aerial photography, these were slow in securing recognition.

These factors, certainly until well into 1916, told heavily against the prospect of a successful offensive on a large scale. The artillery simply could not hit in sufficient numbers those targets it could not directly observe. So when an attack went in, the enemy's guns would have escaped serious damage and could deal harshly with assaulting infantry. And even those targets subject to direct observation, such as trenches and machine-gun posts, rarely suffered such extensive damage as to rendered them ineffective.

VI

What follows from the foregoing survey of weaponry is clear enough. Those seeking to conduct this war faced a conundrum. The war could only be won by offensive action, yet the advantage resting with the defenders was so great as to render offensives unproductive. Somehow the balance of advantage had to be overturned, yet the means of doing this were not readily to hand.

The conundrum gave operations on the Western Front in 1915 and 1916 a decidedly melancholy quality.

2

The Search for a Solution, 1915–1916

I

Twice during 1915 and 1916, attempts were made to resolve the conundrum of the Western Front by the introduction of entirely new weapons of offence. One weapon was poison gas. The other was the armoured fighting vehicle, or tank. These would in due course prove useful supplements to existing weaponry. They would not supply the key that unlocked the door of stalemate.

Poison gas was first employed, at least in a manner that attracted notice, by the Germans at the Second Battle of Ypres in April 1915. Their reward – at the cost of much opprobrium – was a local success but nothing more. That was in part because the German command was only testing a new weapon under favourable conditions, not attempting a major advance. But it was also because poison gas did not have the potential to facilitate a large success. There was an obvious problem about employing gas as a strike weapon. How was it to be delivered? Ultimately the answer would be found in the gas shell, which enabled the attacker to place the gas approximately where he wanted it. But in 1915 each contestant was painfully short of shell cases even for shrapnel and high explosive, and had none to spare for experiments with poison gas. That left one alternative, of questionable efficacy. The gas must be brought to the attacker's front line in cylinders, and released into no man's land when a convenient wind – that is, a wind blowing towards the opposing trenches at not too great a velocity – presented itself.

At Second Ypres, the German command had to wait several days for these conditions. It was not a comfortable interlude. There was no question of bringing up reserves to exploit any success which might attend the use of gas, lest their appearance be detected on the other side and result in a hostile bombardment which (unintentionally) smashed up the cylinders. That is, even had the German command wished to convert Second Ypres into a major operation, there were powerful reasons for abstaining.

The only occasion during the war when gas was employed as a major strike weapon was during the British attack at Loos in September 1915. This operation was delivered in support of a much larger French offensive. The BEF plainly lacked the quantities of shell required for their part in this undertaking, and hoped the employment of poison gas would make good the deficiency. This was a desperate measure. As the attack was to go in on a particular day stipulated by the French, there could be no question of delaying the operation – as had the Germans in April – until the wind was favourable. In the event, the morning of the attack found the wind just appropriate on some parts of the British front and quite inappropriate on others. The attack went ahead anyway. The gas was probably more effective as a smokescreen, concealing British movements in no man's land, than as a means of incapacitating the enemy. Certainly British gas casualties, owing to the perversity of the wind, exceeded those of the Germans.

Problems of delivery were not the only shortcoming of poison gas. Means of combating it were developed within weeks of its first appearance. Early gas masks were uncomfortable to wear, restricted visibility, and lost their efficacy after exposure to gas for more than 30 minutes. But they rendered poison gas, even when delivered in ideal conditions, ineffective as a principal strike weapon.

The other major innovation of the opening years of the First World War, the tank, was a direct response to the problem of getting an attacking force across no man's land without sustaining prohibitive losses from machine-gun and rifle fire. Troops endeavouring to reach the enemy front line might stand a better chance of survival enclosed in a metal box than on their own two legs. Winston Churchill, an early proponent of the tank, actually envisaged it as an infantry carrier, a wildly impractical scheme given the size of vehicle necessary to carry substantial numbers of troops. Later developments under Major Swinton saw the tank emerge as a weapons platform. With its semi-immunity to small-arms fire, it seemed equipped to cross no man's land and subdue trench strongpoints in advance of the attacking infantry.

Two misconceptions are widely entertained concerning the role of the tank in the First World War – that the Allied high command refused to welcome it and that, properly employed, it had the capacity to turn the war around. Neither view is well founded. It was the German command who were not impressed with the tank. Haig, when he took command of the BEF late in 1915 and first learned of plans to construct this weapon, was full of enthusiasm. Indeed he hoped to spearhead his mid-1916 offensive on the Somme with a great flock of these armoured vehicles, failing to recognize that production difficulties (among other things) would render this impracticable.

Even less defensible, though even more widely believed, is the view that the tank had the capability, if properly employed, to break the trench deadlock. Its supposed efficacy follows from the assumption that what dominated no man's land, and brought infantry attacks to a halt, was the deadly fire of machine-guns and rifles. Any instrument immune to a hail of bullets was thought to possess the answer to stalemate on the Western Front.

There is a vital element missing here. Artillery, even more than small-arms fire, was the great destructive force in this war. And the tank enjoyed no immunity from the high explosive shell. On the contrary, although an impressive product of modern industry and technology, the tank – both as it first appeared and as it was modified as the war proceeded – was decidedly vulnerable to established weapons. It was painfully slow moving and subject to mechanical breakdown, so that it was under fire a considerable time. It was also (like cavalry) a conspicuous instrument of attack, and so attracted a disproportionate amount of hostile attention. The number of shells which came its way, along with hand-thrown bombs, meant that – unless the opposition had already been severely dealt with by other means – no great number of tanks was likely to get as far as the enemy trenches.

None of this would deny the tank a role in offensive operations during the second half of the war. But like poison gas its role would be supportive. It would not prove to be the main strike force.

II

Even by early 1915 it was becoming painfully obvious that offensive operations on a large scale were doomed unless supported by large quantities of artillery ammunition. This posed problems for all the great powers, who had exhausted their stocks in 1914. But it presented a particular problem of adjustment for Britain, with its highly developed industrial base but little previous commitment to military (as against naval) preparedness.

On a succession of occasions in 1915 British forces, as part of larger and ill-rewarded French endeavours, launched offensives on the Western Front. (The Germans, by contrast, were by and large standing on the defensive in the west in 1915 owing to their commitments in the east.) Oddly enough, the first of these British actions saw an appropriate amount of weaponry brought to bear in support of the attacking infantry. The remainder did not.

In March 1915 Sir Henry Rawlinson's IV Corps attacked German positions at Neuve Chapelle. In preparation, Rawlinson took note of the length of German trench needing to be subdued, and calculated the number of shells required for the task. The length of trench was not great, and consisted only of a single line. Rawlinson was able to direct against it the required number of shells and the German line was duly overrun. That proved the limit of his advance. It had been assumed that initial success would open the way to exploitation, but events proved otherwise. The Germans brought in reinforcements and created a new defensive line. Rawlinson's artillery had no opportunity to register the position of this line, the shells missed their mark, and all follow-up attacks failed.

Thereafter in 1915, British endeavours on the Western Front proved quite in vain. Aubers Ridge, Givenchy, and Loos are names of unhappy memory in British military annals. The predominant reason for failure lay in the ratio of available artillery to the length of trench under attack. No commander (including Rawlinson) repeated IV Corps's calculation before Neuve Chapelle, presumably because it was feared that the answer would not come out right. But, as mentioned, the deficiency was clearly recognized at Loos, when poison gas was employed in an attempt to make good the shortfall in artillery ammunition.

As early as May 1915, these abortive operations produced outspoken comment on the British home front. One consequence was the formation of the Ministry of Munitions under the political direction of David Lloyd George. Expanding on foundations already laid by the War Office, Lloyd George set in motion the conversion of Britain's existing productive capacity from peacetime to war purposes, the establishment from scratch of whole new enterprises, and the mobilization of labour in the service of the battlefield. The outcome, in the production of weaponry, was within a year decidedly impressive. But it was accompanied by a huge expansion in the size of British forces being sent into battle and by the extent of operations which the British army was being called upon to undertake. Whether there was an appropriate correlation between, on the one hand, the quantity of munitions now available and, on the other, the ambitious ends these munitions were supposed to achieve was a question which nobody in authority seemed to be asking.

III

As 1916 dawned, the conundrum of the Western Front was still unsolved. Now, however, commanders on both sides did not doubt that they possessed the means of its resolution. Poison gas may not have proved the answer, and the tank might be tardy in making its appearance. But big guns and shells, along with mortars and hand grenades and machine-guns (as well as flame-throwers in the case of the Germans), were available in quantities without precedent in warfare. Simply by the unrelenting use of artillery, commanders now proclaimed, it had become a straightforward matter to pulverize trenches into deathtraps. Hence attacks might proceed without prohibitive loss.

This notion – the capacity of artillery employed *en masse* to suppress trench resistance – inspired the two great Western Front campaigns of 1916. The first was the battle of Verdun, launched in February by General Falkenhayn, the German commander-in-chief, against the forces of France. The second was the Allied campaign on the Somme, which opened on 1 July and became, owing to French losses already sustained at Verdun, a predominantly British endeavour under Haig's direction.

On paper, Haig's and Falkenhayn's methods of proceeding looked a good deal different. Haig was convinced that he could deliver a devastating bombardment over a wide front. The extent of frontage was crucial to his plan. It meant that in the centre of the attack, his cavalry – along with assaulting infantry – could drive through the gap free from interference by enemy fire from the flanks. So, at last, they would break out into open country, with all its opportunities for exploitation.

Falkenhayn's *modus operandi* looked rather different. He left the cavalry out. And he chose to attack on a much narrower front than Haig, thereby achieving a far greater concentration of firepower. He argued – anyway after the event – that the capture of territory was less important than the killing and incapacitating of French soldiers. He proposed to devastate the limited area under attack so thoroughly as to render life insupportable within it. His forces could then occupy the blasted stretch of land at little cost to themselves, after which his artillery would move forward and create further devastation followed by further occupation. The cumulative outcome would be the destruction of the French army, the (probable) capture of Verdun, and – in some obscure way – the incapacitation of Britain, which he was not directly engaging but which he regarded as Germany's principal enemy.

In the two horrendous campaigns of 1916 at Verdun and on the Somme, neither Falkenhayn nor Haig accomplished his purpose. Falkenhayn has sometimes been credited with a sort of success, because he did not aspire to achieve as much as Haig and hence did not fail so badly. The British commander, after all, never ruptured the enemy front or made productive use of his cavalry, and never looked like doing so. His forces did, in what developed into a wearing-out campaign, gradually drive the Germans back a few miles, but to no strategic effect and at somewhat greater loss to themselves than to their enemy. Falkenhayn, as long as he talked only of shedding French blood, did at least impose an equal number of casualties on the French as he himself suffered. And he did not need to excuse his failure to accomplish a breakthrough.

Yet Falkenhayn's failure was manifest. He offered the Verdun operation as a means of knocking Britain's 'best sword' from its hand, which was a nonsense (because Britain's best sword now consisted of its own army) and something he certainly did not achieve. He had sought to bleed the French army white while preserving his own forces, and instead had sustained almost as many casualties as his adversaries. And whatever obfuscation he may have offered concerning his objectives, he clearly was out to conquer Verdun – as his conduct of operations made plain – and he did not do so. (Indeed, such limited amounts of territory as he did capture, the French in the latter half of 1916 wrenched back from him.) It requires an odd perspective to see this as a superior performance to that of Haig on the Somme.

IV

Large conclusions have been drawn from these failures to score decisive victories at Verdun and the Somme. It has been assumed that both commanders were wrong in their shared premise that the answer to the conundrum of trench warfare lay in the high-explosive shell employed *en masse*. Victory in this war, it was taken to follow, had to come from new weapons (such as the tank) or from a more imaginative strategy (such as at Palestine or Salonica) or from a campaign directed not against soldiers but against civilians (such as a food blockade or a propaganda offensive). These conclusions are thoroughly wrong-headed, and certainly find no warrant in what went awry for the attacking armies on the Western Front in 1916.

Falkenhayn and Haig were misguided about many things (Haig's obsession about breakthrough, and the employment of cavalry in its accomplishment, is a painfully obvious example). But they were not wrong in the fundamental thing: that, appropriately employed, an amplitude of high-explosive shells could in some measure reverse the dominance of defence over attack on the Western Front. Where they were woefully astray in 1916 was in believing that they already possessed the required abundance of shells, and could straightway accomplish a compelling victory. Wartime mobilization had advanced considerably, but it was still well short of that stage.

The German and British commanders were no doubt mesmerized by the 'unprecedented' quantities of guns and shells now at their disposal.

Plainly these should be able to accomplish large purposes. But whereas Haig chose to employ them to breach the enemy line on a wide front, and Falkenhayn to convert a stretch of opposing territory into a depopulated wasteland, neither was actually calculating how much these accumulated missiles could accomplish.

Haig's miscalculation was the more obvious. For an attack on a 20-mile front against successive lines of elaborately constructed trenches, his supply of shells was anything but overwhelming. Indeed, in terms of yards of trench under attack, his bombardment proved only half as severe as that delivered at Neuve Chapelle more than a year before. As a consequence, the German defences were scarcely dented, and his grand scheme for a breakthrough ended catastrophically on the first day. The campaign on the Somme continued sporadically, for another four and a half months, but now with more limited objectives: to force the defenders back a stage at a time, in the process imposing heavy casualties on them until they became so weakened that a general advance might prove possible. Sometimes, as on 14 July and 25–26 September, the quantities of artillery employed were appropriate for a limited advance. More usually, they were not.

Falkenhayn's self-delusion at Verdun six months earlier had been altogether more subtle. He did not try to convince himself that his huge stockpile of shells was sufficient to eliminate the French defences on a wide front. So he chose a narrow front: eight miles on the right bank of the river Meuse. He planned to obliterate the French troops facing him on just this sector, occupy the devastated region, and then repeat the process. Step by step, over the bodies of dead Frenchmen, he would proceed towards Verdun.

What Falkenhayn was choosing to ignore was the likely response of his opponents in the areas adjacent to his attack. Yet on such a narrow front, his ability to get forward would depend not just on how he dealt with adversaries directly ahead but on how his enemies on the flank chose to respond. Haig, it will be recalled, attacked at the outset on a wide front so as to secure his forces in the centre from the danger of flanking fire. Thereby he spread too thin the artillery resources at his disposal and got virtually nowhere. But at least he was trying to deal with an issue which Falkenhayn, electing to advance on a narrow front, was culpably disregarding. What would be the response of those French forces situated outside the ambit of his assault but in sufficient proximity to direct flanking fire against his whole line of attack?

The importance of Falkenhayn's oversight soon became apparent. After one spellbinding success (the capture of Fort Douaumont), the German advance was brought to a bloody halt by intense French artillery fire from the left bank of the Meuse – that is, from a region which

Falkenhayn, in order to concentrate his bombardment, had chosen to disregard. At this point Falkenhayn's grand plan ended as abruptly as would Haig's on Day One of the Somme. What followed, for the one commander as for the other, was improvisation, halting forward movements to no great purpose, and a steady exchange of slaughter. First Falkenhayn was obliged to suspend his undertaking on the right bank of the Meuse and turn his attention to the Mort Homme region on the left bank, where the French artillery was concentrated. This meant that, contrary to his original premise, he found himself lengthening his front of attack. That endeavour attracted fire from French batteries yet further to his right (Côte 304), forcing him to extend his front once again. By the time he had subdued these trouble spots on the left bank of the Meuse and was in a position to return to his original objectives, all prospect of conducting the sort of campaign originally envisaged had departed. He pressed on, at great pain to the armies of both sides, in the endeavour to secure some respectable acquisitions before the impending Allied offensive on the Somme gave him cause to halt. Even this limited aim was to prove beyond the power of his armies.

V

Pretty evidently, the great offensives on the Western Front in 1916 had been failures. Yet – if from a rather bleak perspective – they did carry some positive messages. Verdun, after all, had robbed the French of a significant segment of their fighting forces, and had forced them to relinquish – if only for a time – some distinct geographical objectives: Fort Douaumont and Fort Vaux on the right bank of the Meuse, the Mort Homme and Côte 304 on the left bank. These French losses fell well short of Falkenhayn's purpose of overrunning Verdun and – without great cost to himself – of bleeding the French army white. But it was evidence that a substantial accumulation of high explosive could so diminish a defending force as to oblige it to give ground. Haig on the Somme repeated the demonstration. His adversaries, despite ferocious resistance and costly counter-attacks, were gradually eroded in fighting strength and driven from their elaborately constructed positions on the ridge. They found themselves on less commanding territory from which they soon executed a large-scale withdrawal.

None of this provided evidence that even a better-supplied and better-executed offensive would fulfil the pipe dreams of 1916: that is, would break through on a wide front and/or annihilate the opposing army. But it did demonstrate that even a well-placed defender could be forced to give ground and surrender lives. And this occurred in circumstances where the quantity of weaponry available to the attacker was at last becoming imposing, and where the means of its effective use were steadily mounting.

During the campaign on the Somme, two expressions scarcely heard before began to gain currency. They concerned the use of artillery in support of an offensive. One was 'creeping barrage'. This reflected attempts to suppress fire from enemy trenches while the attacking infantry was seeking to get forward. By and large, on 1 July 1916 Haig's bombardment had lifted from the German front line as his foot soldiers left their trenches and started to advance. Given that the British had by no means eliminated the defenders, this resulted in fire being rained on the helpless attackers as they endeavoured to cross no man's land.

What the offensive needed was an artillery barrage which moved just ahead of the infantry and so forced the front-line defenders to keep their heads down almost to the moment when they were about to be assaulted. For the gunners this was a taxing assignment. It required high-quality guns and shells which would perform consistently to requirements. And it required gunners with the skill and experience to 'walk' or 'creep' their curtain of shells just ahead of the advancing foot soldiers, neither falling short and killing their own men nor opening too wide a gap and allowing the defenders to rally.

For all its difficulties, by September on the Somme the employment of a creeping barrage in support of an infantry attack was becoming general in the British army. This meant that, when Haig's forces resumed the offensive in 1917, they would be in possession not only of a better-made and more plentiful supply of shells fired by a more highly trained body of gunners, but of a technique for marrying the forward movements of infantry with the artillery's assault upon the enemy's forward positions.

The other expression pertaining to artillery which was becoming current late in 1916 was 'counter-battery'. An attacking force was not just in peril from the fire of front-line defenders. Enemy artillery well behind the lines greeted them with a hurricane of shrapnel and high explosive. Such was the intensity of the German counter-bombardment on 1 July 1916 that numbers of British troops were swept away even before leaving their trenches; while a great many more fell in no man's land to the curtain of fire placed across it by the German gunners, or became victims of the enemy's pounding of their own former front lines when the attacking troops had managed to get that far.

Hitherto, the task of knocking out enemy artillery had appeared so imposing that it had scarcely been addressed. But by late 1916 this was gradually changing. As we have noticed, the gunners were gaining skill and experience, and British industry was producing weapons in increasing numbers. Further, back in Britain the Ministry of Munitions had reinstated quality control – so rashly set aside in 1915 in the interests of increasing output – and was thereby producing more precise weapons better capable of hitting even distant and discrete targets such as an enemy gun or battery.

What remained necessary, and was only beginning to emerge, was a system for pinpointing the whereabouts of enemy guns. The principal means, growing in volume and sophistication, was aerial spotting supplemented by aerial photography. But other methods too were being developed. They included flash spotting, that is visual detection of guns in the act of firing, and sound ranging, whereby the position of a gun could be established by employing microphones which recorded the wave of sound that followed its firing.

What we are observing, then, as 1916 proceeded is a conjunction of factors steadily diminishing the potency of defensive artillery in halting infantry attacks. These, in summary, were the growing volume of offensive guns and shells, the mounting expertise of the gunners, and the development of methods to establish the whereabouts of enemy batteries. The dominance of the defensive was in a measure being undermined. So although 1916 was primarily a year of blighted hopes for those seeking a decision on the Western Front, its message was not quite unqualified.

The problem, as 1917 loomed, was what pointer these mixed signals provided towards future operations. If inadequate weaponry had failed to produce a momentous victory in 1916, just what sort of a victory could be hoped for – and should be aimed at – in the presence of more abundant weapons? Further, were the politicians and soldiers now in charge of Britain's military endeavours, for all their expertise and experience, equipped to recognize what had gone wrong up to now and what might – and might not – be accomplished hereafter?

3

Stratagems: January–May 1917

I

As far as the Western Allies were concerned, decision-making at the start of 1917 would rest on the interaction of four groups: the political leaders and the military leaders of Britain and France. Ultimately, the civilian chiefs would decide, as was their constitutional responsibility. But they would receive advice, and experience pressure, from the heads of the military.

In the closing stages of the Somme campaign, the then military chiefs of France and Britain, Joffre and Haig, had agreed on strategy for the coming year. 'Alternative' strategies, directed not at Germany but at one of its allies, or at some undefined part of Germany remote from the Western Front, did not enter into consideration. With the coming of the new campaigning season, the offensive on the Somme would be resumed. The Asquith government in Britain, like its counterpart in France, having authorized one campaign on the Somme seemed prepared to authorize another.

By January 1917 these simplicities were under challenge. After two years without a victory, Joffre's command had been brought to an end. The French government chose as his successor, not Philippe Pétain the master of the defensive who had rallied France's forces at Verdun, but Robert Nivelle, who had initiated some limited, costly, but strikingly successful counter-attacks at Verdun late in 1916. Nivelle offered what the political rulers of France wanted to hear. He promised, employing his supposedly novel offensive techniques on a much wider front, to rupture the German lines at a sector of the Western Front other than the Somme, and forthwith to expel the invader from the soil of France. The initial breakthrough, he insisted, would occur in the first 24 to 48 hours of the offensive.

In Britain, it was a change not of commander but of government that threw strategy into the melting pot. In December 1916 David Lloyd George, having been successively Chancellor of the Exchequer, Minister of Munitions, and Secretary of State for War, supplanted Asquith as Prime Minister. Lloyd George did not propose any direct change in Britain's military command. But it was recognized that he entertained severe reservations concerning Haig's fitness to direct operations in the west, as he did concerning the competence of Sir William Robertson, the government's principal military adviser; and he clearly opposed resumption of the offensive on the Somme.

During 1915, Lloyd George had evinced a somewhat ill-developed enthusiasm for a Balkans strategy over a Western Front strategy. And during 1916 he did not conceal his preference for French commanders over British commanders in the conduct of operations on the Somme. These positions did not seem to have a lot in common, except that each envisaged operations in which Sir Douglas Haig would not play a key role.

Yet whatever upheavals had taken place in Britain and France by the start of 1917, in essentials there was no change. Political and military leaders were of one mind in believing that the war must be carried on to victory, not abandoned. And for this purpose, the fight must be taken to the enemy. So any differences existed in the context of an unshaken belief that this must remain, in Lloyd George's words, a fight to a finish, to a knock-out.

There was another instance of unanimity. The political and military leaders of Britain and France were agreed that strategy meant the pursuit of large objectives. Joffre may, in the course of his command, have justified his operations on the grounds that he kept nibbling. But that was strictly an after-the-event rationalization of operations that had failed to attain their goals. His purpose had been to deliver such body-blows as would terminate the enemy's powers of resistance. And his failure to do this had cost him his job. At the start of 1917, the rulers of Britain and France remained determined to see that job carried out.

II

For France then, at the start of 1917, a happy unanimity existed in its governing and military circles. There would be no resumption of operations on the Somme. Nivelle would launch a great strike, where the Western Front ran east–west rather than north–south. His chosen area was the Chemin des Dames, scene of the fighting on the Aisne in long-ago 1914 as well as of great endeavours by Joffre in 1915. The British army would not be involved in this region. But it would be asked (or even, if Lloyd George was accommodating, ordered) to launch a subsidiary operation out of Arras, to the north of the Somme region. This would hold German forces away from the principal sector of attack. And it might also enhance Nivelle's triumph. For if Haig's forces managed to break through at Arras and advanced eastwards, they would cut off the line of retreat of the German forces whom Nivelle was driving north.

If France's political and military leaders were – for the moment – of one mind, the same was not true in Britain. At least in private, Lloyd George made clear his determination to curb Haig's predilection for large operations costly in British lives. Haig, it was evident, favoured one or other of two proceedings. As long as the French command was eager, he would resume the joint offensive on the Somme. If they were not, his preference lay with a distinctly British undertaking. Located in Belgium, it was to commence with a breakout from the Ypres salient, but not to stop there. It would continue much further.

Lloyd George was equally averse to both proposals. He resisted schemes involving great numbers of British forces and threatening heavy British casualties, and he distrusted the judgement of Sir Douglas Haig. Determined though he was to carry the war to the enemy, he preferred an operation outside France and Flanders, giving no great role to Haig, and employing mainly non-British troops.

In January 1917 Lloyd George proposed switching the Allied endeavour for the year to the Italian front. For the moment the principal adversaries there were Austro-Hungarians, but it was always possible for the Germans to intervene on this front in strength. Lloyd George was clearly envisaging an operation in which, on the Allied side, the Italians would bear the brunt of the fighting. He argued (in private) that up to now Italy had been behind-hand in contributing manpower to the struggle. And he declared (in public) that with a great infusion of British and French weaponry – along with an indeterminate contribution of British and French fighting men – the Italian army could accomplish great things.

At least from a somewhat partisan perspective, this scheme had much to recommend it. It promised to set in motion a major campaign, but not to place at risk great numbers of British lives. And, without in any sense unseating Haig, it gave him no large part in the conduct of operations.

From a wider perspective, the scheme was badly flawed. The German command might conclude that their Habsburg ally was seriously in danger and send a number of German divisions to Italy from the now-quiescent Western Front. That could place the Italians in considerable peril. Or the German command might decide that the Austro-Hungarians, given their fortunate geographical position, could cope even with a strengthened Italian army. This would mean that the Germans could then pursue their own designs untroubled by the usual Anglo-French offensive.

There were further difficulties about Lloyd George's Italian strategy. The British military command did not approve of it, which – if Lloyd George was determined on his course – did not matter very much. The French government and the French military did not at all care for it, which (in a coalition war) mattered a great deal. Most of all, the directors of Italy's war effort could not fail to recognize the burden – and the potential peril – which the British Prime Minister was seeking to thrust on them. That settled the matter. Lloyd George's preferred course – not at all on account of the attitude of Haig – had ceased to exist. An Allied conference in Rome in January 1917 took no time in seeing it off.

That shifted consideration to the French alternative. Nivelle's proposed proceeding was at least viable, in the sense that, anyway in January, it had the endorsement of the French political and military command. (This proved less the case after March. A change of government in Paris brought to the surface widespread doubts, among civilians and soldiers, about the practicality of what was being proposed. Yet the operation was not cancelled.) The Nivelle scheme possessed a further merit:endorsement from Britain. If not the preferred course of either Lloyd George or Haig, it had attractions for both of them. To Haig (as to Robertson), it constituted a Western Front offensive in the familiar manner, and so rescued strategy from Lloyd George's geographical eccentricities. For Lloyd George, its merits were quite otherwise. It offered an offensive where the British, although a substantial contributor, would not be the main participant or liable to sustain the heaviest losses. To that extent it was akin to his Italian proposal. And it offered an offensive which, although taking place on the Western Front, would not be the brainchild, or under the direction, of the British commander-in-chief.

Lloyd George, in short, was swinging away from the view that what was wrong with British generals was simply commitment to the Western Front. He was now coming down heavily for the position (which he had aired rather tactlessly at one phase of the Somme campaign in 1916) that Western Front operations might be all right as long as they were not directed by British generals.

III

Given that Lloyd George and Haig, if for different reasons, endorsed the Nivelle strategy, they could well have proceeded with a reasonable display of unanimity. But Lloyd George would not have it so: he proved determined to render the arrangement as disagreeable as possible to the British high command.

Having developed a considerable affinity with General Nivelle, Lloyd George set about placing the British army under French control. Unlike the comfortable arrangement whereby Joffre and Haig, while theoretically commanders of independent armies, worked out joint proceedings, Lloyd George determined on a different chain of authority which could only humiliate Haig. The British army would become a unit in a composite Allied force directed by the French commander-in-chief, with Haig as his subordinate. Nor was this arrangement designed just for a single operation or even campaign. Nivelle's command of the British army would continue in perpetuity (assuming, which proved not to be the case, that Nivelle retained command of the French army in perpetuity).

The questionable nature of this arrangement, along with the questionable methods employed to put it into place (the notorious Calais conference), aroused dismay not only within but outside British military circles. This led to some back-tracking. First, Nivelle's command over Britain's forces in France was confined (at least for the moment) to this one campaign. Second, Haig was given the right to appeal to his own government against Nivelle's directives if he believed these were endangering his army. Third, the French commander-in-chief was required to address Haig with more civility than had become his custom. Yet the essence of the proceeding remained: Haig and his forces had become a unit in Nivelle's consolidated army and were subject to his command. The credit for such successes as this operation might accomplish would rest with Nivelle, and also with Lloyd George. It would hardly light upon Haig.

Matters did not work out according to plan. In the British sector, the first day (9 April) of the campaign witnessed a notable success. On Haig's left the Canadians stormed Vimy Ridge, and in the centre the Third Army achieved an advance of 3.5 miles – the greatest distance accomplished at a bound since the onset of trench warfare. Success had been aided by inept placing of counter-attack forces on the part of the Germans, the thorough training of British infantry, and the crashing weight and effective employment of Haig's artillery – which, among other things, fired a preliminary bombardment almost treble the density of that on the Somme prior to 1 July 1916.

But if, for a moment, the BEF seemed poised for the long-awaited breakthrough, this mirage soon vanished. The elaborate artillery contribution to the initial success could not be replicated in short order. The enemy instituted effective counter-measures. In no time at all, the Battle of Arras became the type of slogging match already rendered familiar by the previous year's struggle on the Somme. It was persisted in, at mounting cost, for six largely unfruitful weeks.

But if the British experienced mixed fortunes during their part in the Nivelle offensive, the French experience was hardly mixed at all. Initial French progress was negated by fierce German counter-attacks. And subsequent modest advances – if the equal of Joffre's earlier 'nibbling' operations – bore no resemblance to the grandiose breakthrough promised within 48 hours. Nivelle's position had already become precarious, owing to scepticism about the undertaking among military subordinates and his new political masters. Now it disintegrated as confidence evaporated at every level. Most calamitous was the mounting unwillingness of French rank and file soldiers to continue participating in this much touted and obviously barren undertaking.

Within weeks of the inception of the operation, large sections of the French army had entered a state of collective disobedience. They might be prepared to return to the front in order to ward off attacks but they would no longer be involved in attempts to capture unattainable objectives. These events were decisive. Nivelle was sacked and his place taken by Pétain, devotee of the defensive and a profound pessimist concerning large-scale offensive operations. The Nivelle strategy was abandoned, and the French army moved into a phase of quiescence and recuperation.

For Lloyd George these events could not be other than embarrassing. He had embraced Nivelle with reckless enthusiasm, and placed the British army under his command. And he had managed to perceive great promise in a Western Front strategy. Now Nivelle had been relegated to the lumber-room of history, and Haig was securely back in direction of the BEF. As for Lloyd George's second preferred strategic option, it had proved as insubstantial as his first.

It was in this context that Britain's rulers were obliged to decide on the nation's military strategy for the second half of 1917.

4

Decisions: May–July 1917

I

Clearly, the calamity of the Nivelle offensive had played into Haig's hands. French offensive strategy was discredited, Lloyd George stood humiliated, and Haig was securely restored to command of his own army. As Lloyd George's private secretary noted in her diary on 12 May: 'In the meantime, Nivelle has fallen into disgrace, and let [Lloyd George] down badly . . . Sir Douglas Haig has come out on top in this fight between the two Chiefs, and I fear [Lloyd George] will have to be very careful in future as to his backings of the French against the English.'[1] That seemed to place the British commander-in-chief in a strong position to devise the next military operation.

Lloyd George, for one, began talking as though Haig now occupied the box seat. In early May he attended a conference in Paris to press on the French – as if oblivious to their recent misfortunes – the need to persist with the offensive ('We must go on hitting and hitting with all our might'). He took the opportunity to proclaim that he had no pretensions to being a strategist, that he left such matters to his military advisers, and that Haig had full authority to attack where and when he thought fit. This may have been grotesque, particularly in the light of his conduct during the past four months. But it did suggest that he was now prepared to relegate fundamental decisions concerning British strategy to the military arm.

What Haig would do, if decision-making did indeed rest with him, was not in doubt. Earlier in the year he had extracted an agreement from Nivelle that, should the latter's operations not fulfil expectations, then Haig's preferred option would move centre stage. That option was a campaign in Flanders intended to do more than drive the Germans off the ridges overlooking the Ypres salient (a tall enough order). Its purpose was to expel the enemy from all of Belgium. Primarily this would be accomplished by continuing the advance out of the Ypres salient all the way to the Channel. But that action would be aided by an ambitious landing of forces from the sea, supplemented by a thrust north-east by units situated on the coast.

Events since February seemed to have made such a course more appropriate. For one thing, Ypres did not carry an aura of failure. The BEF had fought two bloody defensive actions there in 1914 and 1915, but had not attempted a major advance. That set Ypres apart from the remainder of the British-occupied sector of the Western Front, most of which had been the scene of costly and barren British offensives. Further, Belgium was proximate to Britain, the BEF's supply base and source of reinforcements (as well as the springboard for an amphibious operation). This was of particular moment given that, for the present, any Western Front campaign was bound to be a largely British under-taking. A further argument for an offensive towards the coast was provided by the U-boat campaign unleashed in February against British and neutral merchant shipping. This rendered desirable the capture of German-occupied ports on the Belgian coast – a consideration, it must be added, that greatly concerned Jellicoe (the First Sea Lord) but did not appear to cut much ice with Haig or Lloyd George.

All in all, then, by May 1917 the ball seemed to rest in Haig's court, and Haig's fixation was with Flanders. That, apparently, provides an explanation for what otherwise would be inexplicable: the decision to go ahead with a Flanders campaign. No one of note other than Haig seemed to be eager for it. Lloyd George's preference – once he rediscov-ered that it was appropriate for him to have one – lay elsewhere: indeed almost anywhere apart from the Ypres salient. Robertson, unlike Lloyd George, was certainly a committed westerner, but he was also deeply alarmed by Haig's vaunting ambitions. Sir Henry Wilson, a maverick military figure whom Lloyd George – if not too many others – found agreeable, disapproved of anything proposed by Haig. (However, as the day of decision approached, Wilson did veer towards giving it a sort of endorsement.) Among leading French military figures, Pétain was averse to any offensive except of the most limited sort, and Ferdinand Foch regarded the low-lying Flanders plain as no area for a major operation. Haig, then, appeared almost alone (outside naval circles) in willing a campaign in Belgium.

So it seems to follow that praise or blame for the inception of the Third Ypres offensive rests with him. Yet that conclusion is specious, for very important reasons. Haig never possessed the authority to launch a major campaign without consent from Britain's principal ally and the clear endorsement of Britain's civilian authorities.

The attitude of the French authorities needs to be spelt out. It is sometimes believed that they were pleading for a British offensive in the west so as to prevent the Germans from assailing their own disintegrating army. This is without substance. The French command were not impressed by Haig's strategic nostrums. And, whatever their problems, they were aware that the enemy was in no position to mount an offensive against them in the foreseeable future. On the contrary, in the early weeks of 1917 the German command had executed a major withdrawal on the Western Front to the secure strongholds of the Hindenburg Line. The intention was to rest on the defensive in the west, embark on wide-scale mobilization of their home front, exploit Russia's mounting difficulties, and eliminate Britain not by a land campaign but by a submarine blockade. The German command, therefore, was not in a position, even if conscious of possible French demoralization, to make the plans, assemble the weapons, and train the forces necessary for a large offensive in the west.

But if the rulers of France were not – on account of their supposed peril – beseeching Britain to launch a Flanders campaign, they certainly had no cause to try and stop one. It was altogether acceptable to them for the British, in these unpropitious times, forcefully to engage the principal enemy just about anywhere. The French were even prepared to make a modest contribution to such an undertaking (and to promise to do a good deal more). Had the political and military leaders of France not provided this much endorsement – had they rather argued passionately against the Ypres campaign – then Britain's rulers would have been obliged to take their objections very seriously.

An even more imposing hurdle had to be surmounted before Haig could embark on his cherished operation – that provided by the nation's civilian rulers, focused in the office of Prime Minister and the recently established War Cabinet. Without their authorization, major operations would not be launched anywhere in this war.

II

It is customary to exaggerate the role played by the military arm in shaping the course of British history between 1914 and 1918. Because the nation was at war, the military had an unusually prominent place in British affairs. Further, these years were beset by instances of decision-making which seem to epitomize military obtuseness and so are adjudged of military origin. Finally, the most prominent figure in British affairs in almost the opening two years of the war was not an established politician but the nation's most prominent Field-Marshal: Lord Kitchener of Khartoum.

The conclusion often drawn from these points, that Britain had fallen under a sort of military direction, is unwarranted. First, from August 1914 until his death in June 1916, Lord Kitchener was occupying a civilian post and wielding civilian authority. There is no evidence here of the military exercising undue influence in British affairs. Second, highly placed civilians proved more than capable of reaching bizarre decisions on military matters, as Gallipoli and Salonica and Lloyd George's Balkans schemes make evident. These civilians were not thereby acting as 'militarists'. Third, and quite fundamentally, the military arm in Britain, though unusually prominent, did not control the levers of power.

The vital decisions taken in Britain between 1914 and 1918 – even decisions with decided military implications – were not initiated and authorized by the military. In the diplomatic crisis of July–August 1914, no one asked the service chiefs whether or not Britain should enter the fray, any more than, in the ensuing weeks, the military command was called on to decide whether Britain should abandon its small-army, 'business as usual', orientation in favour of a mass army and a war economy. Equally, it was as a result of an intense political tussle, not a military diktat, that Britain in 1916 decided to terminate voluntary enlistment and conscript adult males (only) for the armed services – with provision for conscientious objection, a decidedly unmilitary concept. Even in that area of great concern to the military, grand strategy, it was the cabinet and its offshoots which ultimately decided whether Britain would confine itself to operations on the Western Front or, simultaneously or as an alternative, would mount expeditions in Mesopotamia and Gallipoli and Salonica.

If Sir Douglas Haig had been commander of the German army, he might (one can speculate) have played a key role in provoking a great war and waging it for grandiose purposes and by reckless means. Opportunities for such conduct were open to Germany's military leaders under the system of rule bequeathed by Bismarck. Under the British constitution, as it operated not only in peace but during the two great wars of this century, the chance did not exist for the military arm to bring catastrophe upon the British people.

The point needs to be taken further. Haig was not the commander of Britain's army, even in a purely operational sense. He was commander only of British forces in France and Belgium – and only, as Sir John French had discovered, for as long as the nation's civilian rulers chose to retain his services. That is, if the government decided that Britain would raise no great army and would confine itself to a naval and economic war; or if it chose to raise a large military force but employ most of it in the Balkans or the Middle East; then the name of Sir Douglas Haig would be as little remembered as are the names of Britain's commanders in Mesopotamia and Salonica.

Haig, in sum, may have been responsible for much that happened, and much that is open to criticism, in the Great War generally and the Third Ypres campaign in particular. But responsibility for the fact that the Flanders operation of 1917 was ever launched, and ever persisted in, lies elsewhere.

III

If Haig was not responsible for the inception of that operation, it is sometimes argued, then inevitability was. That is, the decision-makers of Britain, little though they cared to recognize it, had no choices: the terrible logic of this war drove them to reach what was actually a pre-determined decision.[2]

We have noted how soon after the outbreak of war it became apparent that the launching of offensives on the Western Front was going to prove a costly and unrewarding business, and yet with what persistence, year after year, the Western Allies embarked on these grisly undertakings. An apparent explanation is that decision-makers and strategists were acting under an irresistible compulsion, whereby no other way of proceeding lay open to them. As far as the Allies were concerned, the war could not be won, in any foreseeable time-span, by blockade at sea, because Germany had a continental land base and kept acquiring further territories. And there could be no question of Britain's resting on the defensive and allowing the enemy to batter themselves senseless against impenetrable defences. If the British tried anything of the sort, the Germans would pick off its allies one by one, expanding territory and resources as they went. If Britain was not to see the alliance of which it was part crumble to nothing, it must play a conspicuous role – with whatever support its allies could provide – in carrying the war to the enemy. That arguably meant, in the summer of 1917, a Flanders campaign. The futilities of extraneous forms of strategy in previous years, and the abrupt repudiation of alternative campaigns in Italy and on the Chemin des Dames in the first half of 1917, had in this view meant that Third Ypres was the one option remaining for the Western Allies. So in the argument from inevitability the Flanders campaign, far from being undertaken thoughtlessly or as a consequence of wild delusion or in disregard of more appropriate choices, had been rendered unavoidable by a succession of misfortunes which had eliminated all other options while not eliminating the need to act.

This is a seductive argument, but it omits important matters. Third Ypres was undertaken on the premise that this war could prosper only as a result of mass offensives directed towards major geographical objectives. Perhaps Verdun and the Somme and the Chemin des Dames and Arras had not yielded great victories or important gains of territory, but they had been the right sort of undertaking. Another of the same sort, hopefully better rewarded, remained the only way to proceed.

Yet if attention is directed to military accomplishment rather than military necessity in Western Front operations so far, a different imperative presents itself. While Verdun and the Somme plainly failed in their main purpose, they did yield to the attacker certain rewards. This point is reinforced by other operations. For example, limited attacks launched by the French at Verdun late in 1916 had restored all the territory earlier captured by the Germans (as well as making Nivelle's reputation as a wonder-worker). And these productive undertakings were reinforced in April 1917 by the stunning opening to the British offensive at Arras, and even by Nivelle's near-simultaneous advance up the Chemin des Dames – before the threatened open-endedness of his undertaking caused the politicians and rank-and-file soldiers of France to call a halt.

These hopeful episodes in the otherwise bleak operations of 1916 and early 1917 seemed to carry a clear message: well-trained and well-equipped forces of infantry, when proceeding with the support of massed artillery, could achieve striking successes. Certainly, success would be limited by the restricted capacity of the gunners to suppress enemy weaponry and to accompany the forward movement of the infantry. That is, the physical limits of achievement were determined by the distance that high-explosive shells could travel.

This sort of accomplishment may not have transfixed Britain's civilian leaders and military commanders, hankering as they were after sweeping advances towards far horizons. But it did offer something appropriate to the war they happened to be waging. That something was attrition, but attrition – bizarre as it may sound – in its creative and hopeful sense: the step-by-step elimination of the enemy's fighting force and will to resist, not cancelled out by a corresponding diminution of one's own fighting strength and resolution.

So if attention had been directed to the positive aspects of recent campaigns, there were indeed choices still open of a hopeful – if hardly momentous – kind. Inevitability had nothing to do with it.

IV

If the civilian rulers had opted for this sort of proceeding, and had refused to entertain Haig's grand design, would they have been terminating their occupancy of office? It is often alleged that Lloyd George's hold on power was so precarious that he could not hope to defy Haig and survive.

Haig, in this view, held the whip hand. He could count on the support of the monarch, of backbench Conservatives, and of powerful elements in the press in any tussle with the civilian chiefs. Lloyd George, by contrast, in order to become Prime Minister had broken with the leaders of the Liberal Party to which he belonged and had formed a coalition government in which he had no secure party base. If he dared to repudiate Haig's strategy, the commander-in-chief would resign, and that would bring down the government.

This scenario is so insubstantial as to approach the absurd. If ever Haig had been prepared to resign, alleging insupportable conduct by the Prime Minister, then Lloyd George's action in February not only in imposing Nivelle's strategy on Haig but in placing the BEF under Nivelle's direction would have given ample cause. In political – and royal – circles the Prime Minister's unorthodox, not to say devious, conduct in this matter created much adverse comment. But it also revealed two further things: that Haig was not inclined to attempt a political coup; and, more importantly, that there was no political grouping in existence (even among Asquith and his followers) eager to unseat Lloyd George – least of all at the behest of the military. It was beyond belief that, by May or June, such a grouping was gestating so as to rescue from War Cabinet opposition Haig's proposal for a vast military undertaking in Belgium – as against, say, limited operations in the manner of Vimy Ridge. As for the speculation that Haig might so much as threaten resignation should his Flanders proposal suffer a rebuff, neither his actions nor his written record support so improbable a suggestion.

Equally without substance is the notion that Lloyd George's position was precarious and might not survive a decision by him to decline Haig's preferred strategy. (There was no question that such a decision by Lloyd George would involve him in seeking Haig's removal as commander-in-chief.) Certainly Lloyd George was not a party leader, or the head of a regular party government. But his position in 1917 was unassailable, thanks to the circumstances that had brought him to power and the conjunction of political forces that had put him there. During 1916 there had been much resistance in political circles (if only on personal grounds) to Lloyd George's elevation to the premiership. But by December it had become too evident that he alone conspicuously possessed the qualities required to carry the nation through these dire times. During 1917, no forces of substance wanted a return to an Asquith regime, or could detect, in or out of office, any other potential war leader of Lloyd George's stature.

Further, if Lloyd George lacked the underpinning of his own party, he had the support of a wide conjunction of political forces. He had come to office with the endorsement of virtually the entire Conservative Party, many Liberals below the leading ranks, and the nascent Labour Party with its potent trade union links. To look at only the last of these, what chance was there that Labour would enter into, or the trade union movement co-operate with, any government formed as a consequence of a political coup against Lloyd George engineered by the military and the monarch? Yet how could a replacement government propose to take office, at this perilous stage of the war, when not assured of the support of organized labour? There is, of course, a further question: when did the King, or Haig, ever give a hint that they were preparing to engage in such political skulduggery? (Haig, it is worth noting, was dismayed a year later when General Maurice publicly condemned the government for presenting misleading information on military matters to the House of Commons. The commander-in-chief did not doubt Maurice's accuracy, but questioned the propriety of even this much intervention by a serving officer in the political process.)

Far from Lloyd George's hold on office being desperately precarious, so that at the last he must betray his views on strategy in order to retain power, the Prime Minister – as long as he was alive and while the war lasted – was indispensable. In the second half of 1917, as very manifestly in the first, the power to decide on strategy rested with him.

Exploration has nowhere further to go. There can be but one explanation as to why Haig was able to embark on the Third Ypres campaign: the civilian rulers of Britain gave their consent. In a situation where, given the defensive posture of the enemy on this front, they could have opted for nothing more reckless than strictly limited operations, they agreed to the inception of a vastly ambitious campaign. For that decision there can be only one reason. Either they were eager for such an undertaking, or (while being less than eager) they preferred it to any other feasible course.

V

The process of decision-making was thrashed out in the War Policy Committee, an offshoot of the War Cabinet which began meeting on 11 June. Its members were the Prime Minister, Lloyd George, two prominent Conservatives in Lords Milner and Curzon, and the South African statesman Jan Christian Smuts. Also often present was the Conservative leader and Chancellor of the Exchequer, Andrew Bonar Law, and the government's chief military adviser General Robertson. Professional experts, such as Haig and Sir John Jellicoe, the First Sea Lord, were called in when appropriate and available. Its secretary was the highly respected Sir Maurice Hankey.

In the course of lengthy meetings, none of the members of the War Policy Committee succeeded in offering clear-headed advice leading to a policy different from that proposed by Haig. They tended to talk at random, and without consistency. So Smuts more often than not spoke in support of Haig's proposal, but on occasion argued for concentration against Turkey (not least because of the effect this might have on Turkey's diplomatic orientation after the war). Milner was equally variable. On 7 June he wrote: 'It may be said that the whole position is so full of uncertainties that no plan is possible. . . . Nevertheless, it cannot be right to go on without any plan at all.' No coherent proposal followed. (There was a suggestion that the Americans, instead of making a contribution of 'another million or two' of soldiers to the Western Front, might make 'an overwhelming effort in the air'. Mercifully for the outcome of the war, nothing more was heard of this.) Then at the War Policy Committee of 19 June, Milner first argued that it would be worth the loss to Britain of half a million soldiers if thereby the Belgian coast was freed from the Germans, and then countered the claim that the Flanders campaign would wear down the enemy by warning that it would wear down the British as well.

One thing emerged with certainty from these nebulous gatherings: had Lloyd George come down decisively against a Flanders campaign on the scale and with the objectives which Haig was proposing, his colleagues would not have tried to overrule him. The buck stopped with the Prime Minister.

Lloyd George put forward three major propositions. The first was that a campaign in Belgium would not prosper. As Hankey, in his diary, recorded the Prime Minister's view:

> Ll. G. objects to [the undertaking] as having no decent chance of success. Russian & French cooperation are too insufficient; our superiority in men & guns too slight; the extent of the advance required in order to secure tangible results (Ostend & Zeebrugge) too great in his opinion to justify the great losses which must be involved, losses which he thinks will jeopardise our chance next year, & cause great depression.

Lloyd George's second proposition concerned a campaign in Italy. To quote Hankey again:

> Ll. G. wants to mass heavy guns on the Italian frontier, making use of Italian manpower, and dealing a blow which will compel Austria in her exhausted state to make peace.[3]

That is, Lloyd George seemed to be setting forth simple alternatives: either a Flanders campaign conducted overwhelmingly by the British; or a campaign in Italy for which Britain would provide much weaponry but few if any men. Essentially, from that straightforward dichotomy he never departed. He might make reference to other possible courses: for example to the 'Pétain' approach, which meant strictly limited operations; or to a policy of delaying the Flanders offensive until 1918 when the Americans might be present in force. But he never engaged these matters. Always, he brought the discussion back to the Italian option as the one meaningful alternative to Flanders.

Lloyd George's third proposition was that the ultimate decision between these courses must rest not with the War Cabinet or War Policy Committee (with whom constitutionally – although Lloyd George did not say this – responsibility clearly belonged) but with the military. In this he was reverting to the position he had adopted in Paris in early May 1917 in the chastened aftermath of the Nivelle fiasco. The minutes of the War Policy Committee record his view

> that the responsibility for advising in regard to military operations must remain with the military advisers. Speaking for himself, and he had little doubt that his colleagues agreed with him in this, he considered it would be too great a responsibility for the War Policy Committee to take the strategy of the War out of the hands of their military advisers.[4]

So, he went on, if the military leaders, having heard his views, 'still adhered to their previous opinion', then the responsibility must rest with them.

This third point was decisive. If told that they had the right to choose, and that the choice lay between their preferred Flanders campaign and Lloyd George's fanciful Italian option, no further word need be uttered. Haig, as he had made clear all along, was wedded to the scheme for a sweep to the Belgian coast. Robertson entertained severe doubts about this, but did not doubt that a Western Front undertaking was preferable to any diversion to Italy. An Italian campaign, he told the War Policy Committee (in Hankey's account), was

> very risky, owing to the danger of a German counter-stroke in the Trentino which will stop our attack and possibly cut off the whole Italian main army including our guns. He dreads to transfer the war to the Italian front, where he considers the Italian army unreliable and our communications inferior to those of the enemy.[5]

Robertson could have argued further: that neither Lloyd George nor himself was in a position to opt for a campaign in Italy. The most they might do was press it on the Italian authorities, who had rejected it in short order back in January. In Lloyd George's view General Cadorna, the Italian commander-in-chief, was now better disposed: but even if true, this was likely to be in circumstances where the Allies were either engaging the Germans on the Western Front or pouring troops into Italy. Italian eagerness to embark on a proceeding which would bring a considerable section of the German army against them was not evident. According to Robertson, the Italians were 'miserably afraid of the Germans' – 'They themselves have confessed as much.'[6]

Two things about all this give cause for dismay. One is Lloyd George's resort to the figment that the British military, not himself, must have the last voice in decision-making. The other is his determination to argue as if only two choices presented themselves: either a great campaign in Italy which it was not even in his power to set in motion, or a great campaign in Flanders which it certainly was. Decidedly, these were not the only choices. The one hopeful aspect of battles during 1916 and again in April 1917 had nothing to do with large strategic operations anywhere. And just at this very time when the War Policy Committee was struggling with the issue of strategy, that hopeful aspect had received stunning confirmation with the British assault on Messines Ridge. By assigning ultimate decision-making to Haig and Robertson, and by offering as the only alternative to Haig's plan not the sort of limited assaults which had already borne fruit but a foray into strategic cloud-cuckoo-land, the Prime Minister was clearing the way for the Flanders campaign.

VI

Yet having gone this far, at the last Lloyd George and the War Policy Committee drew back just a bit. They seem to have been seized by an awareness that, after all, it was not the military's business to do the deciding. What Haig was proposing was a Flanders campaign of unlimited duration. The civilian authorities refused to endorse this, opting for no more than the first stage in such an undertaking. What happened thereafter, they concluded, would be decided by themselves at the appropriate time. If the first phase of the campaign fulfilled what had been promised, the operation would proceed. If it degenerated into a slogging match akin to the Somme, it would be terminated. Attention would turn elsewhere.

So, if late in the day and with the starting pistol raised to fire, the Prime Minister appears to have realized his grave responsibility. He might not be prepared to force upon Haig the only sort of undertaking (limited attacks within artillery range) which wisdom and painful experience appeared to warrant – if only because he was no more enamoured of such undertakings than was Haig. But at least he was asserting his control over the course of operations. Haig would not be free to launch a succession of failed attacks or even to proceed from one meagre advance secured at excessive cost to another and then another. Third Ypres would either start well and consequently secure cabinet authorization to continue, or it would not start well and would be called off by the civilian authorities.

But this move into responsible decision-making, if it was to mean anything, must be accompanied by grim intent. It could only be put into effect by close oversight of what was actually occurring on the battlefield. That alone would facilitate an authoritative decision on whether accomplishment was approaching expectation or whether the command should be bluntly instructed to call a halt. It was by no means certain that a Prime Minister who periodically proclaimed that on matters of strategy the military must exercise the final decision, and whose own strategic inclinations were so little related to reality, would actually monitor Haig's operations with the steely determination which circumstances were going to require.[7]

Part II

Initiation

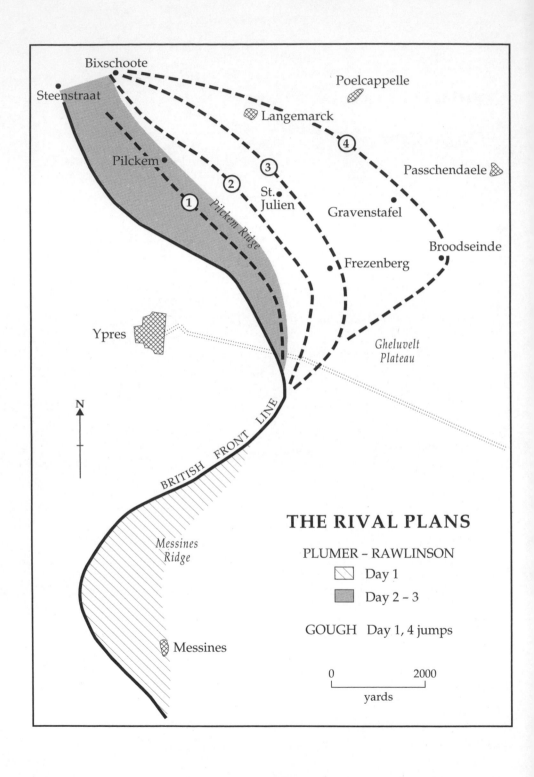

Bixschoote

Steenstraat

Poelcappelle

Langemarck

Pilckem

④

Passchendaele

③

②

St.
Julien

Gravenstafel

①

Pilckem Ridge

Broodseinde

Ypres

Frezenberg

*Gheluvelt
Plateau*

N

BRITISH FRONT LINE

THE RIVAL PLANS

PLUMER – RAWLINSON

Day 1

Day 2 – 3

GOUGH Day 1, 4 jumps

*Messines
Ridge*

Messines

0   2000

yards

5

Making Plans

I

In order to understand what Sir Douglas Haig set out to do, some recapitulation is necessary. The First and Second Battles of Ypres had left the British holding a fragment of Belgium which, on account of its symbolic importance, it was difficult to relinquish, but which placed them in a position of great tactical inferiority. From the Pilckem and Passchendaele Ridges to the north-east of Ypres, through the Gheluvelt Plateau to its east, and down to the Messines Ridge to its south, the Germans held the high ground. They could observe most movements of British troops and guns within the salient and bring down artillery fire upon them. British forces, conversely, had no direct observation over enemy positions, least of all over the great concentration of German guns concealed behind the Gheluvelt Plateau.

But, as we have seen, the Third Battle of Ypres in 1917 was not designed merely to rob the Germans of command of the high ground surrounding the salient and thereby render life more tolerable for Haig's forces within it. Haig certainly intended to capture the immediate ridges, and Passchendaele Ridge beyond that, and Klerken Ridge still further away. But he was not going to stop there. His intention was to thrust north-east to Roulers and Thourout, and then swing due north towards the Belgian coast. Simultaneously with this last phase he would launch two other operations. His forces on the coast around Nieuport would advance against the German positions at Middlekirke. And from the sea an amphibious landing would strike behind the German lines. All three operations would converge on the stretch of Belgian coast that lay between Ostend and Zeebrugge, liberating these ports and at the same time driving the enemy over the Dutch border. Haig's aim, in short, was a great strategic victory.

Planning for this operation began in November 1916. Haig told Sir

Herbert Plumer, whose Second Army had occupied the Ypres salient since 1915, to prepare an offensive from Ypres with the ultimate objective of clearing the Belgian coast.

Plumer's response can hardly have pleased his commander-in-chief. Haig had asked for a scheme which would accomplish an advance to the sea. All that Plumer came up with was a detailed proposal to capture the Messines and Pilckem Ridges, as an 'essential prelude' to operations elsewhere.[1]

Haig, meanwhile, was having his attention diverted by his involvement with the Nivelle offensive. But this did not dampen his enthusiasm for – or belief in the viability of – a large offensive out of Ypres. Indeed, he claimed that the prospects for such an operation were becoming more hopeful. For, he told Plumer early in January, the German army would have become considerably weakened by the blows rained upon it by Nivelle's assaults and by his own action at Arras.[2]

This conviction could only leave Haig dissatisfied with Plumer's limited aspirations, as revealed in the plan drawn up by him. So, despite Plumer's intimate knowledge of the Ypres salient, Haig in January 1917 turned to Sir Henry Rawlinson, who had commanded the Somme campaign in 1916. He told Rawlinson to proceed to Ypres and begin planning an offensive of which Rawlinson was to command at least the northern section.[3]

Haig went further. Just to be on the safe side, he also put to work a special section of his own GHQ staff, under Colonel Macmullen, to produce yet another proposal for an Ypres campaign.[4]

The outcome of all this was curious. Rawlinson's visit to Ypres was not a success. He and Plumer could not even agree on how to divide the salient between them. Hence he produced no plan – although he would in time comment on the plans of others. Plumer, by contrast, produced a second plan, designed to meet some of Haig's objections to his first attempt. He now proposed an initial operation intended to capture Pilckem in the north and Messines in the south, with a small advance east across part of the Gheluvelt Plateau. This would be followed in short order by further advances across the plateau, then by the capture of Passchendaele, and ultimately by a push towards the Belgian coast. He proposed that the attack by the two armies, presumably Rawlinson's in the north of the salient and his own in the south, should occur on the same day. He envisaged employing for it 42 divisions and huge quantities of artillery (some 5,000 guns).[5]

This plan had an evident flaw – there were not so many guns on the entire British sector of the Western Front.[6] So it may have been with some desperation that Haig turned to Colonel Macmullen's plan which appeared two weeks later. Macmullen proved more ambitious than

Plumer but less demanding in the matter of artillery. He would attack all three obstacles – Pilckem, Gheluvelt, and Messines – simultaneously. Concerning the problem of crowding enough artillery and troops into the salient to subdue all the German defences, Macmullen came up with a novel solution. The British artillery would deal only with Pilckem and Messines. The Gheluvelt Plateau would not be bombarded at all. It would be overrun by a mighty force of tanks. He calculated that within three days the British would be on the Passchendaele Ridge.[7]

Haig was delighted with this plan, and especially its proposal to conquer a major obstacle by tanks alone. The tank experts at GHQ, by contrast, were aghast. After investigating Macmullen's scheme they pronounced the Gheluvelt Plateau, with its swamps and dense cluster of shattered woods, utterly unsuitable for large-scale tank operations.[8] (They might have added, but did not, that any tank attack lacking massive artillery support was doomed to failure whatever site was chosen for its execution.) So despite Haig's initial enthusiasm, Macmullen's plan was swiftly shelved. Indeed, it was never heard of again.

In the absence of any offering from Rawlinson, Haig now seemed to have no choice but to accept Plumer's plan. But Plumer himself was having second thoughts. He was coming to the conclusion that an attack in the north, against Pilckem, would not succeed while the high ground at Gheluvelt remained in enemy hands.[9] So instead of opting for a simultaneous attack only in the north and south, he began proposing a staggering of his attacks, beginning with Messines and the western portion of the Gheluvelt Plateau. What he did not specify was the sort of interval that would obtain before he then got on with what, for Haig, was the real job: the capture of Pilckem and the advance to Passchendaele and points east.

So Haig turned again to the silent Rawlinson – who (as far as anyone knew) was still to command the northern half of the attack. Asked to comment on Plumer's views, Rawlinson endorsed Plumer's second version: that the attacks on Pilckem and Messines should not occur simultaneously. The first target should be Messines. If that fell, then the operation should be moved against Gheluvelt and Pilckem. However, Rawlinson was more specific than Plumer in one important respect. Maximum advantage, he argued, should be taken of German confusion following the fall of Messines. Hence there must be no great interval before the second assault was launched against the centre and the north. He recommended a gap of 48–72 hours, the minimum necessary to reorient the artillery.[10]

Rawlinson, although he could hardly have realized it, had just done himself out of a job. Haig would not again consult him on any aspect of the various Ypres plans or invite him to submit one of his own. And gradually it would dawn on Sir Henry that he was not going to be accorded command of the northern aspect of this offensive, as he had been promised. Clearly, he found it hard to discern the nature of his offence. The idea of attacking the preliminary objectives one at a time eliminated the problem of overcrowding in the Ypres salient, and served to reduce Plumer's excessive demands on British artillery. Certainly, Rawlinson's timetable for launching the follow-up attack against Pilckem and Gheluvelt might be criticized as over-optimistic – could the artillery really be repositioned and brought to bear on new targets in two or three days? But at least he was engaging an important issue which Plumer had dodged in his second scheme – how long a delay was it safe to allow the enemy before renewing the attack, once the Messines operation had made it clear that the Ypres salient was to be the scene of a major offensive?

It certainly made sense to pass over Rawlinson in favour of Plumer. Rawlinson's plan was virtually identical to that of the Second Army commander; and it made sense to concentrate the command on an individual who was already familiar with the ground. But this was not the direction in which Haig's thoughts were inclining when he decided to eliminate Rawlinson from his Ypres offensive.

The progress of Haig's thoughts is extraordinary. In discussing the proposed Ypres offensive with Nivelle in March and with Plumer in April, Haig had emphasized one issue: the time-gap between the attack in the south of the salient and that in the north. In March he had seemed to accept Rawlinson's proposal for an interval of a few days.[11] But then in mid-April he pressed Plumer to agree that it might be possible to attack all three objectives simultaneously. Plumer, although making his misgivings clear, went part-way to agreeing. He offered simultaneous operations against two, but not all three, of the obstacles.[12] Did Plumer but realize it, he was about to share a variant of Rawlinson's fate. He would retain a subordinate role in the Ypres undertaking, but he would not be the army commander accorded its overall direction. And Haig would not again ask his views on the timing of its initiation.

II

On 7 May 1917, without a word of warning, Haig produced a new timetable for the inception of Third Ypres. The occasion was an army commanders' conference at Doullens. It took place in ominous circumstances. The Nivelle offensive had failed disastrously. And Hubert Gough, the commander of Haig's Fifth Army, was at that very moment conducting a particularly costly attack at Bullecourt in what would prove to be the last stage of the Arras offensive. As a consequence of all this, the elimination of the German reserves during the Franco-British operation, which Haig had foreseen as rendering an Ypres offensive altogether more viable, had scarcely been accomplished.

The situation was highly ambiguous. Nivelle's catastrophic failure had cleared the way for the campaign nearest to Haig's heart: Third Ypres. It had also rendered more precarious his prospects of success.

In this opaque setting, Haig at Doullens informed his army commanders that the main British effort would be switched to Ypres, 'with the ultimate objective of securing the Belgian Coast and of obtaining other strategical results'. He also told them that he had resolved the dilemma of allowing a gap of some days between attacks on the various ridges or of attempting to deliver them simultaneously. He was now opting for neither. He proposed dividing these operations into two distinct phases. The attack on Messines would take place on 7 June; that on the other objectives, Pilckem and Gheluvelt, would follow 'some weeks later' – in fact, at the end of July.[13] In other words, the issue of whether his forces should attack Pilckem, Gheluvelt, and Messines simultaneously, as he had hitherto urged, or a few days apart, as Rawlinson had suggested and Plumer had dithered about, was being decided in the most startling way. There would be a gap, but it would not be a matter of days. Seven weeks would elapse between the attack on Messines and the attack on the other objectives. No one up to that point, and least of all Haig himself, had contemplated such a proceeding.

How do we explain this change? It is sometimes suggested that the British were obliged to act prematurely at Messines, and so to show their hand regarding the forthcoming operations at Ypres, for one or other of two reasons. The first concerned threatened action by the Germans. Beneath the Messines Ridge Plumer's forces had, over the years, excavated 21 great mines which they had packed with explosive. The detonation of the mines was vital to the attack on Messines, and in this scenario a fear was developing among the British commanders that the enemy were about to discover what was going on. Should this happen it would invalidate the opening phase of the Ypres operation. Hence the attack at Messines went ahead before it was possible to mount the offensive as a whole.

This hypothesis is groundless. There is no evidence that Plumer or Haig were concerned about the security of the mines. The Second Army intelligence files recording the regular interrogation of Germans captured around Messines convey no hint that the enemy were aware of their peril.[14] Nor, during this period, did Haig express to Plumer any anxiety about the mining aspect of his plan.

What is more, if the Germans had suspected the impending detonation of a great many mines under their positions at Messines, their only sensible response would have been immediate withdrawal from the ridge. That would have served Haig's purpose very nicely. Plumer's troops could then have occupied the Messines position without delivering a big attack and so without indicating to the Germans that operations there were the first stage of a major campaign.

The second reason sometimes put forward to explain the long interval which Haig had decided should follow Plumer's strike at Messines focuses on the condition of the French army. In the aftermath of Nivelle's calamitous failure, it is suggested, the French would have crumbled in the face of a German assault. Haig needed by swift action to pin German attention to his own sector of the Western Front.

There is nothing in this. It is true that major sections of the French army had mutinied: that is, had refused to persist in hopeless attacks. It does not follow that the Germans, even had they known anything about this, were in any position to switch from their rigidly defensive posture in the west to an all-out offensive. What is more, it is plain that in early May, when Haig unveiled his new plan to his army commanders, the British commander-in-chief himself knew no more about the parlous state of the French army than did the Germans. He was certainly aware that Nivelle's great offensive had not prospered and was being reconsidered. But Haig had had plenty of experience of being required to call off a failed offensive without there being any suggestion that his army (notwithstanding seemingly good cause) was in a state of mutiny. It was not until the first week of June, by which time the attack at Messines was imminent, that Haig learned from General Debeney that the French army was worn down and its morale seriously impaired.[15]

If Haig was not influenced either by fears for the secrecy of the mines, or by the condition of the French, we can only speculate as to why he chose to act at Messines seven weeks in advance of the main operation. He was certainly anxious to get the campaign under way as soon as possible. And by early June he would have transferred sufficient artillery northwards to be in a position to carry out an attack on one of the ridges. Further, he already had Plumer's plan available. Messines was the obvious first target. The mines were in place, so a large part of the undertaking could proceed expeditiously. And Messines was the pre-eminent high point overlooking the salient.

On the other hand we know that Haig was determined to introduce a new man to command his great offensive – Sir Hubert Gough. In most respects Gough seemed ill-qualified for the task. He had not commanded a major campaign. His recent operations at Bullecourt had proved alarmingly barren. He had no close acquaintance with the Ypres salient.

So his participation in a Belgian campaign hardly seemed so full of promise as to warrant the introduction of a long interval between the attack on Messines and the main offensive – with a consequent loss both of surprise and of good campaigning weather.

But with all this against him, Gough had two qualifications which, in Sir Douglas Haig's scale of values, marked him out for the post of commander at Third Ypres. He was a devotee of the 'hurroosh' – the rapid advance. The essentially 'bite and hold' mentality of Rawlinson and Plumer was not for him, any more than it reflected Haig's cast of mind. Hence whereas the other potential commanders might genuflect towards the Belgian coast before getting down to the serious business of enlarging the Ypres salient, Haig had in Gough a man who – like himself – would actually fix his gaze on distant objectives.

Gough's second qualification for the job was simply his lack of qualifications. His limited experience and indifferent record rendered him, when entrusted with a large undertaking, peculiarly dependent on the commander-in-chief. So Gough would endeavour to carry out to the full Haig's wishes. But of course the choice of the new man meant that time would be needed for him to establish a headquarters, familiarize himself with the ground, and produce a plan. So the introduction of Gough also inexorably meant the introduction of a significant gap between the operation at Messines and the commencement of the main campaign.

Haig managed to convince himself that this was not of consequence. He produced an involved scenario whereby the Germans would not recognize the assault at Messines as being the first stage of a large undertaking, and so would not respond by strengthening defences and massing reserves in that region. He expounded this view at the conference with his army commanders on 7 May where he pointed out that he did not possess sufficient reserves to maintain two offensives simultaneously, namely the offensive he was presently conducting at Arras and the offensive on his preferred front at Ypres. So resources would necessarily be run down at Arras, and ammunition and guns transferred to Ypres. But he intended to convince the enemy (and for that matter his own troops) that 'the main battle front' continued to be that at Arras. And he believed that, even when the attack at Messines was launched early in June, the enemy might still be misled into believing that this was not the first phase of an offensive at Ypres.

To ensure that the enemy failed to realize the significance of the Messines operation, Haig would continue – even after the capture of Messines – to mount attacks at Arras. He would manage to do so by bringing to the Arras sector some of his forces currently on the Somme whom he expected would soon be relieved by the French. And to ensure that the programme of deceit was complete, he would arrange that the transfer of guns and ammunition from the phoney offensive at Arras to the real campaign at Ypres would occur so gradually that the enemy might not detect what was really afoot. Thus, when Haig's forces attacked Pilckem at the end of July, the Germans would (on this hypothesis) be no readier to receive them than they had been prior to Messines early in June.[16]

This deception plan was based on very dubious premises. Haig had already pointed out that he did not have the guns and men to launch offensives at both Arras and Ypres, yet he was expecting the Germans not to notice that he was acting offensively at Arras only with token weaponry and forces hastily assembled. And he was gambling on the enemy's remaining deluded even after the British had struck against the Messines Ridge.

In the event, the plan faded to nothingness in the weeks that followed its unveiling. On the Arras front, because of the rapid displacements of guns northwards and the depleted state of the divisions holding the line, the British kept up attacks there only until the middle of May.[17] They made no attacks at all in June and July. As for the transfer of troops from the Somme, which was supposed to facilitate further token action at Arras, this never took place because the French would not co-operate. Pétain explained to Haig that he could not facilitate substantial relief of British divisions on the Somme. In lieu, he offered six French divisions to operate to the north of the British in Flanders as an integral part of the Ypres attack.[18] Haig immediately accepted this offer. No doubt he was pleased to receive French commitment to his main operation. But he did not seem to notice that Pétain's actions spelt the demise of another aspect of the deception plan. For if British divisions on the Somme could not be relieved, then Haig would have no fresh troops to maintain the impression of an active front at Arras in June and July.

Haig's deception plan, in sum, seemed to have the capacity only to deceive Sir Douglas himself.

III

In sum, Haig's actions in the period of finalizing preparations for Third Ypres were characterized by uncertainty of purpose. He switched planners alarmingly. He vacillated between Rawlinson and Plumer as potential commanders. He altered the timing of operations, first objecting to a gap of as long as three days between the first and second strikes and then opting for an interval of seven weeks.

Yet in the most important respect, there was no uncertainty. Haig was determined on one big thing, and would play fast and loose with plans and timing and commanders to ensure that he got it. The big thing was a campaign designed to burst out of the Ypres salient and sweep all the way to the Belgian coast. The plans of Plumer and Rawlinson, whatever their merits, had one great demerit. While paying lip-service to Haig's grand design, they were actually a set of deliberate steps aimed only at taking in stages the high ground overlooking the salient.

In short, Haig's yearning for a great strategic undertaking at Third Ypres had consequences which introduced an element of jeopardy into the whole campaign. One was the allocation of overall direction to his least qualified army commander. The other was the introduction of an unwarranted interval into what should have been the first two stages of an integrated undertaking.

All this had an immediate result: it raised the distinct possibility that an initial success at Messines would not greatly benefit the subsequent course of the campaign.

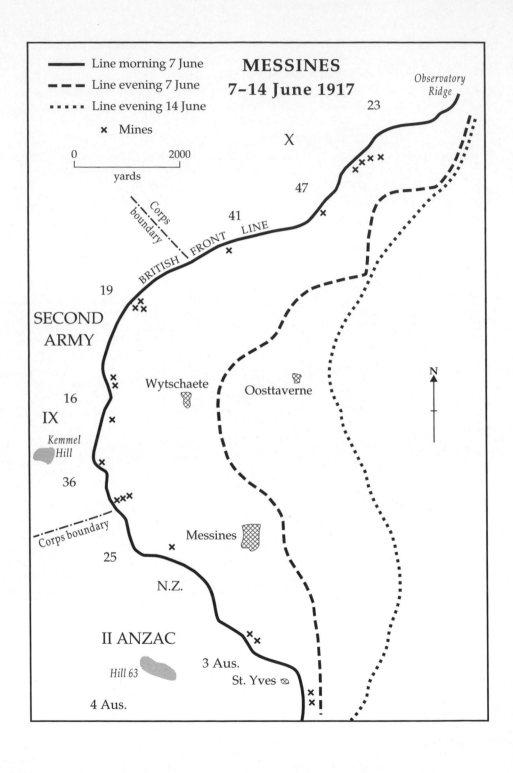

MESSINES
7–14 June 1917

Line morning 7 June
Line evening 7 June
Line evening 14 June
× Mines

0   2000
yards

Observatory Ridge

23

X

47

41

Corps boundary

BRITISH FRONT LINE

19

SECOND ARMY

16

IX

Kemmel Hill

36

Corps boundary

25

N.Z.

II ANZAC

Hill 63

4 Aus.

Wytschaete

Oosttaverne

Messines

3 Aus.

St. Yves

N

6

False Dawn: Messines

I

Haig, it will be recalled, had decided on 7 May to split his northern offensive into two distinct attacks, separated by seven weeks. The first of these was to be conducted by Plumer's Second Army. Its objective was the capture of the Messines Ridge from which 'the Germans could watch every detail of any preparations the British might make for an offensive eastwards between Ypres and the Belgian coast'.[1]

Although the Messines Ridge was a position of considerable strength, earlier battles in 1917 had seen some hopeful developments for limited offensives against objectives of this type. In particular these developments related to artillery.

In March and April the British Third and First Armies had instituted artillery planning in the most meticulous detail for the capture of the Arras and Vimy positions. For Vimy the exact length of trench to be assailed and wire to be cut had been calculated and the appropriate guns and shells assigned to the task.[2] In the matter of troop protection nothing was left to chance. The attacking infantry were not only preceded by a creeping barrage, but in front of that fell further barrages of machine-gun bullets, light howitzer shells, and a final curtain of fire from the medium and heavy howitzers. In all a moving barrage of shells some 500 yards deep fell continuously in front of the infantry for the 7.5 hour duration of the attack. Even then artillery protection did not cease. A standing barrage of 200–300 yards in width continued to shield the infantry from enemy counter-attack until nightfall.[3] A third element in the new thinking related to counter-battery. At the Somme this was usually fired only by those guns which remained after guns had been allocated to other tasks, such as trench destruction. At Arras the reverse was the case. Counter-battery work received absolute priority. Where the German artillery was unexpectedly reinforced, batteries engaged in trench destruction were switched to deal with the newly deployed enemy guns.[4]

Moreover at Arras/Vimy the guns had a greater chance than ever of hitting their targets. Sound-ranging sections were used across the whole front of attack for the first time. In addition flash spotters were employed extensively, as were more traditional methods of artillery spotting such as observation balloons, aircraft, and FOOs. And all these sources of information were to be linked to a central artillery intelligence unit so that the whereabouts of the enemy guns could be disseminated to the appropriate counter-batteries in optimum time.[5]

All this was made possible because, at last, Haig's army had a sufficiency of guns and ammunition. For the spring offensive the First and Third Armies possessed 2,817 guns of which 863 were heavy or medium calibre.[6] For the Vimy sector alone 50,000 tons of ammunition was available for the guns. Moreover, the ammunition was high quality and some of it was equipped with the new 106 fuse which ensured that it exploded on impact, thus making it particularly effective against barbed-wire entanglements.[7] These figures may be compared to those of the Somme, where over a wider front of attack the British had just 1,400 guns, of which 380 were heavy or medium. And at the Somme British ammunition fuses had been notoriously unreliable, 30 per cent of some calibres failing to explode and an alarming number detonating prematurely.

These new artillery methods had been sufficient, on 9 April 1917, to ensure a major advance at Arras and the overrunning of the Vimy Ridge. They could not, however, ensure further successes. The exact position of the more distant German trench lines and fortifications had to be discovered and registered once more by the guns, and the great task of hauling the guns into new positions for a second attack had to be undertaken. Unfortunately for the troops, the British command were persistently of the belief that German morale was on the verge of collapse, and so not of a mind to await these developments. Attacks were ordered before the enemy positions had been reliably established and before adequate artillery preparations could be made. The result was that operations at Arras developed into a slogging match of a type only too familiar from the Somme. So for Plumer, in planning his attack, there was a warning as well as a message of hope to be gleaned from Haig's spring offensive.

There was even a hopeful message to be gained from the Nivelle offensive. That operation is usually seen as a disaster – after all, the French armies did engage in 'collective indiscipline' as a result of it. But the reaction of the French soldiers probably stemmed from the exaggerated claims that Nivelle had been making. It remains the fact that, in his first weeks, Nivelle captured the heights of the Chemin des Dames using methods similar to those employed by the British at Arras/Vimy. At one point in the opening days, so panic-stricken did the Germans become that they voluntarily gave up a considerable amount of ground lest they should be destroyed by the French artillery.[8]

It is a sorry comment on the dissemination of information by the higher commands on the Western Front that the methods used to achieve success by one army commander might be completely unknown to another. However, by 1917 there were many in positions of command who were quite capable of divining for themselves that the limited offensive held the key to a type of success. So while there is no evidence that Plumer received detailed information on the methods employed by the First and Third Armies or by the French, it is clear from his battle preparations that he had grasped the essentials of the new techniques. What remained to be seen was whether his commander-in-chief had also grasped them.

II

As already noted, Plumer had been planning for the Messines operation since January – although until May it had been envisaged as the southern section of near-simultaneous attacks encompassing all of the Ypres salient. His first detailed plan for the Messines aspect of the Ypres campaign reached Haig in mid-March. It called for an attack on the ridge by nine divisions (three each from X, IX, and II Anzac Corps). First there would be a preliminary bombardment lasting four days. Then, at zero, would come the explosion of the 21 mines (containing a total of one million pounds of TNT) which had been placed under the German front line over a long period. The infantry would thereupon advance and occupy these devastated positions.

That was all Plumer intended for the first day. For the following day he proposed that the remaining high ground be captured together with Wytschaete village. At its furthest extent the operation would advance the British line 1,500 yards.[9]

Haig's reply, early in April, showed that he was not satisfied with this modest proposal. For the first day he wanted Plumer to capture not just the high ground he had specified but also the fortified village of Messines. He also wished Plumer to consider advancing on subsequent days to the line Courtrai–Roulers, a distance of between 20 and 30 miles! (These towns, it may be noted in passing, would only fall to the British when the Germans evacuated them late in 1918.) Haig did enter one note of caution. No attack should even commence until the barbed wire had been cut. To allow enough time for this to be accomplished, wire-cutting should commence well before the proposed four-day bombardment. For the Messines attack, Haig offered 635 medium and heavy guns and 600 lighter pieces in addition to the field artillery of the nine assaulting divisions.[10]

Plumer went some way towards meeting Haig's objections. He promised that wire-cutting would commence well in advance of the preliminary bombardment. And he agreed to try and capture Messines and Wytschaete on the first day, providing the initial attack developed according to plan. But regarding an advance on Courtrai–Roulers he remained noncommittal, saying that he needed to know what additional troops were going to be provided.[11]

III

At this point the planning for northern operations halted, as Haig turned his attention to the Arras/Vimy offensive. Only in May did the commander-in-chief return to consideration of Messines. He did not again propose including Courtrai and Roulers among the early objectives, but he clearly still hankered after something more ambitious than Plumer had proposed. To facilitate this, on 5 May he informed Plumer that he was adding over 100 medium and heavy guns to his complement of 635.[12] Their purpose, although not specified in this communication, may be inferred from Plumer's operations order of five days later. Not only was the Second Army to press on to Messines and Wytschaete on the morning of the attack, but during the afternoon of the same day it was to advance beyond them down the far side of the ridge. Its new objective was the capture of the German guns around an intermediate position called the Oostaverne Line.[13]

Haig had thereby doubled (to 3,000 yards) the proposed distance of advance. This entailed the suppression of an additional line of German defences. Plumer, as far as the records reveal, did not protest against the extension of his objectives. Perhaps he concluded that further dispute was pointless. But it is possible that he was coming to agree that, with the additional instruments now to hand, he might achieve Haig's purpose.

IV

The situation confronting the British at Messines was not without some hopeful features. Certainly, the German position on the ridge looked formidable. The front line ran along the high ground from Observatory

Ridge to St Yves. On the top of the ridge itself a second system protected the villages of Messines and Wytschaete, which were themselves fortified. Some 1,000–2,000 yards behind these villages, on the reverse slope of the ridge, lay the Oostaverne Line. All lines were heavily wired and supplemented by concrete pillboxes which could contain machine-guns, or a small garrison of infantry, or both.

Nevertheless the German position was not as strong as these details might suggest. Despite the elevated ground on which the German defences were situated, the British had good observation over some of them from even higher ground around Kemmel Hill and Hill 63, in rear of their own front. Further, the Germans suffered from the disadvantage of occupying a salient. British artillery placed on the northern and southern flanks of the attack could fire in enfilade directly along the German first and second lines, making these positions difficult to hold in strength.

Plumer had additional grounds to be hopeful. To ensure the accuracy of his bombardment, he needed not just the observation posts provided by the high ground behind his front line but a great array of aerial spotters. As preparations for the campaign proceeded, British command of the air – and therefore effective observation for the artillery – became ever more pronounced. By the time the preliminary bombardment opened up, 300 British machines were available – about twice the number opposing them in the area of the battle.[14]

Similarly, a superiority in the key weapon of artillery became steadily apparent. Unlike the major operations on the Somme a year before, but in accordance with the methods employed at Arras in April, the number of guns now provided for a British offensive was carefully calculated according to the amount of wire to be cut, the length of trench to be destroyed, and the number of German batteries to be subdued.[15] In all, it was estimated that 1,510 field and 756 heavy guns would be sufficient to accomplish these tasks.[16] To ensure that the guns would not be idle, 144,000 tons of shell were transported to the Second Army front before zero day.[17]

Against this powerful array, the Germans could dispose merely 344 field and 404 medium and heavy guns.[18] Overall, therefore, they were outnumbered by approximately five to one in field and two to one in heavy artillery.

A factor beyond the control of the British command came to Plumer's aid. Aerial and artillery superiority could count for nothing in poor visibility. Observation of artillery shoots, aerial photography of German positions, and identification of German guns by flash spotting were all dependent on periods of clear weather. In the weeks leading up to the battle one fine day followed another. With this last piece of the jigsaw in place, Plumer had cause for looking towards the coming operation with at least some prospect of success.

The process of wire-cutting, counter-battery fire against the German guns, and the destruction of such German strongholds as Wytschaete and Messines villages began on 21 May and became intense on the 31st.[19] Despite British superiority, the contest was by no means one-sided. As late as 29 May Second Army intelligence reported heavy enemy artillery retaliation along the whole front.[20] Moreover, during the course of the bombardment the Germans reinforced their artillery and much time and resources had to be devoted to locating and neutralizing these new guns.[21] In time, nevertheless, weight of numbers told. Wire was comprehensively cut, trench lines smashed in, and Wytschaete and Messines reduced to rubble. From 1 June enemy artillery fire began to slacken. Before long the Germans' reply to practice barrages for the great attack could be described as feeble. Prisoners taken during the many raids mounted to check on the destruction proved in a stunned condition, and their defences, except for the pillboxes, were described as non-existent.[22]

V

Before these assessments could be put to the test, one particularly anxious moment had to be passed through. It had been intended all along that the infantry would go into the attack in the immediate aftermath of the explosion of the mines. But this scenario was thrown into doubt when, on 29 May, Haig drew Plumer's attention to evidence that the Germans were preparing to evacuate their trenches on the ridge. British troops might, he observed, take the opportunity to occupy these positions once the Germans had gone, but this would mean losing the opportunity to detonate the mines. Perhaps, he argued, the best plan would be to explode the mines immediately, which would have the added advantage of getting the Germans to disclose the whereabouts of guns hitherto silent.[23]

This was a curious response. If the Germans were about to evacuate the ridge, then a large part of Haig's purpose might be achieved without having to mount a large-scale attack. Further positions could then be taken at leisure from the heights on the ridge. Moreover, the intact divisions of the Second Army might be available for more rapid action against the Ypres salient than had been anticipated. In other words it might be possible to bring forward the timetable for the whole summer offensive. None of this seems to have crossed the mind of the commander-in-chief. All that concerned him was that the great effort put into mining operations might go for nothing; he seems to have forgotten that, after all, the aim of those operations was to establish the British on the ridge.

In the event nothing came of this flurry. Plumer assured Haig that the Germans were not about to abandon their front line, and that practice barrages were being added to the artillery programme in an endeavour to induce the Germans to disclose the position of any silent guns.[24] So the plan would proceed as laid down.

VI

At 3.10 a.m. on 7 June 1917, the order was given to explode the mines under the German front positions. Their detonation produced what, up till then, was the largest man-made explosion in recorded history. It reached London in the form of a muffled roar, while 15 miles away in Lille the citizens thought they were experiencing an earthquake. A German account describes the effect on their front positions.

> The ground trembled as in a natural earthquake, heavy concrete shelters rocked, a hurricane of hot air from the explosion swept back for many kilometres, dropping fragments of wood, iron and earth, and gigantic black clouds of smoke and dust spread over the country. The effect on the troops was overpowering and crushing ... the trenches were now the graves of our infantry.[25]

Immediately after the explosions the British artillery opened fire, placing a barrage 700 yards deep ahead of their advancing infantry.

The ensuing battle fell into four phases. The first of them, consisting of the capture of the German front line, was accomplished quickly and with few casualties. The detonation of the mines had buried or destroyed most of the front German garrison. The remainder, in the words of one divisional report, 'fled in all directions'.[26] In consequence, the attacking infantry encountered little of the habitual machine-gun fire.[27] Further, effective British counter-battery fire ensured that German artillery retaliation was feeble.

The only unhappy experience during this phase befell 3 Australian Division attacking on the southern flank. Their approach march to the front happened to coincide with a severe gas shelling by the enemy. Some battalions lost 10 per cent of their force before they even reached the front, and altogether somewhere between 500 and 1,000 men were incapacitated.[28] Even so, the devastation wrought by mines and shelling on the enemy front lines proved so compelling that 'enemy resistance was almost absent' and so the depleted Australians managed to take their first objective.[29]

The second phase, the capture of the crest of the ridge, followed almost immediately. Opposition proved greater, but was generally only patchy. So the New Zealanders did encounter some resistance in Messines village,[30] whereas the rubble that was Wytschaete fell to 16 Division with scarcely a shot being fired.[31] Sometimes the garrisons of pillboxes managed to offer resistance, but because of their isolation they were soon dealt with by outflanking parties. By 9 a.m., less than six hours after the mines had gone off, the ridge was in British hands.

The third phase consisted of consolidation. The troops on the ridge commenced digging trenches and preparing for the assault of the coun-ter-attack divisions. In the event no counter-attacks developed. The enemy had apparently not yet digested the lesson of the opening phase of Arras, and had once again held too far back the forces intended to recover the lost ground. In fact by 8 a.m. the counter-attack regiments were still crossing the river Lys.[32] That was not the only shortcoming in this aspect of German preparations. So intense had been the British preliminary bombardment that two of the designated *Eingraff* (counter-attack) divisions had been diverted to relieving battered front-line units. The formations called in to replace them were unfamiliar with the ground and in their approach to the front allowed themselves to be split into small units. They were easily thrown back by British artillery or, in some cases, by infantry alone.[33]

The way seemed clear for the last phase of the day's operations. This was Haig's addition to the original Plumer proposal: the advance down the far side of the ridge to the Oostaverne Line. But here matters began to go awry. For one thing, German batteries – many of which the British had hoped to capture in their advance – had been removed behind the Oostaverne Line following the commencement of the attack. These now opened fire on the crowded British troops clearly outlined on the crest of the ridge.[34] Casualties began to mount, and units so far largely unscathed found themselves suffering severely. Then as the troops of the reinforcing divisions left the ridge positions and started to advance down towards the Oostaverne Line they were hit by British batteries firing the protective barrage in front of the troops consolidating on the ridge. The advancing formations were forced to fall back, and when these movements were seen by the British artillery observers it was assumed that they were taking place as a result of enemy counter-attack. Consequently the British gunners shortened the range, but by too great a margin. Their fire now landed squarely on the original attacking forces entrenched on the ridge. So by mid-afternoon all British formations on the battle front had been deluged by artillery fire, most of which came from their own guns.[35] By the end of the day one division (25) had suffered 2,750 casualties, 90 per cent of them caused by artillery fire from one side or the other.[36]

The result was that, particularly in the south where German and British fire was heaviest, the Oostaverne Line remained in enemy hands that day. Only in the ensuing week, as the Germans came to realize that this position was becoming increasingly disadvantageous once the British had gained command of the high ground, did they decide to withdraw to a defensive line further back. With Haig's objectives of 7 June in British hands by the 14th, the Messines operations came to an end.[37]

VII

For the Germans, the Messines operation – with its sequence of preliminary bombardment, the ferocious detonation of some nineteen great mines (two having failed to explode), and a savage creeping barrage ahead of an infantry attack – must have been an unpleasant experience from the start. The British experience, arguably, was different. It began as something of a cakewalk, but in the ensuing days became a grim contest conducted with increasing ferocity.

We have some evidence of the savagery of the battle's last phase in a diary account of Private Gallwey, a member of 47 Battalion, 4 Australian Division. This division was engaged in the final, costly, phase of the battle; it had already suffered heavily at Bullecourt earlier in the year and had not expected to be used again so soon in a major encounter. The mood of the troops as they prepared for Messines was therefore pretty grim. Nor did the circumstances in which Gallwey's battalion entered the battle improve matters. As they lay waiting to advance towards the Oostaverne Line they were heavily shelled by German artillery. Then, as they moved forward, Gallwey's section came under machine-gun fire from a blockhouse. His diary now takes up the story.

> The gun in this block house was now silenced by our machine guns so we moved on again. Walked right up to the place and a couple of men went to the entrance where the gun crew was found all huddled up inside. They had evidently been wounded and killed by our fire. No time was lost here however and [our] . . . men fired point blank into the group. There was a noise as though pigs were being killed. They squealed and made guttural noises which gave place to groans after which all was silent. The bodies were all thrown in a heap outside the block house to make sure all were dead. There were five of them altogether. It was a good thing this hornets nest had been cleaned out so easily. Nearly all were young men.

It is an impossibility to leave wounded germans [*sic*] behind us because they are so treacherous. They all have to be killed. Too often after an advance, our men have been shot in the back by the wounded they left on the field. Now to obviate such a thing, we have what is called a 'mopping up party'. This consists of a small number of troops and [they] despatch any of the enemy who might have been passed over in the first rush. Sometimes in our hurry we leave a wounded man and then the duty of the mopping up party is to finish him. Their work would be light today for we are determined to kill every german [*sic*] we come across.[38]

VIII

There was a curious epilogue to the Messines offensive. Before the battle, Haig had drawn Plumer's attention to the fact that it might be possible, in the confusion that would befall the Germans, for the Second Army troops to the north of the battle front (VIII and II Corps) to seize a portion of the Gheluvelt Plateau. This would be a great aid to Gough's subsequent operations in that area. As a result plans were made to exploit any success at Messines by advancing about 700 yards across the Gheluvelt Plateau.[39]

In the immediate aftermath of Messines Haig asked Plumer if he was in a position to carry out these plans. Plumer replied that he was, but that he would need three days in which to get the supporting artillery in place.[40] This was in fact a very optimistic response, considering the confusion into which the British artillery had fallen during the battle. But for inexplicable reasons, Haig considered the delay excessive. On 8 June he ordered Plumer to hand over VIII and II Corps to Gough and instructed the Fifth Army commander to prepare a plan for action on the Gheluvelt Plateau. Gough, not surprisingly, asked for a few days to study the problem. This Haig granted him, though it meant a longer delay than that proposed by Plumer. By the time Gough had considered the operation, six days had elapsed and German defences on the plateau had been considerably strengthened. Gough therefore concluded that further activities here should await his main attack six weeks later. Haig, bewilderingly, concurred.[41] So the only consequence of the commander-in-chief's determination on a hasty sequel to Messines was no action whatever.

IX

The Messines operation had been a noteworthy success. The combination of an ample and well-delivered artillery bombardment, the devastating explosion of the mines, and a creeping barrage capable of providing a degree of protection for the attacking infantry had facilitated the seizure of one of those dominating areas overlooking the Ypres salient.

There was also a pointer here to further fruitful undertakings. Certainly, in one respect Messines was a one-off success. The employment of mines as a springboard for the infantry was simply unrepeatable. It had been the product of a front line that had moved scarcely a yard over more than two years. And detection of mining activities had now become so effective that the war underground was ceasing to be viable. But the artillery aspect of Messines was another story. The massive accumulation of guns and shells, the unrelenting preliminary bombardment of trenches and strongpoints, the employment of aerial spotting and other means of observation to enable counter-battery units to suppress the enemy guns, and the wall of protection accorded the infantry by the creeping barrage, all combined to proclaim an important development in the war of the trenches. An infantry attack launched at objectives within artillery range was not fore-doomed to failure and massive human loss.

Yet Messines was also important for what it had not achieved, or had achieved only partially and at excessive cost. The whole operation had not been cheap, with a British casualty toll of 25,000.[42] And it had proved to hold no potential for opening a way to regions beyond certain limited goals. Plumer, significantly, had originally opted for an advance of 1,500 yards; and on the day he managed to accomplish this with only moderate losses. But Haig was determined on more: an advance on the first day alone of between 3,000 and 4,000 yards. The extra distance was quite another proposition, requiring a week to accomplish and costing Plumer most of his casualties. And by the time the week was out, the operation had clearly yielded all it had to offer. Messines provided no evidence that the Third Ypres campaign was likely to achieve the wide-ranging goals fundamental to Haig's conception. Had it been immediately followed up, it might have aided in further successful limited operations around the salient. It did not point in more grandiose directions.

Messines, then, on account of the nature of the war along with the decision of the high command, proved an isolated event. It had many helpful lessons to teach about the correct marrying of infantry with artillery, as well as a sobering lesson about the limited accomplishment that was to be expected even of a thoroughly prepared operation. What in ensuing weeks would become evident was that these lessons were of equally little interest to Britain's military commanders and to their political masters.

So time and good weather passed. Direction of the main operation moved to an army chief whom Haig had deemed capable of attaining more than Plumer seemed even prepared to contemplate. And the country's political leaders pondered what was being proposed.

Part III
Gough

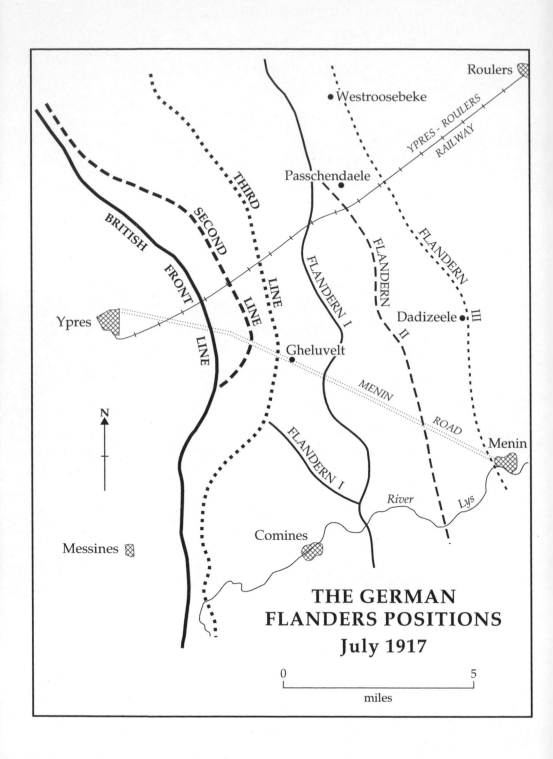

Roulers

• Westroosebeke

YPRES - ROULERS RAILWAY

Passchendaele

BRITISH

SECOND

THIRD

LINE

FLANDERN I

FLANDERN II

FLANDERN III

FRONT

LINE

Ypres

Dadizeele •

Gheluvelt

MENIN ROAD

LINE

Menin

N

FLANDERN I

River   Lys

Messines

Comines

**THE GERMAN
FLANDERS POSITIONS**

July 1917

0   5

miles

7

The New Commander

I

Even before Haig had settled on Gough as commander of the main attack at Ypres, he had chosen Sir Henry Rawlinson to conduct the coastal aspect of the plan. We last encountered Sir Henry back in February as a commentator on the plans of General Plumer. Those comments did not win the approval of the commander-in-chief and Rawlinson had been sidelined. Now, in early April, Rawlinson was informed that after all he would play a role in the campaign – not as the instigator of the main attack but as the commander of the coastal operation that would be launched in time to meet Gough's armies as they debouched from the high ground beyond Roulers and Thourout.

The idea of an operation along the Belgian coast was of long standing. It had been suggested by Sir John French early in 1915. In 1916 it had been revived by Joffre, who brought forth a plan to land five divisions from the sea in conjunction with a coastal advance.[1] The plan appealed to Haig, not as an autonomous operation, but as part of his grand design for Third Ypres. As Gough's armies swept towards Ostend from the south-west, he would propel a force under Rawlinson along the coast. Simultaneously he would land one division (Joffre's plan to employ five divisions took no account of the difficulty of this type of operation or the need for specialized landing craft) from the sea behind enemy lines. All British forces would then link up and advance on Zeebrugge, thereby unhinging the German hold on coastal Belgium.[2]

On 22 June Rawlinson took up his new command at Nieuport. The force assigned to him was the XV Corps. The drive up the coast would be undertaken by two divisions with two in reserve,[3] while one division would land from the sea between Middlekerke and Westende.[4]

The preparations for these operations were soon to be disrupted. The Germans had noted the appearance of XV Corps on the coast and correctly appreciated that it heralded some kind of attack. On 10 July the Germans launched a pre-emptive strike near Lombartzyde. By the end of the day Rawlinson's force had been driven back across the river Yser, except for a small bridgehead to the west of Nieuport. It would be from this cramped position (only a few hundred yards in extent) that any coastal advance would hereafter have to be made.[5]

Despite this setback, preparations continued. The 1st Division was withdrawn from the line for training in amphibious operations. Special pontoons to carry troops and equipment were built, tanks practised climbing the kind of sea walls that would confront them, and shallow-draught monitors which could sail close inshore to engage the many coastal batteries were placed at the ready.[6]

The amphibious aspect of the plan was hazardous in the extreme. The German batteries were numerous, the slow-moving monitors and pontoons unprotected by armour. Moreover, the wall-climbing tanks were a dubious proposition. The walls were 30 feet high, their gradients steep – probably too steep for the traction of the tanks, which in any case were mechanically unreliable. In addition the Germans kept a mobile force of counter-attack troops in the area to deal with just such an operation. As a last resort they could flood the whole area.[7]

However, for the operation to take place at all, Gough's attack from the Ypres salient would first have to make considerable progress. In particular it would need to penetrate the German defences to a considerable depth in the first few days. On the coast, therefore, all depended on Gough.

II

Already by 30 April, Haig had chosen Gough to conduct the Third Ypres offensive. Yet it would be two months before Gough took up his new post. In the interval he conducted, in the Arras sector, the memorably bloody and ill-rewarded Second Battle of Bullecourt.[8] As a result of this prolongation of the Arras offensive, valuable time elapsed during which Gough and his staff might have been familiarizing themselves with the Ypres battlefield.

In the event, Fifth Army headquarters was established on 1 June in Lovie château, 'a large, pretentious, ugly square building' just north of Poperinge.[9] As his chief of staff, Gough took with him Neill Malcolm – a harsh and unsympathetic individual who as the campaign proceeded managed (according to a leading military historian) to poison relations between Gough and his corps commanders.[10] A rather happier choice was that of Major-General Herbert Uniacke, who had been with Gough since the early days of the Somme, as director of Fifth Army's artillery.

III

Gough's prime task was to overwhelm the German defences facing the Fifth Army. This was no small undertaking, for (especially as compared with those at Arras) these defences were truly formidable and becoming more so with every day that passed.

The skeleton of the German defensive system had been in place for some months.[11] In addition to the German front line, there were from early 1917 three trench systems. The second line ran from Bixschoote in the north, along the reverse slope of the Pilckem Ridge, and then across the Gheluvelt Plateau. The third line, located 2,000 yards further back, commenced at Langemarck and proceeded to Gravenstafel, where it turned sharply and joined the second line on the Gheluvelt Plateau near Glencorse Wood. Of some significance, between these lines ran the Steenbeek, a river which on account of constant shelling had by mid-1917 become more an extended bog. Further back still was the so-called Flandern I Line. This ran in front of the Passchendaele Ridge and crossed the Gheluvelt Plateau just in rear of Polygon Wood.

Because of the low-lying nature of the Flanders terrain and the high water table, few deep dugouts had been constructed (in the manner of the Somme on Day One in 1916). Instead the Germans had erected hundreds of pillboxes, low concrete shelters built up several feet above the ground and covered with turf and soil. These could house machine-gun nests or a garrison of between two and forty men. The pillboxes were supplemented by the fortification of the many stone farmhouses which were characteristic of this area of Flanders.

These were indeed formidable defences. They incorporated a rear slope position (the second line), a river that had become a bog, and the imposing observation points provided by the occupation of the Passchendaele Ridge and the Gheluvelt Plateau.

But for Ludendorff this was not enough. The fall of Messines seemed to him salutary warning that his defences should be further strengthened. On 14 June he sent Colonel von Lossburg, his expert on these matters, to the headquarters of the German Fourth Army at Courtrai.

Von Lossburg determined to turn the existing defences into the strongest on the Western Front. To the rear two more lines were commenced: Flandern II from Passchendaele village (where it joined Flandern I) south towards Menin; and Flandern III on the reverse slope of the Passchendaele Ridge. Later an additional position was constructed across the Gheluvelt Plateau from Broodseinde to Becelaire. So at least five lines faced the British, and on the Gheluvelt Plateau the number rose to as many as seven.

For von Lossburg, however, these additional lines were only an interim measure designed for the eventuality of an immediate British attack. Given time he was convinced that he could prevent the British from ever reaching these rearward positions. What he intended was to pack additional defences into the forward area from his own front line to Flandern I. To this end he ordered construction of more pillboxes in each of the lines and of concrete machine-gun nests between them.

IV

By mid-July the whole defensive network was nearing completion. The front system consisted of three lines of breastworks rather than trenches, about 200 yards apart and garrisoned by four companies of infantry.

Two thousand yards back was the second trench system, with ample pillboxes to shelter the support battalions. Between the first and second systems were scattered concrete machine-gun posts holding between two and four guns. The whole area was dubbed the forward battle zone.

A further 2,000 yards back lay the third trench system, in which sheltered the reserve battalions. Between this line and the second lay most of the field guns which would support the front-line troops. Protecting these batteries were more concrete machine-gun posts. The whole area was known as the greater battle zone.

Behind the third line to a distance of 5,000–7,000 yards lay the Flandern I Line – the rearward battle zone. Within this area were located regiments of the counter-attack divisions. From the foremost line to Flandern I constituted a distance of 10,000–12,000 yards (six to seven miles).

Unlike the defensive arrangements he had improvised at Arras, von Lossburg allowed no flexibility or elasticity within the Ypres defences. The task of the garrison of each position was to fight it out *in situ* and to break up the enemy attack as much as possible until help arrived. So the front companies and the support battalions were to remain in place however severe the attack. Their rescue would be accomplished by the reserve battalions and the counter-attack regiments, which would be sent forward as soon as the offensive began.

It was expected that the decisive encounter would take place in the greater battle zone: that is, in the vicinity of the third trench system. There the attacking British force, disorganized by the resistance of Ludendorff's front-line troops, would encounter the relatively fresh troops from the reserve battalions reinforced by the counter-attack formations. The British would thereby be thrown back and forced to relinquish any captured ground.

A significant feature of the German defences was the excellent artillery positions available to them. Most of the heavy guns could be located behind the Gheluvelt Plateau and the Passchendaele Ridge. In these positions they were hidden from direct British observation, yet their fire could be brought to bear on any British target by observers on the German-held ridges.

Manning these defences opposite the nine attacking divisions of the Fifth Army, the Germans had five divisions in the line, four more in close reserve, and another four further back.[12] These troops were supported by approximately 1,150 guns.[13]

What is noteworthy about these defences, apart from their imposing nature, is the timetable of their creation. No small part of them had come into existence during the seven-week interval between Plumer's attack at Messines and the commencement of Gough's operation on 31 July. This was the interval that Haig had introduced into the planning process – disregarding the fact that the deception aspect, which was supposed to justify such an interlude, was the merest fantasy. Haig, in short, had arranged matters in a way which proved greatly to his enemy's advantage.

V

On taking up command in the Ypres salient, Gough set about formulating the outline plan for the coming assault. This required him to decide four things: the duration of the preliminary bombardment; the length of the front to be attacked; the support to be accorded to the Fifth Army by the French on his left and Plumer's Second Army on his right; and the depth of enemy defences into which he hoped to penetrate.

The first matter, the duration of the bombardment, did not admit of argument. So extensive were the German defences that a protracted bombardment was indispensable. It was scheduled to commence on 16 July and continue until the 25th (at this stage the day intended for the commencement of the attack).[14]

The third issue, the role to be played by the flanking armies, would in a measure be dependent on Gough's decision concerning the second issue: the length of front to be attacked. He chose to place the left of his assault on the fringe of the Houthulst Forest – the forest itself being too impenetrable to be included in the operation. This meant that two divisions of the French First Army would actively participate in the assault on the left of the Fifth Army. On the right Gough, following Haig, had intended to place the southern flank of his attack at Observatory Ridge on the Gheluvelt Plateau.[15] He concluded, however, that an advance due east from that ridge would leave his front vulnerable to attack from strongpoints on the right of the plateau, such as Shrewsbury Forest. So with the agreement of Plumer and Haig, the boundary of the Fifth Army was moved a thousand yards south to the Kleine Zillebecke road, thereby encompassing most of the plateau in the attack and adding

to Fifth Army what had been one of Plumer's divisions. This established
the final front of the attack. It would run from the Houthulst Forest in
the north to Kleine Zillebecke in the south, a distance of about 14,000
yards (about eight miles).

Plumer's Second Army, as such, was not to participate directly in the
attack, and the question remained of how it should assist Gough. Haig
requested Plumer to develop ways of securing Gough's right flank, and
the Second Army commander obliged by coming up with a scheme to
open an attack all along his front (from Kleine Zillebecke to Oostaverne
spur). He would not attempt a considerable advance, indeed he would
go little further than the German front line. But Plumer speculated that
his action would lead the enemy to believe that the Second Army was
engaged in the main operation and so would hold troops and guns in
this area, away from the principal British effort.

Like Haig's deception plan for demonstrations at Arras, Plumer's
scheme (although meeting with Gough's approval) had little to recommend it. It required Plumer to spread his guns thin across the whole
Second Army front, instead of concentrating them on Gough's right
flank where they could have provided the Fifth Army with a real
measure of support. And Plumer simply did not possess enough artillery
pieces to convince the enemy that his activities were a central part of the
British attack.[16]

A major decision – the fourth of those enumerated above – remained
for Gough: on the intended depth of penetration on the first day. What
objectives could realistically be set in the aftermath of the preparatory
bombardment?

As we have seen, when Rawlinson and Plumer drew up their plans
early in 1917, they had opted for an advance of 1,500–1,750 yards. At
that time, the German defences had been comparatively rudimentary by
the standards confronting Gough on 31 July. Nevertheless, the Fifth
Army commander opted for something altogether more ambitious: an
advance of 4,000–5,000 yards, to the line Polygon Wood–Broodseinde–
Langemarck. That distance, he came to conclude, could be accomplished in four jumps. The first would capture the enemy's front system,
and after that the Gheluvelt Plateau as far as Shrewsbury Forest and
Bellewaarde; while to the north it would reach the crest of Pilckem
Ridge. There would then be a pause of 30 minutes for consolidation.
The next jump would capture the German second line. There would
then be a considerably longer pause, this time of four hours. The third
jump would carry the British forces beyond the Pilckem Ridge to the
Steenbeek around St Julien, and on the Gheluvelt Plateau an entry would
be forced into Polygon Wood. Once these objectives had been reached
there would be no settled pause, but as soon as opportunities arose the
concluding thrust would be made towards the final objectives.[17]

In all, Gough was contemplating an advance of 3,000 yards in the first three jumps, followed by further progress of between 1,000 and 2,000 yards as and when circumstances admitted. The whole German defensive system, up to and including the greater battle zone, would thereby be overrun.

Three things are noteworthy about this proposal. One, relative to the type of operation with which Gough was identified, is its restrained nature. The Fifth Army commander's major qualification for the command at Third Ypres was his eagerness for the hurroosh: that is, the rupturing of the enemy front and the swift pursuit. Yet for the first day of this campaign, owing to the imposing nature of the terrain to be attacked and the defences arrayed against him, he was certainly not contemplating a breakthrough: this was a bite and hold operation.

The second point is of an opposite nature. It concerns the extent of the advance he was proposing, certainly compared with the plan offered by Plumer and endorsed by Rawlinson. If Gough was making a concession to the realities of warfare on the Western Front, it was highly questionable whether the concession was anywhere near appropriate to the task confronting his army.

The third point concerns Haig. We find him accepting a proposal that, although it might promise an eventual large advance, did not contemplate rupturing the enemy line on the first day. In this, no doubt, First World War realities were imposing themselves on the commander-in-chief as well as on the Fifth Army commander. Moreover Haig could not have failed to notice that Gough's plan went further in the direction of a breakthrough than that offered by anyone else he had consulted. And it may be that Haig nursed a hope that Gough would go on to seize opportunities that might present themselves on the first day, in marked contrast to what he deemed had been the Third Army commander's failure to make the most of openings supposedly offering on the initial day of the Battle of Arras back in April.[18]

VI

It might be speculated that Gough, in offering a more ambitious first stage than Plumer and Rawlinson, was unaware of the enemy's reappraisal of their defensive principles in the light of Arras and Messines, and of the consequent upgrading of their defensive system. But this was not the case. His intelligence appreciations provided him with fairly accurate information on what awaited his forces when he attacked. The location of each of the German systems was known in considerable detail from aerial reconnaissance, and the progress of the new lines (Flandern II and III) was being charted on an almost daily basis.[19]

As GHQ became aware of the imposing obstacles confronting Gough's attack, some therein began questioning the ambitious nature of his plan. Major-General Sir John Davidson, head of the Operations section of Haig's staff, became convinced that too much was being asked of the troops on the first day. Apparently he suspected Gough of hankering after a breakthrough, but in a memorandum to Haig he confined himself to arguing that the attacking troops were being pushed forward into territory they would be unable to hold, thereby sustaining unnecessary casualties.[20]

Davidson recommended an advance of only 1,750 yards (more or less the Plumer–Rawlinson approach). He put forward a series of arguments in favour of this. By and large, they fell under five headings: the need to preserve good communications between rearward headquarters and the advancing troops; the importance of providing the attacking forces with continuous, accurate artillery support; the reduced casualty list that would flow from the setting of realistic goals; the enhanced prospect of relieving exhausted troops; and the beneficial effect on morale resulting from wholly successful operations.

In the course of his exposition Davidson, under the heading 'Concentration in Artillery Preparation', made a crucial point: 'Since the zone of preparation will not be so deep, the artillery fire for the purpose of destruction will be more concentrated.'[21]

What Davidson was saying here deserves to be spelt out. His proposal for an advance of only 1,750 yards, compared with Gough's 4,000–5,000 yards, would have the effect of doubling the quantity of shells falling on the area under attack. Given the advanced state of the German defences by 31 July, this seemed a serious consideration.

It was not, however, one which Gough was prepared to take on board. When he replied to Davidson next day, he countered any suggestion that he was hankering after a breakthrough on the first day by saying he fully realized that a succession of attacks would be required. But he failed to deal with Davidson's point about concentrating his artillery fire on a lesser area, arguing that 'we [should] go as far as we can [on] the first day', and defining that as constituting the objective he had already laid down. His only reference to artillery consisted of a vague assertion that not to take advantage of the long preliminary bombardment would be wasteful.[22]

Fortified by the opinion of one of his corps commanders (Maxse) that some of Davidson's arguments were 'BALLS!!',[23] Gough proceeded to a conference on the matter with Haig, Kiggell, Plumer, and Davidson. It did not take long to reach a decision. Plumer, according to Davidson's subsequent account, came down firmly on Gough's side.[24] But the decisive voice was Haig's. His diary does not mention Davidson's objections, but the matters it did record make it abundantly clear that he was not prepared to accept lesser objectives than Gough was proposing.[25]

Haig also criticized aspects of Gough's plan, but on different grounds from Davidson's. What Haig noted was Gough's failure to pay due attention to the area on the right of his attack which seemed to the commander-in-chief to be fundamental to the whole undertaking. The Gheluvelt Plateau presented especially imposing obstacles to the advance, on account of the nature of the terrain and of the defences which the Germans had in place. Yet it was essential to get forward here, because any attempted advance in the centre could be brought to a halt by enfilade fire from the right, where on the Gheluvelt Plateau the Germans possessed excellent observation. So Haig was at pains to stress the need for a concentration of effort in this region. It is not evident that Gough allowed these views greatly to influence the disposition of his forces.

This exchange between Haig and Gough bears an uncanny resemblance to a disagreement between Haig and Rawlinson a year earlier, in the run-up to the battle of the Somme. Then the issue was whether the preliminary bombardment, on a front of twenty miles and to a depth of 5,000 yards, should be concentrated in a few hours or spread over a week. The point that the British army at the Somme did not have the quantities of shells and guns required to suppress the enemy defences over this depth and length of front, whatever time was employed in the bombardment, appeared to escape both of them. In the approach to 31 July 1917 Haig and Gough were entertaining a difference of opinion on another matter, but with the same failure to confront the essential issue. Gough saw the need to employ a sufficiency of guns along the whole front of attack if his forces were to advance uniformly. Haig saw the need to concentrate guns on a particularly vital and well-defended area of the front under attack. The point that to follow Gough's method of proceeding was to ignore an important matter raised by Haig, whereas to act on Haig's representations meant ignoring the equally important matter that was concerning Gough, simply passed unnoticed. There were just not enough guns and shells on the chosen area of attack to achieve Haig's and Gough's separate purposes.

The necessary supplement of guns and shells was not wanting. Some were to be found with Plumer's Second Army, which was engaged in a largely purposeless diversionary operation. Others were sitting on the Belgian coast. There, supposedly, they would one day play a major part in the accomplishment of Haig's great strategic design. But as a consequence they would not be where they were needed to carry out the first stage of that design, opposite the imposing and absolutely crucial Gheluvelt Plateau.

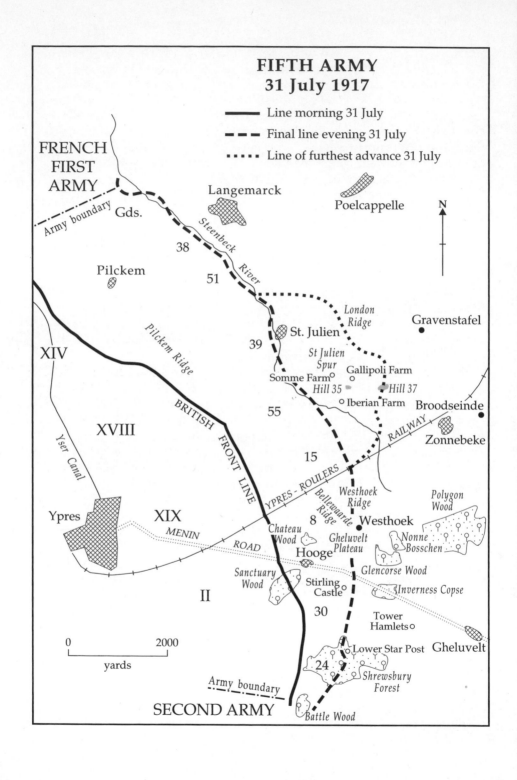

FIFTH ARMY
31 July 1917

— Line morning 31 July

– – – Final line evening 31 July

· · · · · Line of furthest advance 31 July

N

FRENCH
FIRST
ARMY

Army boundary

Gds.

Langemarck

Poelcappelle

38

Steenbeck River

Pilckem

51

39

St. Julien

London Ridge

Gravenstafel

XIV

Pilckem Ridge

St Julien Spur

Somme Farm

Gallipoli Farm

Hill 35

Hill 37

Iberian Farm

Broodseinde

55

XVIII

BRITISH FRONT LINE

Zonnebeke

Yser Canal

15

RAILWAY

Ypres

XIX

MENIN

YPRES - ROULERS

8

Bellewaarde Ridge

Westhoek Ridge

Polygon Wood

Westhoek

Chateau Wood

Gheluvelt Plateau

Nonne Bosschen

ROAD

Hooge

Glencorse Wood

Sanctuary Wood

Stirling Castle

Inverness Copse

II

30

Tower Hamlets

Gheluvelt

0   2000

yards

24

Lower Star Post

Shrewsbury Forest

Army boundary

SECOND ARMY

Battle Wood

8

31 July: The Implements

To achieve his purpose Gough had at hand three implements: the cavalry, the infantry along with their supporting weapons, and the artillery. We shall look at them in ascending order of importance.

I

One thing, in particular, demonstrates that 31 July was not envisaged as an attempt at a breakthrough, but as the first in a series of set-piece attacks. This was the minor role assigned to the cavalry.

Gough may have been an ex-cavalryman, yet for the first day he required little of his mounted soldiers. After the infantry had reached their final objectives, a brigade of cavalry was to scout ahead of the two northern corps.[1] As for the remaining five divisions of cavalry, they were not massed to exploit any rupture of the enemy lines (as on most previous occasions). Even Haig did not press for this. All he did was to place the cavalry on notice that, in the event of a comprehensive German collapse, they were to 'exploit success in the attack on the Passchendaele–Westroosbecke portion of the Ridge'.[2] Otherwise they were not to act.

Consequently, 31 July found the cavalry disposed well behind Gough's front. Reality, in this instance at least, had overwhelmed the instincts of the British high command.

II

On zero day, Gough planned to have in the front line nine divisions of infantry, roughly 100,000 men. In the run-up to the attack, he needed to make provision for their training and equipment.

Training devolved on the four corps commanders. In the event each of

these commanders – Maxse, Watts, Jacob, and Cavan – developed a
similar programme. Hence it is sufficient in describing how they went
about their task to relate the experience of Maxse's corps.

The training schedule devised by Maxse and his staff officer, Captain
Edward Grigg, had three main elements. First, using information
obtained from aerial photographs, from trench raids, and from front-
line observation, a replica of the German trench system to be captured
was marked out on a piece of ground behind the line. The troops then
rehearsed their attack over this practice ground until they were familiar
with the configuration of the trenches and obstacles they would confront
in the assault.[3]

Secondly, the information gleaned from the aerial photographs and
trench raids was used to construct a large model of the section of
battlefield to be traversed by XVIII Corps. The model covered two acres
and according to the corps report, 'Much use was made' of it.[4] That such
models had great practical value was attested to by a member of XIV
Corps:

> Our training ground was a replica, as exact as possible, of the ground we
> were going to take, & each day for over a week we trekked over the
> course, noting the position of trenches, roads, woods, farms etc. This was
> of the utmost value to us all and when we went [into the attack] . . . every
> single man knew the way. . . . Our training ground proved, in the light of
> after events, to be very accurate.[5]

In addition to these measures, Maxse set up special 'battle courses' for
all company commanders taking part in the approaching operation. The
programme of lectures was extensive and included such subjects as
battle formations, topography, weaponry, and all arms co-operation.[6]
As a result of these courses, specialist platoons were trained in methods
of attack on German strongpoints, farmhouses, and pillboxes. On the
day of battle this training would prove valuable.[7]

Corps also attempted to draw on the lessons of previous battles.
Officers were delegated to inspect the captured German defensive
systems at Messines, and notes emanating from the Canadian Corps
regarding what had occurred at Vimy Ridge were circulated among
them.[8]

During this same training period, the corps commanders established
the infantry formations to be employed in the initial attack. The foremost troops would advance in the usual linear formation behind the
creeping barrage, arriving at the enemy front trench simultaneously.
Follow-up troops, however, one of whose main tasks would be the
elimination of surviving strongpoints, were to be deployed differently.

At Arras unsubdued enemy machine-guns had inflicted heavy casualties on the follow-up formations advancing in waves without the support of a creeping barrage. Further, the wave formations had proved too inflexible to deal effectively with the variety of circumstances which awaited these more rearward troops. So it was decided that for 31 July the follow-up units would be deployed variously – sometimes in columns and sometimes in the dispersed erratic fashion referred to as artillery formation. (The latter had the advantage of presenting much smaller targets to the enemy machine-gunners.) This was a more flexible proceeding, enabling follow-up forces either to disperse quickly so as to attack the surviving enemy strongpoints from several directions or to deploy into waves should an advance behind a barrage eventuate.[9]

III

This training would count for little unless the infantry were provided with adequate fire support as they made the perilous crossing of no man's land and closed upon the enemy in their trenches.

By the latter half of 1917 there was quite an array of weapons capable of providing such support. Among these were rifles, grenades, rifle-grenades, Lewis guns, trench mortars, tanks, and the creeping barrage. They varied greatly in their usefulness.

Of least value was the Lee Enfield rifle. It retained a role in repelling counter-attacks once an enemy position had been overrun, but it was difficult to employ during the actual advance on a defended position and anyway was presented with few targets.

Of more use was the hand grenade. Each infantryman carried one or two of these, and the specialist bombers in each battalion carried 10 to 15.[10] These grenades could be thrown about 20 yards and had an explosive force strong enough to kill machine-gunners and occupants of dugouts.

The grenade was a much more effective weapon when fired from a rifle. In 1917 the rifle grenadiers included in each attacking battalion carried 8 to 10 of these bombs.[11] A rifle-grenade might be propelled 200 yards, making it a particularly useful weapon in attacking strongpoints.

These weapons were most effective when employed in combination with Lewis guns and trench mortars. A Lewis gun might pin down enemy defenders in strongpoints while the trench mortar and rifle-grenade units worked around to their unprotected flanks and attacked them from there.

The newest infantry protection weapon was the tank. For the opening day of the Third Ypres campaign Gough employed 120 Mark IV tanks

with 48 more in reserve.[12] The tanks were not expected to lead the attack. They were simply too vulnerable to enemy shell fire, to unfavourable terrain, and to their own mechanical weaknesses. So they were assigned to accompany the rearward waves of infantry and assist in the reduction of unsubdued strongpoints. The circumstances in which they would be operating were not to their advantage. As the tank experts noted, the Mark IV tank could not operate in a swamp, over heavily shelled ground, or through woods.[13] By and large the terrain of the Ypres salient presented just these obstacles.

IV

The weapons reviewed so far could make at best only a limited contribution to an infantry advance against complex and powerfully defended enemy positions. Ultimately, therefore, the infantry's ability to get forward would be determined by the effectiveness of the artillery.

For the battle Gough had assembled 752 heavy and 1,422 field guns.[14] Added to this, the Fifth Army would have the assistance of 300 heavy and 240 field guns from the French to their north and 112 heavy and 210 field guns from the flanking corps of the Second Army to their south.[15]

It is difficult to compare these quantities of artillery with those employed in earlier battles. In round figures Gough's forces seemed marginally better off than had been the British attackers both at Arras/Vimy, where the attack had been supported by 963 heavy and 1,854 field guns,[16] and at Messines where the corresponding figures had been 754 and 1,510.[17] But although the frontages of attack in these three battles were not greatly different, the circumstances obtaining at Third Ypres certainly were. At Arras the British had needed only to deal in the first instance with a conventional linear defence, not a defence in depth. Moreover, the Germans had held their counter-attack forces too far back to intervene when required. At Messines the defences had certainly been deeper, and pillboxes had made their appearance. But the British attack there had received singular support from the massive explosion of ᵗᵉ mines. So the presence of so many guns at Third Ypres did not ᵗᵗitute a guarantee of success.

ᵗat conclusions, then, can be drawn concerning the adequacy of 's artillery resources for the assault of 31 July? He certainly had ᵗeld guns and shells for two main tasks: the removal of the wire ᵗe forward German positions, and the provision of a creeping the first assault troops. But it was less certain that the would be employed appropriately to accomplish these

Luckily for Gough the wire protecting the German first line was not formidable and the field guns could hardly fail to dispose of it. Provision of an appropriate creeping barrage was another matter. This raised two problems: at what rate should it advance, and what quantity of shell should be fired? For 31 July the artillery experts settled on a speed of four minutes per 100 yards, each gun firing four shells per minute.[18] As far as the rate of advance was concerned, this was the same as at Arras, but the number of shells to be fired each minute was being doubled, thus giving the barrage a greater chance of eliminating enemy defenders in shell holes.[19]

Even so, not everyone felt the arrangement was adequate. The commander of 30 Division argued that in the II Corps area the tangled undergrowth and remains of the many woods scattered across the Gheluvelt Plateau rendered a rate of advance of 100 yards in four minutes altogether too ambitious.[20] His words fell on deaf ears, so he repeated his protest on the eve of battle. His advice was not accepted.[21]

What of the heavy guns? Their situation was complicated by the extent of Gough's (and Haig's) objectives. The established tasks of the big guns were trench destruction, the elimination of farmhouse and pillbox strongpoints, and counter-battery fire (to wear down the enemy's artillery resources and to prevent it from operating at least for the period of the battle). These were major aims. But for this occasion the heavy artillery would have to perform additional functions, or else those functions would not be performed. Owing to the depth of the projected advance, the heavy artillery must undertake wire-cutting and the provision of a creeping barrage for troops advancing beyond the range of the field artillery. All this would require (in addition to a high degree of skill) a great many guns and huge quantities of ammunition. Did Gough possess these?

A number of documents demonstrate that Fifth Army artillerymen were indeed endeavouring to calculate the quantities of guns needed to carry out the tasks allotted to the heavy weapons. One produced by XIV Corps is particularly enlightening. In it the staff estimated the total length of enemy trench and wire to be bombarded, the number of shells required to destroy a yard of such trench and wire, the number of strongpoints confronting the corps, and the number of shells needed to destroy each one of them.[22] The document also recognizes that for the infantry to reach its furthest objectives, wire-cutting beyond a certain point must be undertaken not by the field but by the heavy artillery.[23] Ominously, the issue of the provision of a creeping barrage at these further distances is not raised.

What emerges from this XIV Corps document is noteworthy, and not reassuring. The artillerymen calculated that they possessed enough heavy shells, at least for trench destruction and the elimination of wire and strongpoints. But they revealed an insufficiency of heavy guns to fire that quantity of shells in the time allotted. That is, unless the duration of the bombardment was extended, many of the shells needed to wreck the enemy's defences would still be resting on the British side of no man's land when the infantry went into the attack.[24]

This problem could have been mitigated had better use been made of the heavy guns at that moment residing with the Fourth and Second Armies. Rawlinson's force had 189 heavies at its disposal, many more than were needed just to hold the line. Plumer's force possessed 243 heavy howitzers. Of these 112 were to be employed by the corps flanking Fifth Army to support its attack across the Gheluvelt Plateau. The remaining 131, by contrast, were to be used in support of Plumer's diversionary operation further south.[25] These guns were not sufficient ever to deceive the Germans into believing that major action was contemplated in the Second Army area. They would have served more purpose aiding Gough to deliver all of the shells he had available within the time he was allowing for the preliminary bombardment.

There was another considerable deficiency in the artillery preparations for this battle, although it became evident only in retrospect. A crucial function of the heavy artillery was counter-battery: the elimination or neutralization of enemy guns. At Messines this had been accomplished. The 750 heavy guns of Plumer's Second Army had subdued the 200 German batteries opposing them. Gough also had 750 heavies, and his intelligence service reported that ranged against him were 205 German batteries – 185 opposite Fifth Army and 20 opposite the left of Second Army but able to fire on Fifth Army positions.[26] The precedent at Messines therefore suggested that all would be well with Gough's counter-battery preparations for 31 July. Events, however, would not bear this out. Fifth Army intelligence had got its figures wrong. There were almost twice as many German batteries facing Gough's forces as had been reported.[27] This meant that, even if good weather and accurate aerial observation obtained in the run-up to the attack, the German guns were unlikely to have been silenced.

V

Certain conclusions emerge from this survey of Gough's resources for the attack on 31 July. The cavalry could contribute little or nothing unless, first of all, the other arms had been staggeringly successful. The infantry must overrun the designated objectives, but not by their own strength or with the aid solely of the weaponry they could carry with them. Those weapons might help to consolidate, but they could not accomplish, a success. The artillery must suppress enemy guns, remove barbed wire, destroy strongpoints, wreck opposing trenches, and provide the infantry with a protecting creeping barrage which at the very least would confine casualties to a tolerable level.

When we survey the artillery, a decidedly ambiguous picture emerges. The field artillery could certainly destroy the barbed wire guarding the close objectives. It might also, if it did not proceed too quickly, facilitate the infantry's passage across no man's land. As for the heavy artillery, it might fulfil counter-battery objectives to an extent, but not to the extent anticipated: the number of German batteries was much greater than believed, and a proportion of British guns was being wasted on sections of front not directly involved in the battle.

As for the other functions traditional to the heavy guns – trench destruction and the elimination of machine-gun posts and strongpoints – it seems evident that the Fifth Army possessed enough shells to accomplish these purposes, but that its gunners required additional time to fire them because they did not have sufficient guns. That extra time was denied them.

There is a final disturbing point. Direct protection of the advancing infantry was usually provided by the field artillery, who smashed up barbed wire and fired a creeping barrage ahead of the foot soldiers. But that depended on the final objectives of the infantry lying within the range of the field guns. That had been true of the objectives proposed earlier by Rawlinson and Plumer and most recently by Davidson. It was not at all so with the objectives opted for by Gough and required by Haig. How then was the wire to be removed, and protective fire for the infantry provided, in the case of the most distant enemy lines designated to be overrun? Concerning the destruction of barbed wire, something was to be done by the heavy artillery (thereby reducing the number of shells employed for counter-battery and other important purposes). But as for the provision of a creeping barrage for the infantry in the culminating stages of the battle, nothing was said and nothing was being done. The gap between the high command's aspirations and its power to accomplish them could hardly have been clearer.

9

First Strike

I

The preliminary bombardment opened on 16 July. Originally it had been intended to last for nine days, the attack going in on the 25th. In the event two factors postponed the battle until the 31st. First, some of Gough's heavy artillery had been delayed and he requested three extra days in which to complete his bombardment.[1] Secondly, General Anthoine, commander of the French First Army on Gough's northern flank, asked for a further extension because bad weather was hampering his counter-battery programme.[2] Both extensions were granted by Haig.

Anthoine's request has given rise to two allegations: that the French were solely responsible for delaying the attack until the 31st, and that this was of great moment. Indeed, the gap between 25 and 31 July is supposed to have made the difference between attacking in good weather and attacking in bad, and so between success and failure. Gough certainly embraced this view, claiming in his memoirs that Anthoine's intervention was 'fatal to our hopes'.[3]

There is little substance in this. For one thing, the first phase of the delay was instituted by Gough himself, for the good reason that he was awaiting further heavy artillery. For another, although Anthoine did request the second extension, he was not running contrary to British wishes or frittering away excellent campaigning weather. As Haig noted in his diary, three of the four commanders of British corps were grateful for the extra days that Anthoine was seeking, and for the reason Anthoine had put forward: that poor weather was interfering with their counter-battery programme.[4] (The complacent corps commander was Jacob of II Corps. As will be demonstrated shortly, he had no reason for complacency.)[5] So the fact that heavy rain hampered Gough's forces on the 31st is not evidence that climatic conditions had been more promising during the previous week.

Gough in his memoirs seems to be saying that his artillery were able to accomplish the job of suppressing the enemy defences (trenches, blockhouses, strongpoints, and big guns), and that only the delay until the onset of bad weather deprived the infantry of the conditions needed to get forward. This would seem to follow when we notice that, by the commencement of the battle on the 31st, the German defences had been subjected for 15 days to a bombardment of 4.3 million shells.[6]

Nevertheless, not all elements in the enemy defence structure had been suppressed by zero hour. We have noted that even on the front of XIV Corps, which was not facing opposition as formidable as on some other parts of the front, the defences had not been crushed owing to an insufficiency of guns. This factor was made worse by the actual state of the weather (as against the climatic conditions which prevailed in Gough's postwar recollections) during the firing of the bombardment. At the time, Fifth Army intelligence characterized the weather in the run-up to the attack as 'bad' or 'poor' for most of the bombardment period.[7] That rendered largely ineffectual British aerial spotting, which was the only sure guide to the battery commanders that their shells were hitting the German guns concealed behind the Passchendaele Ridge and the Gheluvelt Plateau. Even innovations such as sound ranging were affected by the conditions. The wind blew so strongly from the west that the sound rangers had great difficulty in picking up the detonation of the German guns. In the end no more than 5 per cent of hostile batteries were located by this method.[8]

This combination of inadequate weaponry and unsatisfactory weather ensured that the rearward German blockhouses and machine-gun points remained largely intact. No less than 64 on the left and the centre of the British front confronted such attacking troops as managed to penetrate the front German defences.[9]

There were, nevertheless, some positive aspects of the bombardment on the left and centre. There, the German defences were open to direct observation from the British line, so the damage done by the shelling was considerable. Around the German first and second positions in this area, most of the wire was cut, most trenches destroyed, and pillboxes and farmhouses obliterated. Many German batteries lying in open ground near these positions were also hit or forced to withdraw behind the Passchendaele Ridge.

In short, in the left and centre the bombardment succeeded in neutralizing German defences within 2,000–3,000 yards of the British front. It dealt much less severely with defences further back and failed utterly to silence the concentrations of batteries behind the Passchendaele Ridge.

None of the positive aspects of the bombardment applied on the right. There, in the crucial area of the Gheluvelt Plateau, the preliminary bombardment failed comprehensively. Across the plateau the gunners, who had to contend with the same bad weather as their counterparts in the north, in addition faced difficulties not present on other sectors of the front.

The debris of the shattered woods which littered the plateau concealed many strongpoints and their protecting wire from aerial observation, which anyway was hampered by the poor weather. As a consequence, a considerable proportion of these strongpoints – including 23 pillboxes between the German first and second lines – remained intact on the day of battle.[10]

Equally, most German batteries were difficult to detect because they were either concealed in the remains of the woods or hidden from direct observation behind the Gheluvelt Plateau. The most that II Corps could have done would have been to deluge whole areas with shells in the hope of hitting some of the German guns within them. But it never possessed the huge numbers of shells required for such an undertaking. So (despite Jacob's optimism) II Corps never mastered the German guns.

At the end of the preliminary bombardment, therefore, the condition of the German defences confronting Jacob on the plateau amounted to this: most of the German front line and its protecting wire had been destroyed, but almost nothing else. The hostile pillboxes just behind the German front were intact, as was their protecting wire. Most ominously, the groups of batteries in the woods and the much larger number behind the plateau had hardly been touched.

II

The British command must have been aware that the preliminary bombardment was failing to achieve many of its objectives. Fifth Army intelligence reports made this all too clear. On the 19th they recorded: 'fire [from enemy batteries] continues to be heavy . . . much gas was used'; on the 23rd, 'our battery areas and traffic routes were shelled throughout the whole army front'; on the 26th, '[activity] remained equally intense throughout the whole period'; and on the 30th (the eve of battle), 'the enemy shelled our battery areas and forward communications on all Corps fronts, from time to time firing heavy concentrations'.[11]

Notwithstanding these reports, General Birch, Haig's artillery adviser, discerned on the 28th that the British gunners 'have gained the upper hand over the hostile artillery'.[12] Haig was so impressed by this point that he underlined the entry in his diary. He had, after all, stipulated back in May that offensive operations would 'not go in until we have definitely gained the superiority over the hostile artillery in the area of attack'.[13] The events of 31 July, especially on the Gheluvelt Plateau, would reveal that Birch's conclusion and Haig's confidence did not eliminate what was clear in their own intelligence reports.

III

Zero hour for the big attack had been set by Gough at 3.50 a.m. to take advantage of the first rays of dawn. However, on the day the weather did not oblige. Low, stormy clouds obscured the rising sun. When the men clambered over the top it was still pitch dark.

Success was most complete in the north. Here it was the task of the French First Army to advance 2,500 yards, thereby establishing a defensive flank for Gough's operations. This was accomplished with relative ease. Supported by a greater weight of artillery relative to the front attacked than any French assault yet mounted, the troops swept forward, meeting little resistance up to their final objective.[14] Even beyond that the Germans had insufficient machine-guns to resist a further advance, so that at the end of the day the French were occupying positions beyond those set down.[15] Losses were fewer than 1,000 in each of the divisions involved.[16]

The French official account leaves no doubt as to the cause of this success. 'Unarguably', it states, the troops were able to get forward because of the 'systematic and effective artillery preparation, whose effects, even on enormous concrete shelters and blockhouses . . . made an enormous impression on troops who had failed at the Chemin des Dames'.[17]

To the right of the French, Gough's XIV Corps (Guards, 38 Division) were also completely successful. In this sector of the front much thought had been given by the corps commander (Cavan) to the difficult problem of deploying troops across the Yser Canal. This feature, which ran between the opposing front lines, was a formidable obstacle – 70 feet wide, with a bottom of 'soft and tenacious mud into which a man sank like a stone'.[18] No serious attempt had been made to cross it since 1914. Before the battle the Guards Division had rehearsed the crossing of the canal using long rigid mats and portable wooden bridges.[19] But on the 27th a patrol discovered that the bombardment had proved so overwhelming that it had forced the Germans to evacuate temporarily the front-line trenches. Additional forces were rushed up, and together with the patrol they managed to establish a strong position to the east of the canal before the Germans could return.[20] The XIV Corps could now launch their attack with that obstacle behind them.

In the event, the attack across the Pilckem Ridge by the Guards and 38 Division initially went smoothly. The counter-batteries blanketed the German guns with gas, causing their retaliation to be late and feeble.[21] As the troops crossed into enemy territory some casualties were inflicted by machine-guns hidden in woods and from concrete emplacements.[22] But the opposition, though severe at times, was never so coherent or numerous as to hold up the attack. However, as the advance proceeded towards the Steenbeek, its progress faltered. First, the troops began to lose the protection of the creeping barrage. When the 1st Guards Brigade arrived in the vicinity of the Steenbeek the barrage was in places 800 yards distant, whereas in other areas it was so close that troops could not get forward.[23] Secondly, the preliminary bombardment had failed – as the XIV Corps artillery had anticipated – to subdue the enemy blockhouses and pillboxes to the east of the Steenbeek and these brought Cavan's forces to a halt on the west bank of the river, 1,000 yards short of their final objective. However, an attempt by the Germans to launch a counter-attack against 38 Division was easily driven off.[24]

In all, therefore, XIV Corps, while not achieving what had been anticipated, had captured two German defensive lines and advanced across the Pilckem Ridge to a depth of 3,000 yards.

Losses in this action were, by Western Front standards, moderate: 5,000 casualties including 750 dead, higher than those of the French but lower than any other British corps on 31 July.[25] Yet, as personal records remind us, the concept of moderation in losses is always relative. Lt W. B. St Leger was a company commander in the 2nd Battalion Irish Guards. In the course of the advance he lost his orderly killed by a bullet through the neck, his sergeant (Harris) dispatched by a shell which blew away half of his face, fellow officers Turner and Leggett killed, three friends ('Lucien', Porritt, and Kirk) seriously wounded in, respectively, the stomach, neck, and chest, along with lesser wounds to three more friends, 'Grubby', Day and Publicover. St Leger himself was wounded in the knee and had to be carried from the battlefield on a stretcher.[26] So for this soldier, an action economical by military standards in the lives of the attacking forces involved injury to himself, the death of four friends, terrible wounds to three others, and slighter wounds to a further three. Yet St Leger's battalion was a follow-up formation, not one of those involved in the main attack.

IV

So at the end of the day the northern defensive flank had been secured by the French, and the XIV Corps had taken Pilckem Ridge and were consolidating a position just west of the Steenbeek. When we turn to the situation in the centre and on the right of the attack a somewhat different picture emerges.

In the centre, a measure of success initially attended the action of XVIII Corps (Maxse) and XIX Corps (Watts). On the front of XVIII Corps, 51 and 39 Divisions were to attack north-west, force the crossings of the Steenbeek, and capture the ruined village of St Julien. Then 39 Division was to undertake a further advance on Gravenstafel. This would carry it to within a few thousand yards of the Passchendaele Ridge.[27]

In common with the French and XIV Corps, the attack of the XVIII Corps encountered slight opposition during the opening phase. The enemy's front line had been destroyed, their artillery retaliation was negligible, and the attacking troops advancing just 40 yards behind the creeping barrage overran their first objective with ease.[28]

From then on opposition stiffened. Various concrete machine-gun emplacements dotted about the German second line had survived the bombardment. Hence the struggle developed into a series of actions by companies or platoons against these positions. To some extent this type of resistance had been foreseen and the troops trained to deal with it. The report of 39 Division details how such obstacles (in this instance a fortified farm) were overcome.

> Lewis Guns, Rifle Bombers and Stokes Guns opened a heavy fire on the enemy machine gun emplacements. Two tanks also opened heavy fire at very close range and one of them (G47) advanced through our barrage and rolled out a lane for the infantry in the uncut wire. Meanwhile rifle sections worked round the flanks of the position and, on the barrage lifting, assaulted from both sides and captured the garrison which had been driven into their dugouts.[29]

By such means the defences were steadily overcome and the advance maintained. The tanks, 24 of which accompanied the attack, rendered useful service to the infantry.[30] By 8 a.m., 39 Division had captured St Julien and crossed the Steenbeek on its whole front of attack, while 51 Division had got reconnaissance patrols across the river at two points.[31]

The 39 Division now prepared for its advance on Gravenstafel. However, the situation was not altogether in their favour. For one thing, during the advance to the Steenbeek so many platoons had been detached to subdue strongpoints that much of the division was scattered in penny packets over the battlefield. Few troops remained at the sharp end to press the attack.[32] Then, as 39 Division soon discovered, the barrage which had served the troops so well up to the line of the Steenbeek began to slacken. At the same time fire from the enemy artillery, which had initially been subdued, increased in intensity.[33] Finally, casualties had not been light – just under 6,000 for the corps and 4,000 from 39 Division.[34] So by mid-morning the depleted formations of XVIII Corps found themselves scattered, insufficiently supported by their own guns, and increasingly harassed by fire from the enemy.

To the immediate right of XVIII Corps, the XIX (Watts) was accomplishing the greatest initial advance of the day. On this section of the front the troops had to press forward over three low ridges (Pilckem, St Julien, London), capture three German defensive lines, and push just beyond them. By early afternoon almost all of this had been accomplished. The leading brigades of 55 and 15 Divisions had taken the Pilckem Ridge and were on the St Julien Spur, and the reserve brigades were about to attack through them to the London Ridge.[35] This advance too had not been without cost. The divisions had encountered a group of untouched blockhouses near the German second and third lines which had been subdued only with heavy casualties.[36] As on other fronts, the creeping barrage had thinned as the troops progressed. Nevertheless, the reserve brigades, which to some extent had to fight their way past some blockhouses that were still holding out, advanced towards London Ridge on schedule. Parties of the brigade made rapid progress and reached the vicinity of Gravenstafel.[37] Passchendaele village lay just 4,000 yards away.

Yet the ground gained was proving insecure. For one thing, on the front of 55 Division enemy troops were seen massing for a counter-attack.[38] More ominously, on the right of 15 Division machine-gun fire was being employed against the British forces from the rear.[39] This could have only one implication. All had not gone well with the attack on their right, which Haig had judged the key to the whole operation: that by II Corps against the Gheluvelt Plateau.

V

There is no doubt that the capture of the Gheluvelt Plateau was the most difficult task set any of the corps on 31 July. The tangle of woods which lay astride the line of the British advance and the difficulties they presented have already been described. It was in (at least partial) recognition of these factors that the corps attacked with three divisions (from right to left 8, 30, 24) instead of two, each division being given a narrower front of attack than those to the north.

To begin with, the attack of 8 Division on the left of II Corps enjoyed some success. The leading waves captured Château Wood and the Bellewaarde Ridge and advanced on Westhoek. At this point, however, they were enfiladed by heavy machine-gun fire from the right. Strongpoints in Nonne Boschen and Glencorse Wood had not been captured by 30 Division, so 8 Division had no option but to fall back to a more defensible line.[40]

As with 8 Division, when 30 and 24 Divisions crossed the enemy front line all seemed to be going according to plan. There was little opposition, and very few casualties were suffered.[41] Then the boggy ground and some uncut wire in Shrewsbury Forest and Sanctuary Wood, through which most of the troops were passing, caused them to lose the creeping barrage.[42] Indeed, in some areas so bad was the going that the men could only struggle through the bog by pulling each other out.[43] Thus the pre-battle predictions of the commander of 30 Division, that in the prevailing conditions the creeping barrage was too fast, proved correct.[44]

Soon there were further unpleasant discoveries. While still toiling through the woods elements of both divisions were heavily shelled by German guns.[45] In this area British counter-battery fire had failed utterly. In addition, as the troops emerged from the tangled undergrowth they lacked the protection of their own artillery and came under heavy fire from a series of German strongpoints which had survived the preliminary bombardment. Indeed, so numerous were these centres of resistance that they could bring the whole front of attack under a continuous belt of fire.[46] In some instances this disastrous circumstance was compounded by troops losing their way in the dark. So on the front of 73 Brigade the various battalions lost touch with each other, thereby finding themselves to the north and south of a particularly formidable German strongpoint called Lower Star Post. Enfilade fire from this one point was enough to bring the attack of the entire brigade to a halt.[47] By 7 a.m. the rightward section of II Corps had come to a standstill. Follow-up brigades only added to the casualties.

Little aid was accorded Jacob's men by the endeavours of Plumer's Second Army on their right. X Corps did manage to capture a small section of the plateau to the east of Battle Wood. But, more importantly, along the remainder of the 13,000-yard front Plumer's other corps advanced only 500 yards.[48] No important German positions were captured, no great number of casualties inflicted, and no German troops diverted from the north.

VI

While II Corps stalled on the Gheluvelt Plateau, events elsewhere after midday took some of the gloss off the early gains. The accomplishments of the French and XIV Corps went unchallenged by the Germans. But this was not the case in the centre. There even greater success had been achieved during the morning, XIX Corps and 39 Division of XVIII Corps having advanced over 4,000 yards. These achievements by the British had clearly come as a nasty surprise to the Germans. Their defensive system was designed to allow some penetration, but the speed of the British advance had overwhelmed the local counter-attack formations. As a result Watts's and Maxse's men had driven into the enemy system to a much greater depth than had been anticipated by the German command. There was evidently some panic on the German side, reflected in expressions of fear that the British might break right through to the Passchendaele Ridge.[49] But the major element in the Germans' defensive arrangements continued intact. Their counter-attack formations in the vicinity of Passchendaele village, having survived the bombardment largely unscathed, remained concentrated. Between 11 and 11.30 a.m. three regiments from these formations moved to the attack.[50]

As it happened the troops of Gough's three central divisions (15, 55, 39) against which the counter-attacks were principally directed were not in good shape. For one thing (as noted earlier), the heavy fighting had dispersed the troops across the battlefield. Those who had got furthest forward were few in number and scattered. Secondly, the communications system had failed with telephone wires cut, runners largely ineffective, and visual signalling ceasing to operate on account of the steadily deteriorating weather. Hence no divisional commander on the British side knew with any accuracy the position of his front-line formations or where to direct his reinforcements. Thirdly, the attacking troops had advanced too far for their own artillery to support them with an accurate or dense creeping or standing barrage. As one report stated:

> Throughout the day the greatest difficulty was experienced in finding out where the front line was, and the artillery were very much hampered by this.[51]

As a consequence of all this, the German counter-attacks in the centre achieved a measure of success. No calls for assistance got through to the British artillery, whereas the German forces (as British reports noted) were supported by heavy and accurate artillery fire[52] – made worse for 15 and 55 Divisions by the fact that it came in enfilade from German batteries behind the Gheluvelt Plateau.[53] In these conditions the British troops had little alternative but to withdraw. So on the front of 39 Division St Julien had to be relinquished, while on their right XIX Corps lost all of London Ridge, Somme, Gallipoli and Iberian Farms, and Hills 35 and 37. (These locations would in subsequent weeks take much heavy fighting to recapture.)

Yet this withdrawal was far from being a rout. As the British fell back their artillery somehow became aware that all was not well. The action of 55 Divisional artillery was typical:

> As soon as information was received that the Brigade had reached [i.e. fallen back to] the Black Line the barrage . . . was placed in front of the Black Line and was successful in coming right on to the enemy just as he was trying to force [our front].[54]

Before long this artillery fire, supplemented by a number of machine-guns, halted the German counter-attacks along the line of the Steenbeek on the sector of 39 and 55 Divisions, and before Frezenberg on the front of 15 Division.[55] Exhaustion then settled on the field of battle.

VII

What had been accomplished by the end of the first day of Gough's campaign? The French and XIV Corps on the left, along with XVIII and XIX Corps in the centre, had overrun two German lines and advanced about 3,000 yards. In so doing they had captured the Pilckem Ridge, thus denying the Germans some good observation points over the Ypres salient. This, by Western Front standards, was a substantial achievement – notwithstanding that the XVIII and XIX Corps, having come close to the German third line (which had lain within the day's objectives), had then been driven back.

On the right, assailing the crucial Gheluvelt Plateau, II Corps had achieved less. Even so, it had captured the German front line and advanced about 1,000 yards beyond, depriving the Germans of such observation points as Bellewaarde Ridge and Stirling Castle.

Fifth Army, therefore, could point to some solid achievements. The pre-battle training undertaken by the infantry in most cases proved efficacious. When given a decent chance by the artillery – that is when a fair proportion of strongpoints had been neutralized by the British guns – the combination of Lewis guns, rifle grenades, trench mortars, and occasionally tanks usually managed to deal with those obstacles that remained.

Secondly, although the Fifth Army had suffered 27,000 casualties, it had inflicted an equal number upon the enemy. If this seems a rather negative achievement, it may be compared to the first day of the Somme campaign when the British suffered 57,000 casualties and the Germans one or two thousand.

In another respect Gough's achievements compared favourably with the first day of the Somme campaign. His troops on 31 July captured 18 square miles, including two defensive systems on the left and a certain amount of high ground along the Pilckem Ridge. On 1 July 1916, a mere 3.5 square miles had been captured.

Yet the negative side of the day's results needs to be stressed. The failure to take the Gheluvelt Plateau made the area captured on the left and centre vulnerable to enfilade fire. And the extravagance of Gough's objectives had rendered unduly costly what had been achieved. It had caused his forces in a number of areas to lose the protection of the barrage, suffer unnecessarily high casualties, and succumb to counter-attack.

But the nature of the failure lay much deeper than that. The most that could follow from what had been achieved was a succession of similar operations, carried out spasmodically as guns could be brought forward. This would be a lengthy process. And, if 31 July was any guide, it would carry British forces – probably at mounting cost – only to those commanding points whose possession by the Germans had made life in the Ypres salient so uncomfortable. That is, the only prospect opened up by the favourable aspects of the fighting on 31 July was a limited geographical advantage.

None of this had any bearing on the large plan presented by Haig as justification for the Third Ypres campaign. That plan presumed that the hammer blows of which 31 July was to be the first would result in the wide-scale collapse of German defensive capacity, and the consequent advance by British forces well beyond the range of their artillery support. As a result, important objectives like the Passchendaele and Klerken Ridges would speedily pass into British hands, and the way be opened to significant positions such as Roulers and Thourout, and eventually the Belgian coast.

As a prelude to this scenario Gough's action on 31 July had little to offer. The German resistance, as their unrelenting bombardments and the actions of their counter-attack forces made clear, was not about to crumble. So 31 July held out only a prospect, and that an ambiguous prospect, of a gradual tactical success – in time and at cost – for Gough's forces. It offered no glimpse of Sir Douglas Haig's great strategic objective.

10

Rain

I

As the 17/King's Liverpool Battalion struggled through Shrewsbury Forest on the opening day of the battle, its commander noted at noon precisely, 'Rain Starts'.[1] It was not to stop for seven days.[2] In fact, during the month of August there were only three days (7, 19, 22) when no rain at all was recorded. The total rainfall for the month was 127 millimetres, almost double the August average of 70 millimetres. Most of the rain fell in four periods:

Rainfall – Selected Periods, August 1917, Ypres

Period	Rain in mm.
1–4	40.7
8–12	18.4
14–15	25.9
26–29	38.4
Total	123.4

Even the intervals between the downpours were by no means fine. Between 16 and 25 August, although only 2–3 millimetres of rain fell, some rain was recorded on eight of the ten days. What this meant was that there was no extended period of fine weather during which the ground could dry.

The unfriendly weather hampered the attack in two ways. The low cloud precluded systematic observation for the artillery, either from the ground or from the air, and the condition of the ground was prohibitive of any speedy advance by the infantry and tanks.

On 7 August an observer from a field ambulance, Sergeant McKay, described the scene:

Bringing the wounded down from the front line today. Conditions
terrible. The ground between Weltje and where the infantry are is simply
a quagmire, and shell holes filled with water. Every place is in full view of
the enemy who are on the ridge. There is neither the appearance of a road
or path and it requires six men to every stretcher, two of these being
constantly employed helping the others out of the holes; the mud in some
cases is up to our waists. A couple of journeys . . . and the strongest men
are ready to collapse.[3]

Not only the infantry were affected. At about the same time that
Sergeant McKay was struggling through the mud of the Pilckem Ridge,
Captain Hever was trying to transfer his guns to a safer place. He was
in command of a battery of the 18 Division artillery which was finding
itself under such heavy shelling that it had just lost all its officers in one
bombardment, and was hit three times the day he took command. He
immediately ordered his battery to move, but found this no easy matter
to arrange. So thick was the ooze and slime that it took 6.5 hours to drag
just one of the battery's six 18-pounders – the lightest gun then in use by
the British – a distance of 250 yards. The total time needed to move the
battery is not recorded but it could not have been much less than two
days.[4]

Conditions deteriorated as the month progressed. On 26 August a
junior officer lying in his pillbox headquarters heard 'sobbing moans of
agony, and despairing shrieks' from no man's land, casualties from a
failed British attack. Among the wounded were four of his friends and
he realized that their agonies had a new and horrible dimension. Many
of them had crawled into shell holes for safety and were now slowly
drowning as the driving rain filled the holes. He could do nothing to
help them. The ground was so boggy that unencumbered movement
was almost impossible. In any case the German barrage precluded any
venture into no man's land.[5]

II

It might be thought the conditions just described would have halted all
military operations until the ground had dried. But on the evening of the
first day Gough issued orders for two operations. One involved a limited
advance by II Corps on 2 August across the Gheluvelt Plateau to capture
the original second objective. The other, to take place on the 4th,
required his other three corps to retake those objectives which had been
lost to counter attack on the opening day.[6]

Haig was quick to agree with these instructions,[7] but a dissenting

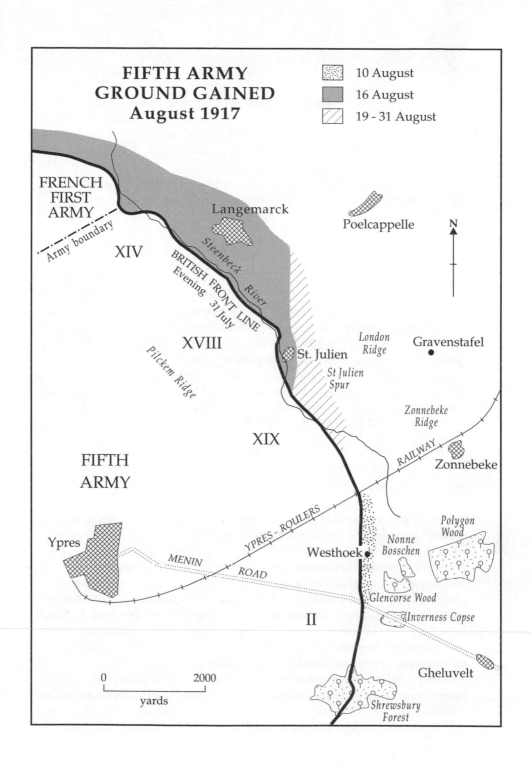

FIFTH ARMY
GROUND GAINED
August 1917

10 August
16 August
19 - 31 August

N

FRENCH
FIRST
ARMY

Langemarck

Poelcappelle

Army boundary

XIV

BRITISH FRONT LINE
Evening 31 July

Steenbeck River

XVIII

Pilckem Ridge

London Ridge

Gravenstafel

St. Julien

St Julien Spur

Zonnebeke Ridge

XIX

RAILWAY

Zonnebeke

FIFTH
ARMY

YPRES - ROULERS

Polygon Wood

Ypres

MENIN ROAD

Westhoek

Nonne Bosschen

Glencorse Wood

Inverness Copse

II

Gheluvelt

0   2000
yards

Shrewsbury Forest

note, as regards the Gheluvelt Plateau, was sounded by Davidson. He deplored the prospect of hurried preparations, the employment of 'part worn' troops, and inadequate artillery support. What was required was three fresh infantry divisions, two or more good days of flying weather, and 'very careful control and accurate shooting'.[8] By the next day Haig seemed to be agreeing with Davidson. He told Gough that he must 'have patience, and not put in his infantry attack until after two or three days of fine weather, to enable our guns to get the upper hand and to dry the ground'. In addition he sought to delay Gough's attempts to advance in the centre, pending progress on the right.[9]

Gough was not responsive. On 3 August he issued a series of operations orders. These envisaged first the capture of the small section of the Gheluvelt Plateau which had constituted his second objective on 31 July, then a more broadly based attack across a large section or all of the front.[10] As the weather continued unfavourable, for a while he postponed these actions. But when at last he launched them little had improved as far as the weather was concerned. Certainly there had been no such improvement as met Haig's and Davidson's strictures 'to have patience' and 'wait for fine weather'. So the first attack (on the 10th), though preceded by some fine days, occurred after a downpour two days earlier from which the ground could not possibly have recovered. And the second larger attack (on the 16th) succeeded two days of heavy rain. There was no prospect here of an operation over 'dry ground' in the aftermath of the guns having got 'the upper hand'.

III

The first of these operations, designed just to capture Gough's second objective on the Gheluvelt Plateau which Jacob's forces had failed to secure on 31 July, was delivered by 18 and 25 Divisions on 10 August. The attacking troops were heavily shelled by the unsubdued German guns even before they went over the top. And although they initially made progress against demoralized German forces that had been left too long in the line, this was soon negated by local enemy counter-attack formations aided by fire from several strongpoints in Inverness Copse. As a result the British suffered 2,200 casualties (amounting in the case of one brigade to half its strength) and gained no ground on the right and a mere 450 yards on the left.[11]

Thus, Gough's first operation following on the major attack of 31 July had not been a conspicuous success. The inability, consequent on bad weather, to provide effective artillery support had cost him lives and failed to make good even the second objective of his initial attack. The one redeeming feature of the operation had been its concentration on the vital Gheluvelt Plateau.

Gough's next endeavour, the attack on 16 August, would not be blessed with even this virtue. It would once again be made in inappropriate weather conditions, but Gough would also ignore Haig's urgings for concentration against a single objective. Instead, he sought to advance over the same broad front as on 31 July. Haig lamely acquiesced. Even though back on 2 August he had urged concentration just on the right of the front, he now stated 'that he left this matter entirely to General Gough's discretion'.[12] Davidson, presumably in despair, kept his own counsel. The outcome would do more than call in question this self-effacement by the commander-in-chief. It would raise serious doubts about Haig's initial decision to place Gough in charge of a major Western Front campaign.

IV

The barrage for Gough's broad front attack on the 16th opened at 4.45 a.m. By the end of the day the French on the left of the front, along with the British forces adjoining them (XIV Corps and the left of XVIII Corps), had captured almost all their objectives, including the village of Langemarck. But in the centre and on the right, hardly a yard of ground had been gained. The Gheluvelt Plateau, so often stressed as the main objective of British endeavours, remained firmly in enemy hands. Not even the second line, which had been the objective of the limited assault on 10 August, was secured.

The success of the French is not difficult to explain. They were endowed with formidable artillery resources – well in excess of what was available to Gough's formations. Further, compared with the Fifth Army their objectives were limited and the German defences not as imposing. So they were able to secure the northern flank at a cost of only 350 casualties.[13]

On Anthoine's right, Cavan's XIV Corps (20, 29, and 11 Divisions), after a thorough artillery preparation which enabled the infantry to bring to bear their Stokes mortars and Lewis guns against the blockhouses, captured all their objectives. So rapid was the advance that the German commanding officer of the battalion defending Langemarck fell into British hands.[14]

An additional factor aiding Cavan's forces was the 'utmost confusion' (in the words of a 20 Division operational report)[15] among the German forces opposing them. Most of the enemy units in this sector had been in the line since 4 August[16] and had been much battered by a series of operations designed to secure the Steenbeek crossings in advance of the main attack and by the bombardment preceding this operation.[17] They were being relieved in the early morning of the 16th when the British attack went in.

Even in this successful operation it should not be thought that all went smoothly. When 20 Division attempted to advance through Langemarck the leading formations came under a withering fire from some machine-gun posts missed by the bombardment. Before they could beat a hasty retreat they had suffered 70 per cent casualties.[18]

On the right of XIV Corps, the preliminary bombardment of Maxse's XVIII Corps had been nowhere near so successful. It had not suppressed the German artillery, as becomes apparent from the fact that 81 per cent of the wounds suffered by one of the attacking divisions resulted from shell fire.[19] Furthermore, a considerable number of strongpoints survived the bombardment. Nevertheless, 11 Division on the left, aided by the progress of XIV Corps, did capture most of its objectives.[20] Maxse's other division (48) fell victim to severe artillery opposition and machine-gun fire from unsuppressed enemy strongpoints. By midday 48 Division had managed to get forward only 100 yards.[21]

The failure of 48 Division demonstrates how badly matters could go wrong even in the best-trained units. Maxse, in whose corps the division fought, was a meticulous trainer. His troops were well drilled and rehearsed before each battle. The courses he ran on leadership, weaponry, and the co-ordination of infantry and artillery tactics were models of their kind. Yet in the attack on 16 August the following incident occurred. The 145 Brigade failed for 12 hours to achieve any advance due to fire from unsubdued machine-gun posts and strongpoints. Then the brigade commander ordered the reserve battalion from 144 Brigade, 1/7 Worcesters, to make a further attempt on these German positions 'without artillery protection'. The result was that the attackers, in the words of the battalion narrative, 'were nearly all wiped out'.[22]

To the right of 48 Division, Watts's XIX Corps faced a particularly difficult problem. The troops of this corps (16 and 36 Divisions) had been in the line for a considerable length of time, under heavy and continuous shell fire. Even before they went over the top, one of the divisions had suffered over 2,000 casualties.[23] It attacked with a strength of 330 men per battalion instead of the regulation 750.[24]

Facing Watts's weary and under-strength divisions, on the bare slopes of the Zonnebecke Ridge, was an impressive array of fortified farmhouses constituting a mutually supporting defensive system. Watts's artillery had failed to eliminate even one of these fortifications prior to the attack. Hence, soon after they set off, the leading battalions of the two Irish divisions which made up this corps had ceased to exist as fighting formations. In one of them, only two officers and three other ranks survived out of 330. The follow-up troops did slightly better, actually managing to eliminate some of the foremost strongpoints. But thereafter the boggy ground and uncut wire caused them to lose the creeping barrage just as they encountered a further sequence of strongpoints. At this moment they were severely counter-attacked and driven back to their own front line.[25]

The official history of one of these divisions (36) is scathing on the causes of defeat. Noting that this had been the first time in the course of the war that the division had failed to reach its objective, the history made the following points: that before the attack the division had already been in the line for 13 days, and during that time as many as 1,000 men per day had been required for carrying work in the forward areas under constant shell fire; that when the attack was launched the state of the ground was such that the men could hardly drag themselves through it; that it was clear the artillery bombardment was not touching the German defences or the enemy artillery; and finally that when the shortcomings of the bombardment were pointed out to counter-battery officers they were not believed.[26]

The sacrifice made by these Irish divisions needs to be spelt out. From the time they entered the line to the end of the battle, the 36 and 16 Divisions sustained 7,800 casualties, more than 50 per cent of their number.[27] Their sacrifice earned them no gratitude. Haig noted in his diary that Gough 'was not pleased with the action of the Irish divisions. . . . They seem to have gone forward but failed to keep what they had won. . . . The men are Irish and apparently did not like the enemy's shelling, so Gough said.'[28] Comment seems superfluous.

The most rightward of the British corps (II) once more faced the formidable defences on the Gheluvelt Plateau. On the left, 8 Division made good progress, advancing almost to their final objective. Then two things happened. First, at 7 a.m. these forces came under heavy enfilade fire resulting from the lack of progress of the attacking troops on either side of them. Secondly, it became evident that the German front had been held lightly and that the real enemy resistance consisted of support and reserve battalions being employed in counter-attack.[29] At 8 a.m. the much reduced and weary ranks of 8 Division were subjected to fierce counter-blows by these German formations and driven back to their original position.[30]

As mentioned, the rebuff to 8 Division was in part the result of failure of forces on both its flanks: on its left by 16 Division, as already recorded, and on its right by the remaining division of II Corps, the 56. The latter attacked on a three-brigade front. The left of these, 169 Brigade, got forward early, even managing to overcome strongpoints in

Nonne Boschen and Glencorse Wood, but then were destroyed by counter-attacks as they entered Polygon Wood. To their right, 167 Brigade encountered a different problem which halted them almost from the start. North of Nonne Boschen they ran into a belt of mud 30 yards wide and 4.5 feet deep.[31] This caused them to lose the barrage, so laying them open to fire from hostile strongpoints – including 'a vital strongpoint' in Inverness Copse 'unaccountably ignored in the bombardment'.[32] Counter-attacks then drove them back to the start line.

The 'vital strongpoint' fell in the sector of the most rightward of the attacking brigades, the 53rd. Its commander, General Higginson, had in earlier encounters rendered himself noteworthy by his frank appraisal of his troops' prospects, and again in the run-up to this attack he stressed on no fewer than four occasions that his men were 'not fresh enough to carry out an attack'.[33] In the event the worn down condition of his forces scarcely counted. They were sent into action against unsuppressed strongpoints and then bombarded by their own artillery. Not surprisingly, their attack had to be abandoned.[34]

The outcome of these endeavours is easily summarized. On the left, the French, along with XIV Corps and part of XVIII Corps, had advanced between 1,000 and 1,500 yards. In the centre, the right of XVIII Corps and all of XIX Corps had advanced hardly at all. On the right, II Corps had made absolutely no progress across the Gheluvelt Plateau. These meagre gains had cost Gough's forces 15,000 casualties.

V

Immediately following the battle, Haig was inclined to put the best interpretation on what had occurred. He wrote in his diary late that day: 'Our attack today was most successful on the left (French) and centre (XIV and XVIII Corps), but only a moderate advance was made on the right (XIX and II Corps). Many Germans have been killed.'[35] When Haig had had time for further reflection he was less impressed. He was still happy with Cavan's achievements on the left, but he acknowledged the measure of failure in the centre, and was not impressed by Gough's attempt to play the Irish card as a means of explanation. He noted that these men had been used in a way that reduced them to exhaustion and that the artillery had failed to remove some of the major obstacles facing them.

Regarding events on the right, Haig discussed the operation with Jacob. He did not appear to dispute Jacob's (inaccurate) assertion that 'a certain amount of important ground' had been captured. But he did remark on the effectiveness of the enemy's artillery. And he noted

Jacob's statement that for the moment II Corps would only attempt to advance hereafter by means of small-scale attacks, making piecemeal assaults on objectives such as Inverness Copse and Nonne Boschen.

In addition, Haig was starting to recollect his strong feelings against the initiation of attacks without regard to the effects of weather on artillery preparations. He wrote:

> The cause of the failure to advance on the right centre of the attack of the Fifth Army is due, I think, to commanders being in too great a hurry!! Three more days should have been allowed in which (if fine and observation good) the artillery would have dominated the enemy's artillery and destroyed his concreted defences![36]

It seems appropriate to comment that Haig was not saying anything about the causes of failure that he had not discerned before the attack was launched. And as not only a commander but the commander-in-chief, he had been well placed to prevent his subordinates from launching attacks in conditions where the artillery could not do its job. One 'cause of failure', in other words, was his refusal to act on his insight and assert his authority.

Gough too was reflecting on the battle. But his conclusions were at variance with Haig's. The Fifth Army commander was more inclined to blame his men than his own decision to attack in bad weather and so deny them the needed measure of artillery support. At a conference with his corps commanders on the 17th, he complained of the inability of the troops to hold on to the ground they had gained and speculated that it might be necessary to court-martial some 'glaring instances' of this type of behaviour by officers or NCOs.[37] He also reached the remarkable conclusion that his divisions were being relieved in the line too soon, thus causing an unnecessary waste of fresh divisions. This practice must stop, he announced, 'or we should run short of troops'.[38]

This was as far as Gough's reflecting went. The remainder of the conference was concerned with forthcoming operations. Each corps commander was asked for his proposals. The results were then summed up and approved by Gough. What was decided upon was a series of operations which would bring the Fifth Army within striking distance of the Passchendaele Ridge. First, on the 19, 21, and 22 August, attacks would be launched by the XVIII, XIX, and II Corps respectively to secure the objectives which had eluded them on the 16th. Then on the 25th, the XIV, XVIII, and XIX Corps would simultaneously attack the Gheluvelt–Langemarck Line, followed later in the day by an assault by II Corps on the same objective. This would be succeeded on an unspecified date by an operation launched across the whole front.[39]

It is necessary to grasp the import of all this. In total, six operations were being proposed. First, the centre–left corps would attack, and two days later the rightward corps. One day after that the corps on the right-centre would move. A pause of three days would then intervene, where-upon all corps would attack on the same day but not at the same time. Finally, after a further three days an advance would be made across the whole front.

What we are looking at are five piecemeal, narrow-front attacks of a sort that had been tried in 1915, 1916, and early 1917 with singular lack of success. Clearly, if the Fifth Army ran 'short of troops', it would not be the result of keeping men too brief a time in the line.

In the event most of Gough's projected operations were abandoned, although not for the obvious reason that they made no military sense. It was found that the shattered divisions of XIX and II Corps simply could not be employed again; nor could they be replaced by fresh troops expeditiously enough to meet Gough's timetable.

So it was decided that XVIII Corps would attack on 19 August to secure objectives not attained on the 16th. Then all corps (except XIV) would attack on the 22nd to capture positions within striking distance of the Gheluvelt–Langemarck Line.

Maxse's first operation went ahead on 19 August and was almost entirely successful. The objectives consisted of a group of fortified farms within a few hundred yards of the XVIII Corps front line.

These positions had inflicted heavy casualties on Maxse's divisions on the 16th, so on this occasion Maxse decided on a novel stratagem. Although by and large the battlefield still resembled a swamp, most of the hostile farms were located near major roads which had been kept in good repair by the Germans, and fine weather since the 16th had firmed these roads sufficiently to permit the passage of tanks. Twelve of these vehicles were assembled in St Julien on the night before the attack. At first light on the 19th the British gunners put down an intense smoke barrage, successfully blinding the German artillery on the near ridges. Behind the barrage rolled the tanks. Slightly in rear followed just 240 infantry. The tanks worked around the rear of the strongpoints and opened fire. This was too much for the defenders, who surrendered or fled. Infantry casualties amounted to 15, those from the Tank Corps 13. Five hitherto formidable strongpoints had been captured in a little over two hours.[40]

This operation, however, had no long-term significance as a method of proceeding. In spite of the success on 19 August, tanks had no general utility in the Ypres salient. This became evident three days later, when XVIII Corps participated as the most leftward element of Gough's wide-front attack of 22 August. Maxse's divisions were again accompanied by tanks, but on this occasion many of the strongpoints could not be brought under fire from the few serviceable roads available. As soon as the tanks ventured from the roads they sank in the slime. XVIII Corps's operation failed to gain any significant ground.[41]

Nor did XIX Corps, operating on the right of XVIII, achieve any greater success. The German strongpoints on the bare slopes of the St Julien Spur took a devastating toll on the infantry of 15 and 61 Divisions as they toiled through the heavy going. Three thousand casualties were suffered; no important gains made.[42] A report from one of the assaulting brigades tersely summed up the causes of failure: the creeping barrage had 'little effect' on the pillboxes; the strength of the enemy defences was 'not fully realised and not sufficiently dealt with by the Heavy Artillery'; and early losses so reduced the attackers' ranks that insufficient men remained to rush even those strongpoints whose garrisons seemed inclined to surrender.[43]

Further to the right, the third attempt by II Corps to secure Inverness Copse also proved futile. (It may be speculated that their efforts were not aided by attacking two hours after the corps to their left, sufficient time to place all the German defenders on the Gheluvelt Plateau in a state of readiness.) Once more, strongpoints had been missed by the artillery, German gunfire was intense, and counter-attacks could not be withstood by the depleted ranks of 14 Division. Bitter fighting over the next two days did not improve the situation. When the battle died down not a yard of ground had been gained on the plateau.[44]

This series of setbacks, and an alarming deterioration in the weather (rain started to fall on 23 August and by the 26th was torrential), provided good reason for halting the attack. But Gough was determined to press on. Information provided to him by his intelligence branch on 24 August encouraged him to do so. It alerted him to the real nature of German defensive arrangements. The enemy forces under attack did not occupy a single line but were distributed chequerboard. As for the counter-attack formations, these were being held beyond the reach of the British guns. Gough proposed two solutions to these difficulties. The percentage of moppers-up to follow the main assault was increased, thereby ensuring the neutralization of such enemy positions as were overrun. And he decided to employ greater numbers of troops in his assaults so as to withstand the expected counter-attacks.

These 'improvements', however, did not address the essence of Gough's difficulties. The Fifth Army was unable to supply fire of sufficient accuracy and density to carry the troops through the German defences at moderate cost. Nor could it maintain those that did get forward on their objective in the face of unsuppressed German artillery operating in conjunction with the counter-attack forces.

Hence, the assaults mounted by Gough in the aftermath of the failures of 22 August enjoyed no greater success. On 27 August the farmhouses and strongpoints on the St Julien Spur were missed by the artillery, as were the German guns. Inverness Copse withstood a fourth assault on the same day.

By the close of fighting on the 27th, Gough's forces were worn out. Since the abortive attacks on 16 August, Maxse's divisions had been employed in three subsequent attacks, Watts's in two, and Jacob's in two. Rain was falling steadily. The case against proceeding for the moment seemed irresistible. Yet Gough ordered another attack for the 31st. The question now emerging was whether Sir Douglas Haig would continue to leave matters 'entirely to General Gough's discretion'.

VI

Haig's ability to perceive the essentials of what had been happening so far, and what needed to be done to put matters to rights, remained as variable and self-contradictory as ever. At a meeting with his senior staff officers on 19 August, he made so wildly optimistic a judgement as to suggest that he was quite unaware of what had been occurring. He told his commanders: 'that our armies' efforts this year have brought final victory nearer. Indeed, I think that, if we can keep up our effort, final victory may be won in December.'[45]

Yet only two days earlier he had taken a very disenchanted view of the operation of 16 August, attributing the failure of Gough's divisions to the inadequacy of his artillery preparations, stressing the folly of launching attacks when the gunners could not suppress the enemy batteries and concrete defences, and castigating commanders who acted in 'too great a hurry!!' This bizarre mixture of wild optimism and realistic appraisal would affect his judgement on Gough's exercise of command in two conflicting ways. The first, as if he was convinced of Gough's inadequacies, was to replace him by Plumer in the key area of the Gheluvelt Plateau. But then, as if this was not happening, for a further period he allowed Gough to proceed as if all had been going well.

So after the failure on the 24th, Haig arranged to interview Gough and Plumer the next day. First Haig saw Plumer, informing him that the front of the Second Army was to be extended leftwards to encompass the area of II Corps. This would entail operations against the Gheluvelt Plateau now being conducted not under Gough's command but under Plumer.[46] Later in the day Haig explained the change of course to Gough. He told him that the next major attack would be along the whole front, but with Plumer and the Second Army responsible for the

Gheluvelt Plateau phase of it.[47] Gough later claimed that he first recommended this manner of proceeding, although there is no contemporary evidence for this.[48]

These arrangements were embodied in an order to Gough on 28 August which stated that the new army boundaries would operate from early September. But, puzzlingly, until this revision came into effect Gough was empowered to undertake attacks against objectives on the plateau which he had so far failed to capture. Haig wrote to him:

> In the present circumstances your operations may be limited to gaining a line including Inverness Copse and Glencorse and Nonne Boschen Woods, and to securing possession, by methodical and well-combined attacks on such farms and other tactical features in front of your line further north as will facilitate the delivery of a general attack later in combination with the Second Army.[49]

Luckily for the troops on the plateau, Haig soon had second thoughts. At a conference on 30 August, when Gough announced his intention to capture on 3 September the belt of woods referred to in Haig's letter, Haig demurred. He now stated that no attack should take place in this area 'until the general conditions were sufficiently satisfactory to offer a good prospect of success'.[50] The next day all prospect that the Fifth Army might continue operations against the plateau vanished. Haig agreed to a request from Plumer that these woods be included in the Second Army's objectives for the first day of the main attack.[51]

These rearrangements, however, did not lessen Gough's enthusiasm for a repetition of his August operations. The XIX Corps, which remained under Gough's command, was employed repeatedly in early September in penny-packet attacks against the fortified farmhouses on the St Julien Spur. Not one was captured.[52] After the fourth of these failures Haig again felt moved to intervene. On 9 September he spoke to Gough about discontinuing small-scale operations. As recorded by Haig, Gough's reply is remarkable:

> [Gough] said that [the two divisions which had carried out the previous attacks] were shortly leaving the front, and that for the sake of training and moral[e] they ought not to go without having taken the two points which they recently attacked with one or two companies, but failed to hold after they had taken them.[53]

Haig once more climbed down, lamely agreeing to further attacks, 'provided that the troops themselves felt equal to the task.'[54] Pretty clearly, this exchange would not open the way to consultations with rank-and-file soldiers about the desirability of attacking objectives which had proved beyond them on four previous occasions. Indeed, it was an entirely meaningless proviso. So, on 10 September, a fifth attack was delivered. The results were summed up by the report of one of the attacking brigades.

> As our men topped the rise they were met by a severe and rapid rifle fire – point blank range. This fire, together with the flanking fire of M.G.'s from [three farms on the flanks of the attack] was more than they could face. In spite of determined efforts on the part of officers and individual men to advance further, the attack collapsed. . . . It does not seem of much avail to launch large masses of men against this type of defensive position.[55]

After this fiasco, Haig became concerned that 'Gough's subordinates' (by whom he presumably meant Neill Malcolm) were keeping the true state of the divisions from the army commander. So he undertook to visit the divisional commanders directly. They gave him contradictory advice. One (Fanshawe) suggested that there was no good prospect of success, the other (McKenzie) that he was certain that his men could take the objectives before leaving the line. Haig inclined to Fanshawe's view. He sought out Gough and urged (but did not order) him to cancel any attacks that were not necessary as a preliminary for the success of the main operation (now scheduled for the 20th).[56] Under this belated pressure, Gough at last decided to abandon all Fifth Army operations scheduled in advance of the main attack.[57] Whether he, or for that matter Haig, realized it or not, Gough's exercise of overall command in the Third Ypres campaign was at an end. Plumer's moment was now at hand.

Part IV
Plumer

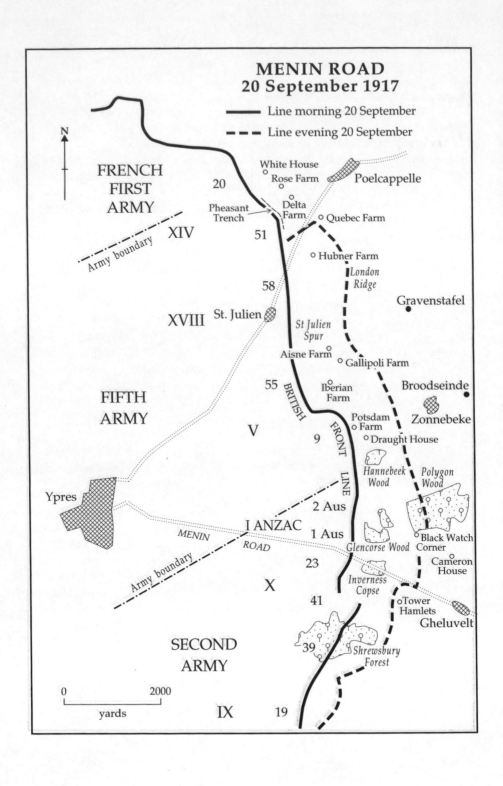

MENIN ROAD
20 September 1917

——— Line morning 20 September

- - - Line evening 20 September

N

FRENCH
FIRST
ARMY

White House
Rose Farm
Poelcappelle

20

Pheasant
Trench
Delta
Farm
Quebec Farm

Army boundary
XIV
51

Hubner Farm

London
Ridge

58
Gravenstafel

XVIII
St. Julien
St Julien
Spur

Aisne Farm
Gallipoli Farm
Broodseinde

FIFTH
ARMY
55
Iberian
Farm
Zonnebeke

BRITISH
Potsdam
Farm
Draught House

V
9
Hannebeek
Wood
Polygon
Wood

FRONT
LINE

Ypres
2 Aus

I ANZAC
1 Aus
Black Watch
Corner

MENIN
Glencorse Wood
Cameron
House

ROAD
23
Inverness
Copse

Army boundary
X
41
Tower
Hamlets
Gheluvelt

SECOND
ARMY
39
Shrewsbury
Forest

0   2000

yards
IX   19

11

Menin Road

I

Plumer's scheme for future operations was submitted to the commander-in-chief on 29 August 1917. It called for a series of steps with a strictly limited objective. Each step was designed to advance the Second Army about 1,500 yards, until the Gheluvelt Plateau was in British hands.[1] It seems safe to speculate that this scheme owed much to Plumer's experience at Messines. At that battle, it will be recalled, Plumer had originally intended to advance just 1,500 yards. Then Haig had extended the objectives to 3,000–4,000 yards. During the course of the battle Plumer's original objective had been taken with relative ease. Later advances had broken down in a welter of muddle and confusion which resulted in heavy casualties. Eventually most of Haig's objectives had been captured, but Plumer must have reflected that this result could have been achieved at a much lower cost had the operation been divided into a series of deliberate steps. This caution can only have been reinforced by observing Gough's increasingly futile attempts against the strong German defences on the plateau during August.

So the Second Army would now fully engage the German defenders on and behind the plateau. At the same time, to the north, Gough's Fifth Army, spared the enfilade fire which had hampered it up to this point, was also intended to proceed by a series of steps. Its objective was the capture of the Passchendaele Ridge, after which it would exploit strategically any large opportunities that might occur.[2]

In this scenario, Plumer would for the moment be the main player, would command the greater number of troops and weapons, and would be dictating the nature of operations. This did not necessarily mean that, in Haig's scheme of things, Plumer would continue to generate operations right to the end of Third Ypres. If Plumer succeeded in capturing the Gheluvelt Plateau with Second Army and the Passchendaele Ridge with Fifth Army, then it would still be possible for Haig to restore Gough to overall direction. So Fifth Army might even yet become Haig's instrument for sweeping across the green fields beyond the salient and claiming those distant objectives which all along had been the *raison d'être* of the campaign.

II

The purpose of Plumer's first move was the capture of those strongpoints and woods on the Gheluvelt Plateau – Nonne Boschen, Glencorse Wood, Inverness Copse, Polygon Wood, and Tower Hamlets – which had held up the Fifth Army throughout August. On Plumer's left, Gough would advance in line and to a similar distance, capturing the complex of fortified farms on the St Julien Spur.

Barring the progress of the British were those formidable defensive arrangements which they had attacked in vain during August. Six German divisions held these positions, distributed in depth and supported by three counter-attack divisions about 5,000–7,000 yards behind their front line.[3]

Supporting their infantry the Germans could call upon 750 guns.[4] The great bulk of these (about 550) faced Plumer, leaving 200 arrayed against Gough.[5] All enemy guns had been carefully sited to prevent easy detection. Most of the heavy pieces lay behind the reverse slope of the Passchendaele Ridge and the Gheluvelt Plateau, with the remainder scattered in small camouflaged groups right across the front. A large number of gun-pits had been constructed by the Germans to facilitate the transfer of batteries from one position to another in order to confuse British observers.

III

Operating against these defences Plumer and Gough had available nine divisions from four corps, aided by the flanking fire of two more corps. Three of the attacking corps and their constituent divisions were new to the battle. From the south, the Second Army had X Corps (Morland) with 39, 41, and 23 Divisions and 1 Anzac Corps (Birdwood) with 1 and 2 Australian Divisions. Further north, Fifth Army had V Corps (Fanshawe) with 9 and 55 Divisions and the battle-experienced XVIII Corps (Maxse) with 58 and 51 Divisions. Flanking fire would be provided to the Second Army by IX Corps (19 Division) and to the Fifth Army by XIV Corps (20 Division).[6]

   As in most First World War battles, it would not be the infantry – fresh or otherwise – that would prove the critical ingredient. To achieve his purpose Plumer called for an artillery concentration that was unprecedented for the length of front to be attacked. The Second Army would dispose 575 heavy and 720 field guns for an attack on a 5,000-yard front. The Fifth Army employed about 300 heavy and 600 field guns for a similar front of attack.[7] These guns would not want for ammunition. No less than 3.5 million shells were available to Plumer, of which he fired 1.65 million in the preliminary bombardment.[8] This gave him a concentration of shells three times higher than that employed on 31 July. Gough was not so lavishly supplied, but even he achieved twice the shell concentration of the opening day.[9]

   The purpose of all this weaponry was to destroy or neutralize a substantial proportion of both the enemy strongpoints and their protecting artillery.[10]

   For the strongpoints – concrete machine-gun nests, pillboxes, fortified farmhouses – destructive fire was to commence at the end of August and proceed until the day of battle. The heaviest guns (9.2-inch, 12-inch, and 15-inch howitzers) were to be used against these structures, high-explosive shell being supplemented with armour-piercing against the most powerful of them.[11]

   In order to ensure the destruction or neutralization of hostile guns, the counter-battery activities (employing aerial observation, sound ranging, and flash spotting) needed to begin early in September and intensify in the week preceding the infantry attack on 20 September. Then at zero hour all known battery positions were to be subjected to a continuous rain of gas shells.[12]

   To protect the attacking infantry from such strongpoints as did survive this amount of attention Plumer arranged a creeping barrage, with the added refinement this time that, as the infantry progressed from one objective to another, the barrage would slow by stages from a rate of advance of 100 yards every four minutes to 100 yards every eight minutes.[13]

   As at Messines, Plumer was not content with these measures of infantry protection. Four more barrages, each 200 yards in depth, would be placed ahead of the creeping barrage to provide a moving curtain of fire of about 1,000 yards.[14] That is, almost the entire zone to be assaulted by the British would be under continuous artillery fire for the duration of the attack.

   Nor would the bombardment cease when the infantry had secured their final objective. The entire 1,000-yard barrage would continue to fall in front of the new British front line for a further nine hours, enabling the troops to consolidate possession of the captured ground free from large-scale counter-attack operations.[15]

IV

During the first 19 days of September, the usual round of infantry training was proceeding. The training took familiar forms. The troops rehearsed their attacks over ground resembling, as far as possible, that to be assailed. Models of the battlefield were constructed and studied by most of the officers involved in the attack.[16]

All this was done with great efficiency. Nevertheless, it was recognized by at least the more perceptive observers at the time that the endeavours of the foot soldiers would not be decisive in accomplishing the objectives of the operation. After attending a practice attack carried out by Australian troops, Captain McGrigor, ADC to General Birdwood, commented:

> Very interesting it was too, but it did bring home to one how appallingly mechanical everything is now, and how every man must conform to the advance of the barrage. Initiative and dash must to a certain extent be fettered as every forward movement is worked out so carefully and mathematically and must not be exceeded or the barrage fail to be reached, otherwise the effect of the carefully thought out barrage is lost and the attack is possibly beaten off or an entire failure.[17]

McGrigor's remarks highlight the distinction between Third Ypres operations hitherto and the type of attack which Plumer was about to launch. Gough on 31 July had stipulated an advance of 4,000 yards not because this was the effective range of his artillery but because his troops needed to get so far so as to place themselves within striking distance of the Passchendaele Ridge. The Second Army commander, by contrast, did not set his sights on some desired geographical objective. He calculated the distance over which his artillery could provide a safe passage for his advancing infantry. As the suppression of German counter-attack activities must be accomplished by his field artillery, the range of these weapons would establish the extent of his planned advance.

V

In a widely held judgement, the preliminary bombardment which preceded the Menin Road battle on 20 September achieved a crushing success. The activity of the German guns, in this view, had been almost completely silenced. The reality was otherwise. Despite the overwhelming superiority in numbers of the British guns, they were hard put to it to overcome their adversaries by the time the British infantry went forward. The history of the 33rd Divisional artillery, supporting 23 Division, makes this clear. It states that losses inflicted upon it by enemy fire during the period of the preliminary bombardment were 'heavy' and that by the time the attack went in 'there was not one detachment [of guns] which had not already been seriously depleted in numbers'.[18] In the area to the immediate south of these batteries, Captain Yoxall (from whom we will hear again) noted that enemy retaliation to British artillery fire was usually delivered within a minute and could inflict heavy casualties.[19]

Likewise, in Gough's command, 9 Division recorded that its battery positions were 'fiercely bombarded' day and night during this period.[20] One battery commander in this area noted that his guns often had to be left unfired because of the hail of 4.2-inch and 5.9-inch shell directed at them.[21]

To this evidence may be added the more formal assessments of army intelligence reports. The Second Army noted heavy fire against at least some of its battery positions on five of the seven days, and the Fifth Army on six of the seven days, of the preliminary bombardment.[22] It is also clear from these reports that the British were not progressively mastering the German guns. Retaliatory fire was as heavy on the eve of battle as on the days the preliminary bombardment commenced.[23] Even bad weather scarcely hampered the Germans: so densely packed were the British guns that good observation was hardly necessary to secure the enemy numerous hits.

So even an artillery superiority of four to one failed speedily to quell the German batteries. It is easy to see why: for most of the period of the preliminary bombardment low cloud and rain hampered aerial observation of enemy guns grouped behind the lee of the Passchendaele Ridge and the Gheluvelt Plateau.

These difficulties were not aided by the action of some British artillery officers, especially those in the Fifth Army. They failed to locate their own batteries on the map with any accuracy, thus making map shooting at enemy guns a matter of chance. These deficiencies were finally realized by the artillery commanders Uniake and Birch, but not until 18 September when most of the preliminary bombardment had been fired.[24]

The vagaries of the weather and the slackness of British artillery officers were not the only problems confronting the gunners. The Germans were active in moving their guns about, so that an enemy battery was not necessarily still in the place located by the time British shells began to fall.[25] Further, a percentage of enemy guns remained silent so as to escape the attention of the British sound rangers and flash spotters.

Hence, although the British bombardment of 1.6 million shells inflicted great damage on the German batteries, it was not the case that only trivial numbers of enemy guns survived. Many remained to engage in counter-battery fire during the preliminary bombardment and to fire on the British infantry both as they formed up and as they endeavoured to cross no man's land.

VI

During the night of the 19th, 65,000 men from the eighteen assault brigades slowly moved into position. Around midnight rain began to fall. The approach march became increasingly difficult as the churned-up ground turned to mud and the shell holes began to fill with water. Gough, perhaps reflecting on his own failure to halt the numerous rain-hampered attacks in August, suggested to Plumer that operations be postponed.[26] But Plumer, after consulting his corps commanders, demurred.[27] The attack would go ahead as planned.

In the event the deteriorating weather, while hampering the approach of the troops, may have served to their advantage by concealing their arrival from the enemy. Only in the area of 1 Anzac Corps was enemy artillery fire a serious factor. Here 1 Australian Division suffered particularly heavy losses, one of its battalions losing all its company commanders and half its junior officers before reaching the front line.[28]

The operations on the far right and left, designed to secure the flanks of the main attack, met with mixed fortunes. That in the north largely failed. There, the main obstacle was a strong trench running between embankments about eight feet high. Its destruction called for pinpoint accuracy by the artillery. This was not accomplished for, in a bizarre judgement, the divisional commander decided to do away with conventional artillery fire altogether and attack it with burning drums of oil thrown from slingshot devices known as Lievens Projectors – noted for their extreme inaccuracy. The result was predictable. The drums missed the trench and the attacking infantry were cut down in great numbers by the unimpaired German defence. At the end of the day the trench remained in enemy hands.[29]

On the southern flank more success was gained, if at high cost. The bombardment in this area had missed a number of strong machine-gun posts directly in the path of the advancing infantry. The leading waves were shot down; subsequent troops attacked without the protection of the creeping barrage which had disappeared into the distance as though the initial attack had been completely successful. In the end the Germans were only overwhelmed by weight of numbers used in repeated frontal assaults. All told, this subsidiary operation, in accomplishing an advance of 500 yards, cost 3,000 casualties.[30]

These flanking operations did not, in the event, affect the course of the battle. The attack by eight out of the nine divisions making the assault in the centre had by mid-afternoon reached almost all their objectives. The two divisions each from XVIII and V Corps had advanced their line about 1,000 yards, and 1 Anzac and 23 Division of X Corps were 1,500 yards from their start line.

It is noteworthy that the reports of this action written at the time and those in the official histories treat the Menin Road battle as largely an artillery victory. So the Australian Official History, a work which usually makes much of the travails of the infantry, here attributes success to the gunners:

The advancing barrage won the ground; the infantry merely occupied it, pouncing on any points where resistance survived. Whereas the artillery was generally spoken of as supporting the infantry, in this battle the infantry were little more than a necessary adjunct to the artillery's effort.[31]

Yet none of this should be taken to mean that the Menin Road battle was an easy victory or that the British forces did not pay a heavy price to secure it. We have already noted the losses among the artillery during the preliminary bombardment and the losses of the flanking divisions on the day of the attack. Heavy casualties were also suffered in the centre, where the attack was most successful. Despite statements in the operation reports about the Germans offering 'little resistance' and causing 'very little trouble',[32] the casualty figures disclosed by these documents tell a different story. At the end of the day XVIII Corps had suffered over 2,500 casualties, V Corps 4,000, 1 Anzac 5,000, and X Corps 5,500.[33] Thus 17,000 casualties had been suffered by the centre divisions. If the flank divisions' casualties are added, the advance cost the British about 21,000 men killed and wounded for the capture of 5.5 square miles – about 3,800 casualties per square mile. To place this in some perspective, on the first day of battle, 31 July, Gough's forces suffered 27,000 casualties and captured 18 square miles, 1,500 casualties per square mile.

The Menin Road battle, that is, was not an easy success but a triumph over adversity. This is made clear by a close reading of the operational reports. The 1 Anzac Corps had no sooner left their trenches than they were subjected to heavy fire from long-range artillery, from machine-guns situated in Hannebeek Wood, Nonne Boschen, Glencorse Wood, Draught House, Black Watch Corner, and Cameron House, and from various scattered pillboxes. They were then shelled by their own artillery.[34]

Similarly, in the Fifth Army sector, the troops of XVIII Corps encountered fire from Schuler and Hubner Farms, Pheasant Trench, Points 48 and 85, Quebec Farm, the White House, and Rose and Delta Farms, as well as a number of machine-guns on the Poelcappelle Road.[35] In fact in this sector so fierce was the machine-gun fire from these strongpoints that some battalions were forced to retreat. Only energetic work by individual officers managed to rally these men on their original front line and drive them forward again. In time their objectives were taken, but at high cost.

The fighting in V Corps area was even more desperate. On the right, 55 Division came under such heavy fire from Iberian, Gallipoli, and Aisne Farms that the creeping barrage was lost. Casualties in some battalions reached 80 per cent and it was only with resolute action by the follow-up formations (accompanied this time by the barrage, which had been brought back) that the final objectives were taken.[36]

On the left, only a novel artillery stratagem by 9 Division allowed it to get forward. Before the battle the divisional commander had been concerned that the strongpoints in Hannebeek Wood which lay directly in the path of the advance were not being eliminated by the preliminary bombardment. So he arranged that the wood be kept under a hail of fire by the heavy artillery until the infantry was in a position to surround it and mount converging attacks. This proved to be a wise precaution. When the wood was entered it was found to be bristling with pillboxes and machine-gun nests which had survived the preliminary bombardment. These positions were rushed by the infantry when the bombardment lifted and thus taken with tolerable losses.[37]

In other areas on the left, casualties were higher. An imposing strongpoint known as Potsdam Farm had been missed by the bombardment and its German defenders took a fearful toll of the attacking troops before they were finally overcome. Despite these mishaps, by mid-afternoon the following waves were able to secure all of the division's final objectives.[38]

What is apparent from all this is that, despite the severity of the artillery's contribution in preparation and on the day of battle, many German guns were still in operation, and along with a scattered machine-gun defence these were able to offer stiff resistance to the British attack. Nevertheless, they proved unable to provide a defence so coherent as to bar the progress of an attack whose objectives lay not far distant from the jumping-off point and well within the range of artillery support.

There was one division on 20 September (41 Division, X Corps) which suffered a different experience and one unusual enough to warrant closer scrutiny. This experience, it should be noted, cannot be reconstructed from the usual array of reports and battle narratives in the war diaries. For this division, on that day, none survive. This gap in the record can be rectified by the personal diary of one who participated in the battle. Captain Harry Yoxall was an intelligence officer attached to one of the division's attacking brigades. At zero hour Yoxall found himself at forward brigade headquarters. There he witnessed the usual arrival of the walking wounded from the first waves of the attack. Satisfactory progress was reported. Then

a terrible thing happened. An enormous crowd of 124th Bde suddenly appeared, retiring in disorder. We formed a battle stop with headquarters officers & men . . . & drove lots of them back. What things we did & what language we used during that hateful half hour I do not remember. We stopped as many as we could but many got around us. A hundred & fifty were collected [as far back as] Bde Hqurs.[39]

What had caused this rout? Apparently the brigade, at the very beginning of their attack, had run into a line of machine-guns which had emerged unscathed from the British bombardment. The assault immediately collapsed under a welter of casualties. The remainder of the brigade fled.[40] These constituted the mob which Yoxall encountered. Later attempts to rectify the position only added to the casualty list. Finally, an outflanking move by the brigade to the north enabled the machine-guns to be overcome, and the first objective was captured. But the division was incapable of further effort and in this part of the line the final objective remained in German hands. Three thousand casualties had been suffered and the brigade finished as a fighting formation.[41]

VII

Notwithstanding heavy casualties all along the front and some episodes of disaster as well, Plumer's and Gough's men had been successful in advancing across the plateau to an average depth of 1,250 yards. Could they now withstand the inevitable German counter-attacks?

Second and Fifth Army intelligence had accurately estimated that the Germans had three counter-attack divisions available that day, about seven miles behind the front.[42] From noon to 7 p.m. these formations launched, or attempted to launch, 11 counter-attacks. Of these, ten failed completely and one only managed to drive the British line back a few hundred yards. The reason for the Germans' failure was clear. The counter-attack troops had been held too far back, and so approached the British line only after consolidation had taken place. But even more, as long as the British advance was not at all ambitious, their artillery did not need to reposition itself in order to ward off the German forces. So enemy counter-attack formations had to thread their way through a standing barrage 1,000 yards in depth covering the newly captured line. That this caused the counter-attacks to become dislocated can be seen by the experience of the German 236 Division. During the course of the afternoon it launched four counter-attacks but at three different times, in four different locations, and in strengths which varied from one battalion to eight.[43] This gave them no chance of success. One British participant summed up the German experience:

> At 6.5 pm the enemy's shelling . . . began to increase and developed into a heavy barrage heralding the expected counter attack. Shortly after [the infantry signalled for artillery support which soon] began to pour destruction into the German territory. Huge clouds of smoke and dust rapidly filled the air forward of our position, and the flashes of our bursting shells only served to make the maelstrom behind the enemy lines more terrible. . . . Our guns continued to pour a tremendous weight of metal over until 8.30 pm. This counter attack failed to develop.[44]

VIII

As noted earlier, in terms of casualties suffered for ground gained the Menin Road battle compared unfavourably with the initial attack on 31 July. This was despite the fact that Plumer possessed many more guns absolutely than had Gough and, prior to the attack, had enjoyed the advantage of much better weather for observing the fall of shot. As for possession of aerial superiority, and of volume of guns *vis-à-vis* those of the Germans, his position was at least as favourable as Gough's had been. Only in one respect – the Germans' peculiar opportunity to conceal their guns when Plumer attacked – was the Second Army commander at a disadvantage compared with Gough three weeks earlier.

It is noteworthy that with such relative advantages, Plumer did not manage to vanquish the German artillery which consequently inflicted on his forces a higher rate of casualties than Gough had suffered in his initial attack (the only day when Gough's operations had enjoyed tolerable weather). And even on the Gheluvelt Plateau, where Gough had fared least well on 31 July, Plumer nevertheless captured less ground on 20 September.

How then do we explain the aclaim that Plumer has since received compared with the less than lavish enthusiasm bestowed on Gough's endeavours?

First, Gough's accomplishment on 31 July has been judged, not in terms of a limited advance even though that was all he was attempting, but of the large expectations of a breakthrough to the Belgian coast which Haig had aroused (and the War Cabinet had found irresistible). No such expectations accompanied Plumer's operation seven weeks later. Secondly, Gough – while capturing more territory on 31 July than did Plumer on 20 September – did not achieve even his stated objective of an advance of 4,000 yards and was driven back by German counter-attacks from some of the territory his forces had initially occupied. This seemed a more ambiguous success than Plumer's operation, with its attainment of smaller objectives but with their retention in the face of German counter-attack. Thirdly, Gough's achievement on 31 July was completely overshadowed by his abysmal operations during August. Fourthly, Plumer had advanced across ground that the commander-in-chief had deemed vital for future British success – the Gheluvelt Plateau. This Gough had signally failed to do (or at times even attempt) in the five weeks during which he had been in sole control of the battle.

What, above all, emerges from this is that the satisfaction generated by Plumer's attack stems less from the extent of his achievement than from the diminishing expectations accompanying the campaign. Gough had failed to strike the sort of blow that would shatter the enemy morale and open his way to the Belgian coast. Nobody noted that Plumer also failed to do this, because no one expected him to do so much. So his quite modest achievement was deemed cause for celebration.

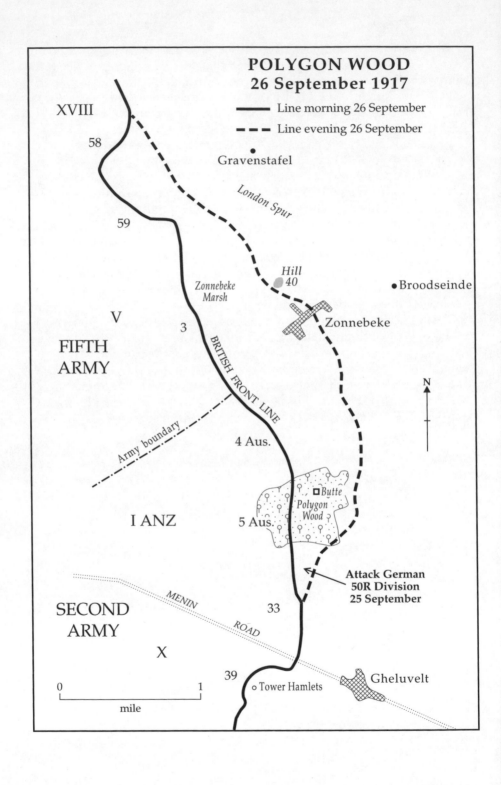

POLYGON WOOD
26 September 1917

——— Line morning 26 September

- - - - Line evening 26 September

XVIII

58

• Gravenstafel

London Spur

59

Zonnebeke Marsh

Hill 40

• Broodseinde

V

3

Zonnebeke

FIFTH ARMY

BRITISH FRONT LINE

Army boundary

4 Aus.

□ *Butte*
Polygon Wood

I ANZ

5 Aus.

N

Attack German
50R Division
25 September

SECOND ARMY

MENIN ROAD

33

X

39

o Tower Hamlets

Gheluvelt

0 ——————— 1
mile

12

Polygon Wood

I

At advanced GHQ Haig took the success of the Menin Road battle as a portent of great things. He immediately issued instructions for the second stage of the plan to commence on the 26th, adding (with a certain circularity):

the attack is to be carried out on as wide a front as possible . . . in order to obtain the tactical advantages of attacking on a wide front.[1]

While his army commanders were doing their best to digest this wisdom, Haig delivered to them a map on which he sketched out the projected stages of the campaign. On the 26th Polygon Wood and Zonnebecke were to be captured. Later (about 4 October) the remainder of the Gheluvelt Plateau including Broodseinde would be taken, along with Poelcappelle to the north. 'Subsequent operations' (time not specified) would capture the Passchendaele Ridge.[2]

Haig – as has sometimes not been noticed – did not intend to stop there. The wide-ranging objectives laid down in the original July plan were now revived. Admiral Bacon was summoned from Dover for consultations on the coastal operation and the seaborne landing. Haig instructed him to place his forces in a state of readiness: they were to act as soon as 'we get on to the ridges above Roulers and Thourout (as we may well do)'.[3] Bacon replied that he could see no difficulty from the naval point of view – favourable tides lasted until 5 November.[4]

Haig's renewed approach to Bacon makes strange reading in the light of what had been achieved so far. In seven weeks' campaigning since 31 July, the British armies had advanced 3.5 miles and had sustained about 86,000 casualties. Haig was now proposing a further advance of 3.5 miles within just one or two weeks, to be followed shortly thereafter by a 12 to 17 mile advance on Roulers and Thourout. After that, to coincide with Guy Fawkes Day and a favourable tide, he anticipated a 30-mile progress to the Belgian coast.

Not entering into these speculations, apparently, was any consideration of the weather. September had proved mercifully dry. Yet even so (on account of the high water table and the destruction of the drainage system by shelling), just 5 millimetres of rain before the Menin Road attack had turned parts of the moonscape-battlefield into a quagmire. Now the end of the campaigning season was nigh. In October the average rainfall was 75 millimetres, with results for the condition of the ground which were bound to be severe. Yet there is no evidence that Haig, in adhering to the project for a large-scale advance, was making provision for this eventuality.[5]

II

Haig's expectations appeared to require the early collapse of German opposition in the Flanders area. Yet events at the front in the ensuing days revealed the enemy to be making an ordered and effective response to the Menin Road setback.

One of the shortcomings of Plumer's step-by-step approach was that the shallowness of the steps did not allow for the capture of any of the German guns. Nor, as we have seen, did the British artillery yet have the accuracy to destroy significant numbers of enemy artillery pieces. Further, in the interval before Plumer's next attack, the enemy proved quite able to replace such guns as had been damaged. That is, far from the British confronting a declining adversary, they would at their next attempt have to contend with guns and troops as formidable as those encountered at the Menin Road.[6]

There was a further severe problem facing the British – one which was inherent in Plumer's plan for a quick succession of small steps across the plateau. In the interval between 20 and 25 September, the British were unable to maintain a counter-battery programme of great intensity. In the aftermath of Menin Road a proportion of the British guns had to be moved forward to new positions for the coming battle, thus temporarily removing them from counter-battery activity.[7] Hence the artillery equation became slightly more favourable to the Germans in the run-up to Polygon Wood than it had been before Plumer's initial operation.

It is clear from British intelligence reports that the Germans made good use of these favourable circumstances. The Second Army reported that from 22 to 25 September the enemy bombardment of their battery positions was 'severe' or 'heavy'.[8] In this area the 33rd Divisional

Artillery preparations on the 21st were 'continually interrupted by hostile shell storms which inflicted many casualties'.[9] Nor did this ordeal slacken as the battle approached. On the 24th the gunners were reporting shell storms 'of *increasing* violence delivered upon every area where any of our batteries were to be found'.[10] Fifth Army Intelligence Reports indicate that their supporting batteries were receiving similar treatment.[11]

The force of these reports is underlined by the casualties being sustained by the British artillery. They were twice as heavy as those suffered in the run-up to the Menin Road battle.[12]

If further demonstration was needed that the Germans were far from being a spent force, it was provided by the events of the 25th. Prince Rupprecht, the commander of the group of armies facing Plumer and Gough, was well aware that the British would soon attempt to follow up the Menin Road victory. He ordered a strong counter-attack to the south of Polygon Wood by two regiments of the recently arrived 50 Reserve Division.[13] The object of this attack was to recapture the German defensive line in front of Polygon Wood, and no doubt to disrupt the preparations for the renewal of Plumer's offensive.

The timing of this attack could hardly have been more unfavourable for the British. When the Germans attacked at 5.45 a.m. 33 Division was in the process of taking over the front from 23 Division.[14] The assault was accompanied by a bombardment of extreme ferocity.[15] Shells from no less than 44 field batteries and 20 heavy batteries rained down on the hapless British.[16] One authority has described this as the heaviest artillery concentration supporting the attack of a single German division in the course of the war.[17]

On the left of the 33rd Divisional front this deluge of shells enabled the Germans to penetrate to a depth of 700 yards. However, on the right the assault made no progress, for the enemy troops lost their way in the mist and joined the forces attacking on the left. Hence, when the mist lifted the elements of 33 Division on the unattacked right were able to pour a withering fire into the crowded forces on the left and so bring the German attack to a halt.[18]

Simultaneously, on the left of the German advance, 5 Australian Division, as they became aware of the seriousness of the situation, managed to establish a defensive flank which was also able to subject the Germans to an intense enfilade fire.[19]

Finally, as the weather cleared around mid-morning, the British artillery commenced a barrage of such intensity on the old German front line that the enemy were unable to reinforce their forward troops. As a result the attack withered from lack of support.

Nevertheless, 98 Brigade of 33 Division had suffered heavy casualties and all attempts to retake the ground lost ended in failure,[20] so impairing the attack which Plumer was about to launch on the following day. Further, this German operation should have put paid to any notion that the enemy was now a waning force and might as a result of persistent pressure be susceptible to abrupt collapse.

III

The plan for the second-step advance had been settled by Plumer and Gough soon after the 20th. The front of attack was to be 8,500 yards, much narrower than for the Menin Road battle (14,500 yards). The advance would also be shallower – 1,000 to 1,250 yards compared to 1,500 to 1,700 yards.[21] These more modest dimensions resulted from the difficulty in getting sufficient artillery forward to support a larger attack. So in a continuing display of sanity, the infantry plan was reduced to what could be supported by the artillery. As the number of shells fired by the British for the attack on the 26th was only 60 per cent of that fired for the advance on the 20th, so the length of front attacked and the depth of advance projected was reduced accordingly.[22] This meant that the artillery *concentration* was just about identical for the two battles.

So on 26 September in the north XVIII Corps with 58 Division would establish a defensive flank near Aviatik Farm. On their right V Corps would overrun London Spur including the ruins of Zonnebecke village and the high ground around Hill 40. On their right 1 Anzac Corps (4 and 5 Australian Divisions) would complete the capture of Polygon Wood and the section of the Gheluvelt Plateau to its north. Further yet to the right, X Corps with 39 Division would secure the southern defensive flank by seizing the high ground around Tower Hamlets. The other division in X Corps, 33 Division, was originally intended to advance in step with the Anzacs to the south of Polygon Wood. However, because of the German counter-attack on the 25th, their objectives were limited to an advance of just 500 yards – enough to cover the flank of the 5th Australian Division.[23]

IV

In general terms the battle of Polygon Wood was a success. Almost all the objectives were captured, despite stiff German resistance from specific strongpoints.

This is not to say that all went smoothly. On the northern flank the mist was so bad that it was impossible to see more than 30 yards. As a consequence, the attacking troops lost the barrage and all cohesion. By the end of the day the line had been advanced only 100 yards.[24]

To the south the ground proved so boggy that 39 Division could not keep pace with the barrage and were shot down in large numbers just short of their objective. Not surprisingly, the tanks sent to assist them failed to penetrate the morass. Consequently the Tower Hamlets Spur remained in German hands. The 39 Division had suffered over 1,500 casualties.[25]

Even more dislocation was experienced in the area of 33 Division as a result of the previous day's counter-attack. The 98 Brigade of this division, which was supposed to advance in concert with 15 Australian Brigade on its left, was nowhere to be seen at zero hour on account of its experience on the 25th.[26] But the situation was retrieved by the Australians, who managed to capture their first objective and then use follow-up formations to sidestep to the right, thus capturing much of the territory assigned to 98 Brigade.[27]

To the north, in the area of the Fifth Army, the troops of V Corps eventually managed to capture all their objectives but only after experiencing some difficulty. In the area of 3 Division the troops lost their way in the mist and then encountered the impassable Zonnebecke marsh. In trying to negotiate a way around this obstacle they lost the barrage and suffered heavy casualties from the German defenders of Hill 40, which remained uncaptured for most of the day. Only a second attack arranged towards evening with appropriate artillery support secured this object for the British.[28]

Further north, 59 Division had an easier time of it. The barrage was good, the ground was firm, and the division even had the luxury of help from two sections of tanks in assisting to take some strongpoints. All objectives were captured according to timetable and no serious opposition was encountered.[29]

The key objective for the day lay in the centre of the attack. There the high ground encompassing the ruins of Polygon Wood was to be captured by 1 Anzac Corps. In the centre of the wood lay a large mound known as the Butte which gave good observation to the defence and which it was feared was honeycombed with bunkers and tunnels that might conceal a considerable number of machine-gun detachments. It was to be attacked by 5 Australian Division, one of whose battalion commanders has left a detailed account of the fighting.

Punctually at Zero Hour (5. 50 a.m.) our barrage opened and the Battalion immediately rose and doubled across 'No Man's land' till reaching about 60 yards short of the barrage where the men knelt down waiting for it to begin to creep forward. [As the battalion advanced it began to encounter the first line of German fortifications but] the formations and methods of attacking strong posts as laid down and practised proved entirely satisfactory and effective. . . . Resistance from 'Pill Boxes' and Strong Posts was encountered almost immediately, but in no case was the advance checked. In one case a strong post was encountered and machine gun fire opened on the attackers. Immediately a CSM [company sergeant major] and about half a dozen men worked round the flanks while a Lewis Gun team opened direct fire on the position drawing the enemy fire off the enveloping parties who were then easily able to work round, rush the position with bombs and the bayonet, and accounted for the occupants and captured the gun.

In spite of a fairly heavy mist[,] direction was well maintained by working on compass bearings which had previously been taken. On reaching the Butte the two platoons which had been previously detailed to occupy it rushed the position and established themselves on the top after slight fighting. Sentries were placed on all entrances to the dug-outs and bombing parties were organised and worked down the passages, several of these were met with fire from inside the dug-out and retaliated with grenades, eventually driving the occupants into one compartment, and as they still continued firing[,] grenades were thrown amongst them and several wounded; the remainder consisting of two officers and 56 others then surrendered.

So one of the strongest German positions on the whole front of attack was captured for a cost of two officers and ten other ranks. Subsequently, other battalions leap-frogged through this position to capture the final objective. In this phase of the battle casualties were higher as more distant strongpoints were found to be still intact. Nevertheless, the final objective, just beyond the eastern end of Polygon Wood, was reached at about 8.50 a.m. and consolidation begun.[30]

Similarly, 4 Australian Division, operating to the north of the 5th and to the north of the plateau, had little trouble in capturing its objectives, although here some confusion was caused by troops losing direction in the dust kicked up by shells hitting the dry, crusty ground.

Even in such a well-ordered advance as this, things could go badly awry. In 15 Battalion (4 Australian Division) the watches of the officers had not been synchronized. Consequently some parties moved off directly into the creeping barrage. These groups had to be brought back and rearranged before a coherent attack could take place. It was fortunate for the Australians that in this area the German defenders had been so cowed by the preliminary bombardment that they were not able to take advantage of the momentary confusion. Most surrendered without a fight.[31]

So by mid-morning on the 26th the troops of the Second and Fifth Armies were on their final objective, with the exception of the ground around Hill 40 (which as already noted was to fall later in the day) and the ground on the extreme right and left flanks of the front of attack. By then the mist had lifted and visibility was good. The artillery was therefore in an excellent position to deal with the expected German counter-attacks. Between 10.30 a.m. and 7 p.m. the Germans launched nine counter-attacks – three against the Fifth Army and six against the Second Army. Five of these were broken up by the British artillery before the enemy troops could close with the new front line. Two smaller attacks were beaten off by the infantry. In only two areas did the Germans make progress and in each their gains were small and costly. In the north they seized two fortified farms previously taken by XVIII Corps, and in the confused area of 33 Division they were also able to recapture several strongpoints.[32]

So once more Plumer's tactics had advanced the British line and had inflicted heavy losses on the counter-attack formations. The victory of the Menin Road had been repeated. Nevertheless, there were several cautionary aspects inherent in these operations.

First, Plumer's methods were only working when aided by the state of the ground. In the area of 3 and 39 Divisions the boggy nature of the terrain had caused the troops to lose the protection of the creeping barrage and so fail to get forward. Only where the ground was dry, in the sectors of 1 Anzac Corps and 59 Division, could the troops make full use of their artillery support.

Secondly, Plumer's method did not allow for the capture of the German guns; the advances were too shallow even to overrun the close-support enemy field artillery. Given that British counter-battery fire was not destroying more enemy guns than could be replaced between battles, there was no prospect here of a seriously diminishing German resistance.

Thirdly, the British victory at Polygon Wood had not been cheap. In all, the attacking divisions suffered 15,375 casualties[33] for the capture of just 3.5 square miles of territory (a 1,250-yard advance on an 8,500-yard front). That represented a cost of nearly 4,400 casualties per square mile, 50 per cent higher than at the Menin Road. The two victories in September had now cost a total of 36,000 casualties for an advance of 2,750 yards. And Passchendaele Ridge was still over 4,500 yards away.

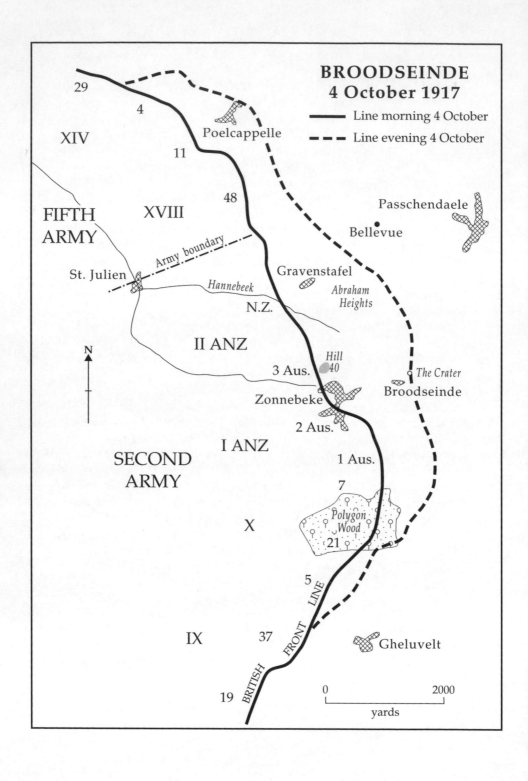

BROODSEINDE
4 October 1917

——— Line morning 4 October

- - - - Line evening 4 October

29

4

XIV

Poelcappelle

11

FIFTH
ARMY

XVIII

48

Passchendaele

Bellevue

Army boundary

St. Julien

Hannebeek

Gravenstafel

*Abraham
Heights*

N.Z.

II ANZ

N

Hill
40

3 Aus.

The Crater

Zonnebeke

Broodseinde

2 Aus.

I ANZ

1 Aus.

SECOND
ARMY

7

X

*Polygon
Wood*

21

5

IX

37

Gheluvelt

19

BRITISH FRONT LINE

0   2000

yards

13

Broodseinde

I

Polygon Wood merely confirmed for Haig the optimism engendered by Menin Road. 'Decisive results', he recorded in his diary, were now possible.[1] The commander-in-chief immediately called a conference at Second Army Headquarters. The Germans clearly had no answer to the tactics being employed against them. The third stage of Plumer's campaign would be brought forward from 6 October to the 4th to take advantage of the fine weather and the state of the enemy.[2]

Haig's thoughts were running beyond immediate events. He saw the Germans as being in an advanced state of demoralization. The moment was approaching when operations of an unlimited nature could be contemplated. By 10 October, so he instructed his army commanders, reserves equipped for rapid action must be concentrated behind the front of attack. Such forces should include the cavalry, which would have opportunities for exploitation in the direction of Moorslede, Staden, and Roulers.[3] Haig was thus contemplating an advance of 20 miles, more than double the distance so far achieved. Nor was the coastal aspect of the plan forgotten. Haig informed Jellicoe and Rawlinson that he might require action by the British divisions on the coast in concert with a landing from the sea towards the end of the month.[4]

It might have been expected that the cautious Plumer would have strongly dissented from these optimistic forecasts. Indeed, in replying to Haig, Plumer did warn that no German collapse could be expected by 10 October. However, he went on to indicate that he expected enemy demoralization to set in immediately the Germans were driven from the Passchendaele Ridge, an event that might be expected to occur around the middle of the month. He suggested that the cavalry should be ready about three or four days after the 10th.[5] Gough agreed; with a minor variation in timing. He considered that the cavalry could operate with a reasonable chance of success only after the 16th.[6]

In the event, Haig was not willing to tolerate even the minor dissent expressed by Plumer and Gough. A further conference was called for 2 October. Haig warned his army commanders not to underestimate the decline in enemy morale. In what must be deemed a monumental irrelevance, he stressed that the Germans had failed to exploit their opportunities in the salient on 31 October 1914! On that occasion, he claimed, one more well-directed attack could have broken the British line. He was not going to make a similar mistake. Each army must ensure that reserve brigades of infantry, supported by cavalry, tanks, and mobile artillery, were concentrated behind their fronts by 10 October. For his part, he would ensure that the entire Cavalry Corps was ready behind the Yser Canal for exploitation beyond the Passchendaele Ridge.[7]

Plumer and Gough did not dissent; they moved immediately to put Haig's wishes into effect. Seven brigades of infantry plus field artillery and some heavier guns were concentrated behind the Second Army front. Two divisions of cavalry were ready behind Ypres. Smaller concentrations of similarly constituted groupings were gathered behind the Fifth Army.[8] All that was needed was a German collapse.

II

The Germans were showing few signs of providing the disintegration required. Nevertheless, under Plumer's assaults their leaders were revealing a good deal of concern. Following 26 September the command of the German Fourth Army, opposite the British, held a series of conferences to find possible explanations for the enemy's success. The conclusions they reached were remarkable. The British advances were being facilitated by the thinly held German forward zone. To counter this, more troops and machine-guns should be concentrated in that area. The Germans also rethought the placement of their counter-attack divisions. As it stood, these divisions were coming forward too late. By the time they arrived on the battlefield (usually late afternoon) they were required to assemble and attack while under the heavy fire of the British standing barrage. It was decided to hold back these formations on the day of battle. They could then be concentrated at night and sent forward early on the following day.[9]

These recommendations certainly prove that the British command held no monopoly on muddle-headedness. Packing troops into a forward zone certain to be deluged by high explosive and shrapnel was bound to ensure increased casualties. Holding back counter-attack divisions until the following day, by which time the new British line would be established and protected by artillery, would achieve a similar result.

III

Plumer's third step, the battle of Broodseinde, opened at 6 a.m. on 4 October. The main attack was carried out by I Anzac Corps and II Anzac Corps (which had taken over the line from V Corps) from Second Army and by XVIII Corps from Fifth Army. Flank protection in the south was provided by X Corps and in the north by XIV Corps.[10]

With what was becoming monotonous regularity, the flanking operations proved the most costly for the amount of ground gained and any protection offered to the main advance. In the north XIV Corps, encountering low-lying territory which the shelling had converted into a bog, lost the rather feeble barrage, and were then forced back by concentrated machine-gun fire from unattacked German troops on the edges of the Houthulst Forest. The corps lost 1,700 men and advanced the line not a yard.[11]

In the south, X Corps achieved its objectives but only at high cost. In some areas the mud and tangled wire in the woods was so bad that the troops immediately lost the protection of the barrage and were subjected to heavy machine-gun fire from the pillbox defences. In other areas the creeping barrage could hardly be distinguished from the heavy enemy bombardment from unsubdued guns on the right of the attack. Only by repeated frontal assaults was the line advanced the required 800 yards. The total casualty list was 8,000 men. [12]

In the centre, operations were more successful: I Anzac Corps (1 and 2 Australian Divisions) managed to capture all its objectives and advance the line to the Broodseinde Ridge. However, even here the fighting was far from easy. As the troops formed up on their start line they encountered a heavy German bombardment. The reason for this soon became apparent: the Germans too had been planning to attack on 4 October. The 6 Guards Division had been brought forward to recapture the high ground near Zonnebecke, but their plan came to nothing. When the British bombardment opened at 6 a.m. it caught these troops forming up. Most were too stunned to put up much resistance and they were overrun by the advancing Australians.[13]

Once more the general level of success masks the complexity of battle. The terrible contingency that was a part of all assaults is well illustrated by a series of platoon reports from 3 Australian Battalion which formed part of the 1 Division attack. There were 12 platoons in this battalion, each consisting of about 50 men. During the advance to the Broodseinde Ridge six of these platoons reported practically no opposition (one losing just a single soldier), four reported moderate opposition, which in the event hardly resulted in any serious casualties, one lost 30 per cent of its strength, and the last ran directly into an unsubdued German pillbox and lost over 70 per cent of its men, just 11 of the original 50 rallying on the final objective.[14]

Also engaged in the 1 Division area was the 2nd Australian Brigade. This formation was hit by the German bombardment as it formed up, was protected by only a 'thin and ragged' barrage as it moved forward, came under heavy machine-gun fire from the left flank, encountered a marsh which had to be skirted and the line then reorganized, ran into a nest of pillboxes which put up 'stubborn resistance' until the garrisons were rushed and bayoneted, engaged in heavy fighting with a company of Germans endeavouring to protect a battery of 77 millimetre guns (this was eventually captured), and finished the day in 'desperate hand-to-hand fighting' with the garrison of a large German strongpoint on the Broodseinde Ridge known as the Crater. All told, this brigade suffered 1,000 casualties, about a third of its total strength.[15] Nevertheless, the Germans had once more proved incapable of stopping an offensive directed towards a strictly limited objective. At the end of the fighting I Anzac Corps had captured the Broodseinde Ridge at a cost of 4,500 casualties.

To the north, II Anzac (3 Australian Division and the New Zealand Division) also secured all their objectives. Here the opposition was rather less fierce. Even so, the New Zealanders were heavily shelled at the beginning of their attack, encountered heavy opposition from some German pillboxes, were forced to negotiate the Hannebeek swamp (which caused them momentarily to lose the barrage), found it necesary to organize concerted attacks with trench mortars on some strongpoints beyond Gravenstafel, and endured sustained shell fire on the bare slopes of the Abraham Heights which were their final objective.[16]

In this area 3 Australian Division, after encountering similar opposition, also made good progress.[17] Their final line was just below the Bellevue Spur, half a mile beyond which lay Passchendaele village.

In the Fifth Army area, the main attack was carried out by Maxse's XVIII Corps (11 and 48 Divisions). Their tasks were to keep pace with the New Zealanders on the right and to capture the village of Poelcappelle on the left. The German defences in this sector were not so strong as to require a preliminary bombardment, so Maxse opted for a hurricane bombardment to begin at zero. All objectives, with the exception of the northern portion of Poelcappelle village, fell to XVIII Corps at a relatively low cost – just over 2,000 men.[18] The only novelty in this action came with the employment by Maxse of tanks. In all, 12 accompanied the advance. Despite the rain which had fallen on the 3rd, the going was just good enough to permit the vehicles to operate. In the event the machines performed well. One strongpoint after another fell to the six-pounder guns of the tanks, the following infantry often finishing off the fleeing garrisons with Lewis gun fire. In other cases the Germans surrendered at the mere sight of the armoured vehicles. In the words of the corps report:

> The moral[e] effect of Tanks was emphasized by the statement of a captured German Officer, who, on being asked the reason for his surrender, said 'There were Tanks – so my Company surrendered – I also.'[19]

IV

So ended the Battle of Broodseinde. At a cost of just over 20,000 men the British line had been advanced about 1,000 yards closer to the Passchendaele Ridge. Almost all the Gheluvelt Plateau had now been secured. More than any other action in the salient, Broodseinde made a powerful impression on those present. As they viewed the scene they felt themselves to be in the presence of a great victory: 5,000 Germans had been taken prisoner; enemy dead littered the battlefield. There seemed to be a certain inevitability about Plumer's steps.

Historians since have accepted this view. Bean speaks of an 'overwhelming blow'.[20] Edmonds quotes him with approval.[21] So do John Terraine and Plumer's latest biographer.[22] Yet it may be wondered whether Broodseinde constituted a model of irresistible progress. Some of its features were the product of ill-judgement and sheer bad luck on the part of the enemy. These were unlikely to be regular features of future operations. For example, it was improbable that the enemy would once again pack additional men into the front zone to be numbered among the dead and prisoners. And Plumer could hardly bank on the Germans again being about to launch an attack of their own when the British bombardment commenced.

More importantly, the success of the battle obscured – at the time and ever since – fundamental problems which were likely to become of greater moment as events developed. One was the state of the ground. Despite the fact that there had been exceptionally dry weather in September, the continuous shelling had destroyed the drainage system of the many small streams which were characteristic of the area. Even without rain these watercourses had become bogs or swamps that provided obstacles for attacking troops. On 4 October units from 5, 21, 3 Australian, and NZ Divisions, along with XIV Corps, had reported losing the barrage because of bad going. Without exception, all of these formations suffered heavy casualties as a result.[23]

This problem was hardly likely to improve. Rain had started to fall on the night of the 3rd and even this small amount had made the going in the non-swampy areas 'heavy and slippery'. And this had occurred after a September which had experienced extremely light falls. If anything like the October average – 75 millimetres of rain – should actually fall, the whole battlefield would become a morass.[24]

Furthermore, the British were approaching an area exceptionally low-lying and so prone to flooding. This ran from just north of Gravenstafel to Passchendaele village and from the edge of the Houthulst Forest to the north-east of Passchendaele. In such an area tanks, which had so aided XVIII Corps on 4 October, were unlikely to be of much utility.

There was a second problem which had been foreshadowed in the Broodseinde operation. The area into which the British were attacking was becoming narrower. Instead of striking due east, Plumer was being called on to drive north-east into a salient. This was diminishing the area in which to place the guns needed to overwhelm enemy artillery and provide a substantial creeping barrage. That is, the intended direction of the British advance ran counter to the emphasis on artillery dominance which had hitherto underlain Plumer's step-by-step successes. And it was laying the British infantry open to attack from an extended arc of enfilade fire from the enemy artillery.

Thirdly, the pace of Plumer's attacks was quickening, and so telling against his forces' preparedness. In order to ensure artillery supremacy, his first strike had taken place not only in appropriate weather but after a full three weeks of preparation. His third, although requiring considerable movement forward and registration of guns, was launched after only eight days: not sufficient, as events proved, for a full complement of guns to be brought into position and to fire a counter-battery programme. Now for his fourth attack, Plumer was prepared to act in deteriorating weather and after an interval of just five days – a proceeding incompatible with the establishment of that artillery dominance which had been the overwhelming feature of his earlier successes.

These considerations reveal the fundamental dichotomy between what 'bite and hold' operations could achieve and the sort of success Haig was determined to accomplish. For a brief spell, Plumer had been able to conduct bite and hold attacks and still advance Haig's purpose. That was no longer the case. Further successes on the lines of Menin Road and Polygon Wood required fine weather, orientation of attacks due east, and a sufficiency of time for the assembly and employment of artillery. But the sort of large success on which the high command was bent now required something different. Attacks must occur in rapid succession, not at a deliberate pace, and at intervals which paid no regard to the need for fine weather and the concentration of artillery in appropriate positions. This was for two reasons. One sprang from the hypothetical impending collapse of German morale: the enemy, on this reading, must not be given time to recover. The other followed from the great purpose which Haig had set for the whole undertaking: not just the wearing down of German fighting strength, but a strategic advance to the sea according to a timetable which also involved troop movements along the coast, amphibious operations across the Channel, and the phases of the moon.

It would be comfortable to summarize this divergence between Plumer's step-by-step operations and Haig's projected dash for the coast as reflecting a dichotomy between the Second Army commander and the commander-in-chief. But this would be to oversimplify. No doubt Plumer, in different circumstances, would readily have agreed to persist in a 'bite and hold' approach. So he would have avoided rushing his next attack, acted only in tolerable weather, and – by orienting his operations due east – avoided funnelling his troops into a salient. Yet there is no evidence that Plumer regarded the Passchendaele Ridge as a less than sensible objective, and none that he doubted the impending collapse of German morale. To Haig's instincts that the enemy might collapse by 10 October, Plumer did not counter that there were no grounds for this. At most he demurred on the matter of timing. He predicted that the collapse would occur slightly later than Haig believed – with the capture of Passchendaele Ridge which he anticipated about the middle of October.

So as the sun ceased to shine and circumstances for even piecemeal advances became markedly less hopeful, not even the commander of Second Army seemed eager to urge caution upon the undiminished enthusiasm of his chief. If any caution was to be brought to bear, therefore, it would have to be imposed by Haig's political masters.

Part V
Political Interlude (i)

14

Deciding and Not Deciding: The War Cabinet and the War Policy Committee, August–November 1917

I

Ever since the termination of the Third Ypres campaign, historians and biographers and memoir-writers and journalists have asked the same questions. How did the political leaders of Britain come to authorize it? Why did they agree to unleash a campaign which, for trivial gains, would go on week after week at terrible cost?

In an important respect, these questions are simply wrong-headed. They are seeking to explain why, late in July, the War Policy Committee endorsed a campaign which would continue until mid-November. As we have seen, the Prime Minister and his colleagues never gave such authorization. On the contrary, they explicitly refused to do so. All they authorized was the opening phase of that campaign. If that phase gave promise of much success, a continuation was probable. If it did not, and only a Somme-style slogging match seemed to be developing, then there would be no second phase. Attention would turn to Lloyd George's Italian option.

This decision appeared to show the country's civilian rulers to be exercising – as was their duty – a firm control over military strategy. But for appearance to accord with reality, a consequent scenario was called for. Either the War Policy Committee must go on meeting and deciding, or the War Cabinet must assume the responsibility of exercising oversight. By one instrument or the other, the country's rulers must scrutinize the first strike at the Gheluvelt Plateau on 31 July, and the actions that succeeded it. Certainly after a month they would want to know if the Klerken Ridge had been taken and whether the coastal operation was about to commence. If no large progress had been made or was in the offing, and if Gough had not shown himself a great improvement on the Rawlinson of 1916, then the Flanders campaign would be halted. All attention (assuming no one was remembering the Pétain alternative) would turn to Cadorna and Italy.

Nothing of the sort occurred. Throughout August and the first three weeks of September the War Policy Committee – the body which had authorized the initiation of the Flanders campaign – never assembled. That left it up to the War Cabinet, which was of nearly identical composition and was meeting regularly, to oversee the progress of the campaign. But this did not happen. The War Cabinet, when it was not dealing with the matter of air raids on Britain (which seemed to occupy an inordinate amount of its attention) and a wide range of other issues, did review aspects of military operations. It even rehearsed the debate over alternative strategies. But it never turned a magnifying glass upon the progress of the Flanders campaign.

This omission did not escape the (private) censure of the secretary of the War Cabinet, Sir Maurice Hankey. So in his diary for 11 August, Hankey lamented the manner in which the War Cabinet devoted four hours just to drafting a letter of rebuke to Arthur Henderson, who had resigned from that body. Hankey called this proceeding

A good example of the way time is wasted. Yet the days are slipping by, it is time to reconsider whether Haig's offensive should be permitted to continue in the bad weather conditions, and whether the alternative plan for a great offensive on the Italian front should not be adopted. . . . But the Cabinet is entirely engrossed in this personal question, and can think of nothing else![1]

II

On 31 July, Robertson gave the War Cabinet a brief account of the first day's attack in Flanders. It was 'progressing successfully, and the first objective had been achieved', he told them. The War Cabinet promptly turned its attention to other matters, especially what course to take should Russia collapse utterly. In that eventuality Robertson urged (as always) total concentration on the Western Front (although more in a defensive than an offensive framework). Others – presumably including Lloyd George – proposed mitigating the effects of Russia's withdrawal by striking down one of Germany's allies.[2]

On 2 August, Robertson again conveyed to the War Cabinet the consequences of operations in Flanders. Haig had captured the Pilckem Ridge, but had failed to achieve the key objectives on the right. On 17 August he told a similar tale, about progress on the left and less progress on the right. On 22 August the War Cabinet learned that the Canadians

The Commanders

1. Field-Marshal Sir Douglas Haig.

2. Lloyd George (with A. J. Balfour) at an Allied conference in Paris.

The Commanders

3. General Sir Hubert Gough

4. General Sir Herbert Plumer with King
George V.

5. 'The Empire's Might': a twelve-inch howitzer on a railroad mounting.

6. Forward Observation Officers directing the fall of shot on enemy positions.

7. A dump of used shell cases on the Ypres-Menin Road, providing stark evidence of the part played by industrial mobilization in the battle.

8. *(top)* One of the huge mine craters formed on the morning of the battle: 'the trenches were now the graves of (German) infantry' (see page 60).

9. A German blockhouse, of the type captured by Private Gallwey's battalion (see pages 62–3).

10. A field battery moving into position for the attack on Pilckem Ridge.

11. German dead on Pilckem Ridge.

12. (*top*) A German shell bursting near a British gun position on 16 August – evidence of the inadequacy of British counter-battery fire.

13. Hauling a field gun out of the mire, as experienced by Captain Hever (see page 98).

14. (*top*) French and British troops digging trenches on a captured section of Pilckem Ridge.

15. A 9.2-inch gun firing on 23 August – one of the inadequate number of guns that managed to get forward to support the British attack.

16. One of the 575 heavy guns assisting Plumer's attack at the Menin Road.

17. The Menin Road battlefield, near Zonnebecke.

18. German defences captured by 9 Division during the Battle of the Menin Road.

19. A fifteen-inch howitzer, the largest employed by Haig's forces, coming into play at Polygon Wood.

20. Some of the 5,000 Germans taken prisoner at Broodseinde, helping to convince Haig that he was on the verge of a great victory.

21. The crowding of guns resulting from the increasingly water-logged state of the ground and the narrowing of the salient.

22. The battlefield approaching Passchendaele: an aerial photograph.

23. Canadians carrying duckboards across 'a desolate wilderness of water-filled shell craters' (see page 175).

had good prospects of taking Lens, and that the Germans were fighting hard to retain the Klerken Ridge: 'If we gained that objective, of which the military authorities were hopeful, ... we ought to have a good chance of gaining a substantial success.'

Three things are noteworthy here. First, Robertson was doing his best to draw the War Cabinet's attention to the progress of the Flanders campaign. Second, he was giving clear indications of only moderate advances but trying to cover this up by large and questionable promises. (Haig's forces were not within cooeeing distance of the Klerken Ridge.) Third, the War Cabinet was failing utterly either to comment upon Robertson's reports or to probe his promises. It was not that the government's military adviser was trying to distract civilian attention from events on the Flanders battlefield. He could not get the civilian rulers to attend.

Only the issue of alternative strategies caused some members of the War Cabinet to give voice. As early as 6 August, at an Allied conference, Lloyd George referred to the desirability of straightway sending large numbers of men and guns to Italy (although not, as far as can be told, as a result of halting operations in Flanders). But he did so in the course of a gathering which, in Marshal Foch's view (as reported by Sir Henry Wilson), was 'an absolute fiasco' on account of Lloyd George's inept chairmanship and tired and peevish manner. According to Henry Wilson: 'Foch thinks Lloyd George is beaten.'[3] Certainly Lloyd George was not providing firm leadership. Repeatedly during August he disparaged Haig's endeavours in Flanders, and spoke longingly of a campaign in Italy with substantial British support. What he rarely seemed to do was tie these positions together: by advocating the cessation of the Ypres offensive and its replacement either by limited operations on the Western Front or by the transfer of British resources to Italy. Least of all did he enquire of the Italians whether they were prepared to continue with their operations against the Austrians once the British had ceased tying down the Germans by large attacks on the Western Front.

So neither in what he deplored nor in what he favoured was Lloyd George generating any sort of action. On 15 August, when Hankey pressed him concerning a possible transfer of endeavours from Flanders to Italy, the Prime Minister proved 'unresponsive'.[4]

These matters came to some sort of head late in August. On the 27th, Lloyd George sent a message to the War Cabinet (from which he was taking a short vacation) urging the dispatch of guns to Italy, to enable General Cadorna to gain a decisive victory on the Isonzo. The War Cabinet also received a riposte to this from Robertson – another absentee – arguing that the successes of the Italians, like the recent French gains in a limited operation at Verdun, were the result of British attacks in Flanders pinning the Germans to the northern sector. A transfer of guns to Italy, Robertson argued, would require the abandonment of the Ypres offensive, constituting a blow to the morale of British troops and tantamount to an admission of defeat.

A day later Robertson was back in person, and insisting on a review of the whole issue of strategy. The War Cabinet, he affirmed, had all along exercised the deciding voice in this matter. So it had been the Asquith cabinet which late in 1916 had opted for a Flanders operation, the Lloyd George cabinet early in 1917 which had chosen Nivelle's (rather than an Italian) undertaking, and the present body which in July had come down for Third Ypres. Now it must decide again. Either it should stick with Flanders or it should end that episode and turn to Italy. So again it was the military representative who was trying to bring cabinet ministers to discuss the achievements of Third Ypres so far; not civilian ministers who were trying to oblige him to do so.

So challenged, the War Cabinet refused to confront the issue. It announced itself impressed with Cadorna's unexpected successes against the Austrians. But it would not override military opinion if the latter concluded that events in Italy did not warrant the abandonment of Third Ypres. The point that events in Italy had no bearing whatever on the achievements or effective failure of the Third Ypres campaign so far escaped the War Cabinet's attention.

Lloyd George continued to be absent from these exchanges. He was resting at the residence of the newspaper magnate Lord Riddell, and sometimes was even – on account of stormy weather – out of telephone communication with London.[5] By letter he conveyed his great enthusiasm for Cadorna's operations, urging the dispatch to Italy of 300 British guns and appropriate ammunition (but not, apparently, any British soldiers) even at the cost of suspending Haig's offensive. Yet when he embarked on direct intervention, it proved as nebulous as that of the War Cabinet. He drew Robertson, along with his off-sider General Maurice, down to the Riddell residence. What resulted was a telegram (principally drafted by Milner) to the British ambassador in Rome, who had written approvingly of Italian operations. It pointed out that Britain could assist the successful campaign of the Italians only at the expense of abandoning the Flanders operation, an action which would be hailed as a victory by the Germans; and that although Britain's leaders were prepared to face this prospect, they could only do so

> if we were assured that a really great victory could be won with our aid on the Italian Front; but that we knew by experience the optimism of generals, and we should therefore require a convincing appreciation.

To whom, and in what terms, the British ambassador was expected to convey this uncomfortable communication is not clear. Nor was it evident what sort of response might emerge from 'optimistic' Italian generals that would carry conviction among doubting British authorities. Robertson only put his signature to the telegram, in the judgement of Hankey, 'because he was sure that the Italians could not convince us'.

That was all that the Prime Minister and the War Cabinet had to say about the course of the Flanders offensive during its first month: a period during which the Gheluvelt Plateau did not fall, Gough's command appeared seriously flawed, the campaign assumed the likeness of a Somme-type battle of attrition, and the projected attack from the sea retreated into limbo. (On 5 September, Henry Wilson learned with relief from Rawlinson that the latter did not think that the 'mad' landings on the coast would ever come off.)[6] Two things are noteworthy about the War Cabinet proceedings: it rarely discussed military operations at all, and it never discussed the actual course of the Flanders campaign. It might consider alternative strategies. It would not do so in the context of what the strategy it had adopted was achieving (and failing to achieve) during its first month. Certainly, the question was never engaged of simply calling off the existing operation because of its meagre results, whether or not anything better was offering.

III

During the first three weeks of September, the pattern of August was maintained. Italy, not Flanders, engaged the War Cabinet's attention. (Rather bewilderingly, in mid-September Lloyd George – along with Milner – also began talking with favour about a British campaign against Turkey as preferable to continued action on the Western Front.) Early in the month General Foch proposed sending to the Italians 100 guns drawn from the French First Army on Haig's left. According to Foch, these guns were not needed for operations in Flanders. According to Haig, they most certainly were.

This wrangle once more enabled the War Cabinet to ponder whether Italy held the promise of a major Allied success – without ever considering what successes, if any, were being accomplished at Ypres. As if to stress the War Cabinet's refusal to deal with the fundamental military question of what was happening in Flanders, Lloyd George made great play of the 'diplomatic' and 'political' aspects of the transfer of artillery to Cadorna. It would be very embarrassing to Britain's relations with Italy, he said, if the War Cabinet appeared reluctant to send the guns when the French were proving eager to do so: 'The French had arranged rather astutely to place us in a dilemma.' By way of emphasizing the irrelevance of all this to the major battle front, Lloyd George insisted that he was talking about 'a comparatively insignificant number of guns compared with the large numbers disposed of in the Western theatre'. In the outcome Haig agreed to contribute from his own front half of the guns to go to Italy. Lloyd George praised the commander-in-chief's self-sacrifice fulsomely.

This saga of a 'comparatively insignificant number of guns' destined for Italy belongs in the story of the Third Ypres campaign only because it occupied a key role in an event which might have significantly affected the future of that operation: the recall of the War Policy Committee. On 21 September the pipe dream that Cadorna and a handful of Allied guns might initiate a new strategic scenario vanished abruptly.

The meeting of the War Cabinet on that day heard news from two fronts. Robertson recounted the complete success of Plumer's first assault in Flanders. True to form, the War Cabinet did not comment. What excited it was news from Italy. The 100 guns had now arrived there, but they were not to play a part in any great events. For, as Robertson informed the War Cabinet, information of a serious nature was to hand. Cadorna had modified his plans, and did not propose to launch another offensive for the rest of the year.

This news produced expressions of bafflement from Lord Derby, the Secretary of State for War, who had been in Italy the week before and had found everything ready for an attack. The War Cabinet decided to send a message to the Italians. It expressed extreme surprise at this inexplicable abandonment of Cadorna's offensive, and described the decision as very embarrassing to Allied operations on other fronts.

On 24 September the War Cabinet reassembled. A message was to hand from Cadorna saying that, five days earlier, the Italian government had taken the decision to launch no more offensives. The Austrians, he said, were showing signs of strengthening themselves on his front, and his forces would counter-attack if this was required. 'He expressed the opinion that a more passive attitude on the part of the Italian troops would not prejudice Allied operations elsewhere.' The War Cabinet responded by deciding to reconvene, that very afternoon, the War Policy Committee. This would be its first meeting since the opening of Third Ypres, yet the meeting would not be taking place to assess the progress of Third Ypres. Its task would be 'to go into the whole question of shipments, reinforcements, and military operations in the *Turkish* theatres' (emphasis added).

This hasty decision places it beyond doubt that the War Policy Committee, despite its quiescence for a period of seven weeks, was quite ready to reassemble whenever strategic matters deemed of importance required consideration. A change of tack by the Italian command concerning operations against Austria was regarded as such a matter. The continuation or termination of the Flanders offensive, apparently, was not.

So the committee gathered on 24 September to devise a response to Italy's back-sliding. The guns dispatched to Cadorna would be removed from him, for as Lloyd George observed: 'General Cadorna had not acted in the way in which he had led us to believe . . . the guns were sent him for an offensive against the Hermada positions.'[7] Graeme Thompson, the director of Transports and Shipping, was quizzed about the possibility of moving guns and troops from Marseilles and Italy to eastern parts of the Mediterranean. (Exotic places like Ayas Bay and Alexandretta were mentioned.)

Disenchantment with the Italian command was speedily accompanied by the growth of doubts as to whether, anyway, the Habsburg Empire was really the easy game it had sometimes been portrayed. A second meeting of the committee on 3 October considered the manpower of the enemy states. As regards Austria-Hungary, Germany, and Bulgaria, this situation appeared ominous from the Allied point of view. Only in respect to Turkey, it was concluded, did the Allies have an advantage.

This reassessment of Austria-Hungary's powers of endurance, along with Italy's disinclination to fulfil Lloyd George's expectations, directed the Prime Minister's attentions firmly towards Turkey. This was a noteworthy change. Up to now Turkey had never been his preferred target – as he continued to insist, he had always opposed the Gallipoli operation (even though he was now prepared to argue that that campaign had failed for want of resources). But Germany, he insisted, could not be defeated until it had been isolated. And Turkey was now emerging as the one adversary which might speedily be driven from Germany's entourage.

How was the elimination of Turkey to be accomplished? Lloyd George argued for a sharp military rebuff – a winter campaign in Palestine – to the Turks followed by the offer of generous terms (Milner spoke of peace 'at any price'). Such terms, admittedly, would be inconsistent with undertakings to France earlier entered into by Britain, but it was hoped that war-weariness would reconcile the French to fewer acquisitions at Turkey's expense than had once been thought attainable. Should Turkey be persuaded by this combination of stick and carrot to leave the war, Lloyd George affirmed, Britain would renew the existing campaign on the Western Front in the spring, in more favourable weather. (The fact that the 'isolation' of Germany would be far from complete excited no comment.)

The logic underlying this proposed course was as follows. Action against Turkey would be a first step – and the only step feasible – in depriving Germany of its allies. The British public, facing the total collapse of Russia, badly needed something to carry them through the winter, and 'a successful attack in Palestine would resurrect the war spirit in the country': 'our policy should be to make peace with the Turks, and then get the forces back to France by the Spring'. To make a certainty of the Palestine operation, guns originally intended for Italy, along with two divisions from France (but not necessarily from Flanders), would be sent to Allenby during the winter months – when, perforce, operations would be suspended in northern Europe.

What was all this saying about the Flanders offensive? That undertaking, let it be recalled, had elicited so sceptical a response at the outset that Lloyd George had reserved the option to close it down. Nothing that had happened in its first two months had caused him to take a more hopeful view. Certainly, when he returned from France late in September he spoke of the poor condition of the German prisoners he had seen on the 26th, and contrasted this with the good spirit evident among the members of the British army he had met and conversed with. But the main messages he brought back from his visit to the Western Front were entirely negative. First, the French were not fighting and would not do so. On 1 September, and again on 25–26 September, the French had been meant to launch attacks to coincide with British operations. These attacks had not eventuated. Now the French were claiming they would act on 10 October. 'No doubt when October 10th arrived some reason for a further postponement would be found, and so on until the end of the fighting season.'

But the Prime Minister's scepticism went further. He felt that Haig's promises of large advances were also worthless, and he informed the War Policy Committee that he was 'very doubtful' if even the Klerken Ridge would be reached.

Only one Western Front operation in 1917 enjoyed Lloyd George's approval: the Nivelle offensive, which had included the British attacks at Vimy Ridge and Arras. At the War Policy Committee meeting on 3 October, the Prime Minister was stung by a comment of Robertson(who was not present), relayed by Smuts, that the War Cabinet early in 1917 had changed the plans of the military. Lloyd George denied that he had imposed operations on the military authorities, claiming that Nivelle and Haig 'had arranged their own plan for the Western Front' and that 'the only thing that the Cabinet had insisted upon was that the two Armies during the offensive must be placed under one Command'. Lloyd George followed this decidedly slanted account with a novel summation of what the Nivelle campaign had accomplished:

He stated that that offensive had yielded the biggest result this year, Arras and Vimy being part of the plan, and, though the French did not accomplish all they attempted, nothing that had since been achieved had been in any way comparable to the results then obtained.

On this it may be remarked that Nivelle's accomplishment was indeed singular: no subsequent operation had reduced one of the major armies on the Western Front to mutiny. But that, plainly, was not Lloyd George's meaning. And it did not augur well for the deliberations of Britain's chief decision-making body that the Prime Minister could seriously make such observations and that they passed without challenge.

Having eulogized Nivelle's accomplishments, Lloyd George turned to the Flanders offensive. At the earlier meeting on 24 September, held in the presence of Robertson and in the immediate aftermath of Plumer's first attack, the Prime Minister had not been wholly condemnatory of the Ypres campaign. He had simply remarked – very much *inter alia* and in the course of arguing for a large reinforcement to Allenby 'to make sure of one offensive being successful' – that Plumer's gains would not bring much benefit. For a war-weary country, 'the effect of an advance such as the recent one in Flanders did not last long'.

At the meeting on 3 October, with Robertson absent and despite a second Plumer 'advance', Lloyd George was less circumspect. Having described the yield of the Nivelle offensive as 'the biggest result this year', he turned to Third Ypres:

> He would have no hesitation in comparing the present offensive with the predictions he made about it. We had not got the Klerken Ridge, and he had always insisted that the French promised to fight but [they] had not carried out that promise.

Curzon intervened to point out that Haig had been handicapped by a month of bad weather, but Lloyd George was not to be deflected:

> he gathered that the Military Authorities in France did not expect to get the Klerken Ridge this year, but thought that they might get about half-way, namely, to Paschendael. Mr Lloyd George remarked that, in considering the present offensive, they had been guided by the very confident Paper they had received from General Haig, and he (the Prime Minister) thought that no-one would have voted for that offensive if they had not been considerably influenced by his optimism.

Lloyd George here makes three points which seem to lead to a single conclusion: the French had not assisted in the campaign, which had been a prime condition of the British decision to embark on it; Haig had misled them by his wildly optimistic predictions; and the military were now admitting that they would not, this year, reach even their first objective, the Klerken Ridge. What appeared irresistibly to follow was that the War Policy Committee would now put its foot down and terminate the Flanders campaign.

Yet that proved not to be Lloyd George's destination. His only conclusion was that the military authorities should be obliged, under the full weight of War Cabinet authority, to agree to an operation elsewhere during the winter months (when activity anyway must cease in Flanders). So:

> Mr Lloyd George continued that it was imperative that we should get into the minds of the soldiers that action should be taken in some theatre of war during the coming winter, and that we should imitate the German practice of undertaking operations during the winter in some theatre when climatic conditions permitted; further, that we should not look to an offensive on the Western Front before next May, so as to be more sure of the weather.[8] He suggested that the War Cabinet should decide on some definite action, taken on the advice of the Chief of the Imperial General Staff [!], which would inflict such a defeat on the Turkish Army as would force the Turkish Government to consider peace.

That is, the desultory results of the Ypres campaign, along with the exposure of Haig's misjudgements and French deceptions, might have consequences. But they would not be in Flanders. No suggestion was being made to halt the Ypres offensive this side of winter, and there was even a promise of its resumption in the spring.

Such infirmity of intent regarding the only military campaign that mattered surfaced yet again on 11 October, when the War Policy Committee met for the last time in 1917. The circumstances of its gathering were less than happy. Three days earlier, the committee had brought into its midst General Lynden-Bell, former chief of staff in Egypt, to offer advice and encouragement regarding a winter campaign against the Turks in Palestine. But the general had failed to oblige. His judgement on such an undertaking had been cautious and largely negative.

So when the committee resumed on 11 October, it devoted much time to attacking Lynden-Bell and discounting his opinions. Lloyd George argued that all the officers commanding in outlying districts were the same. General Milne (commander of British forces at Salonika) 'never asked for any assistance at all'. General Murray (Allenby's predecessor in Egypt) may have asked for assistance but he had always stressed the primacy of the Western Front. In Lloyd George's view:

> This was the great difference between military officers and politicians. Military officers were dependent for their future promotion upon their superiors, and could not express independent views without jeopardising their future. Politicians always had their public to appeal to.[9]

Lloyd George's conclusion, taken in the absence of Robertson, seemed clearly to establish the nature of civil–military relations. Even though, as he pointed out, all but one of those present (the exception being Smuts) were civilians, 'a decision should be taken [by the War Policy Committee] that the Turk was to be defeated in Palestine, and that the General Staff should be informed of this'.

Lloyd George's reaffirmation of the Palestine option was strongly endorsed by Milner and received at least guarded support from Smuts and Curzon. The only doubts were raised by Bonar Law, who was 'less hopeful' about an expedition there after hearing Lynden-Bell and after reading what Robertson had had to say. He feared 'a repetition of the Dardanelles operation'. But Law was not committing himself solely to Flanders. In response to statements by Smuts that 'we must take the offensive somewhere' (an observation redolent of 1915's strategic misadventures) and that the Western Front 'had always presented an insoluble problem', Bonar Law pointed in a direction which not long before would have won much endorsement. Was not Italy, he asked, 'a more promising field than Turkey'? Smuts replied for the other members:

> after the failure of General Cadorna to make the best of his opportunities, he doubted if it would be safe to place any reliance upon the Italian Front.

It would have to be Turkey, that is, because there was nowhere else.

What bearing had all this on Third Ypres? By 11 October it had been raining steadily in Flanders for a week. There could be no reason for taking a more hopeful view of operations there than when Lloyd George, before the weather had broken, had spoken so disparagingly on the subject eight days earlier. Nor was the Prime Minister inclined to do so. He harked back to the only Western Front offensive that had ever aroused his enthusiasm:

> The Prime Minister suggested that the effects of General Nivelle's operation had been underrated by the General Staff. Actually it had been the

most successful operation undertaken by the Allies this year, if measured from the point of view of captures in prisoners and guns.

Third Ypres, in Lloyd George's judgement, was proving altogether more barren.

After stating that the proposed Palestine campaign 'was the only operation to undertake', he went on to make this prediction concerning Flanders:

we would not capture the Klerken Ridge and he would call the War Cabinet's attention to this in three weeks' time. In fact, he believed that he himself had taken too sanguine a view of Sir Douglas Haig's prospects in the Flanders offensive. Unless something of the kind now contemplated were done in Turkey, in a year's time we should find ourselves in exactly the same position as we were in now.

As for a new memo by Robertson urging that 'we should confine our main efforts to the Western front', Lloyd George offered the judgement that it 'merely repeated exactly what General Joffre and all the Military Commanders on the Western Front had always said'.

Nobody appeared to dissent from this bleak view of the Flanders offensive. Curzon was 'ready to assume that Field Marshal Haig and General Robertson were wrong in their views about the Western front'. And Smuts held that the Western Front 'had always presented an insoluble problem' which, should Russia go out, 'would become a hopeless problem'. (Whether anyone managed to divine the difference between 'insoluble' and 'hopeless' is not recorded.) Yet this blunt speaking produced no decision to halt the Flanders operation. In truth, as far as Third Ypres was concerned it produced nothing at all. This meant that during October and November the offensive would continue.

Lloyd George did throw out one suggestion presumably intended, eventually, to circumvent Haig and Robertson. But it promised no immediate action, and it signalled a retreat from his earlier affirmation that the civilian War Cabinet, not military experts, should determine strategy. He recalled that in August 1914, immediately following the outbreak of war, Asquith as Prime Minister had consulted military advisers *in addition to* the commander-in-chief and the Chief of Imperial General Staff (CIGS). And he speculated that if a patient was very sick, no one would take the advice only of the family doctor. The patient would seek a second opinion. 'He suggested that this might be advisable in this case also.' On this limp proposal – not that the War Policy Committee should bring to heel unsatisfactory military advisers but that the Prime Minister might recruit additional military authorities to give different advice – the War Policy Committee passed into history.

What seizes the attention in all this is not what is being said but what is not being said; not the conclusions reached about Palestine but the unspoken decisions being made regarding the Western Front. In the absence of Robertson, no one at this meeting felt obliged to suggest that anything worth while had been achieved in Flanders since 31 July. That is, Plumer's three minor successes had made no impact on Lloyd George and his colleagues or caused them to think that they might take a more hopeful view of the Third Ypres operation. The Flanders campaign had accomplished nothing, and would accomplish nothing by the end of the year. So Lloyd George declined to be misled by Haig's optimism a moment longer. (The record hardly reveals that he ever had been, but that is by the way.) Far from being hopeful, the Prime Minister predicted failure in the attempt to capture even the Klerken Ridge. He 'would call the War Cabinet's attention to this in three weeks' time'.

There is a terrible omission here. None of Lloyd George or Smuts or Curzon or Milner or Bonar Law seemed to be noticing that the Flanders campaign was his responsibility. It would continue not another day if they denied it authorization. They understood well enough their power to initiate and halt operations in Palestine: there they would take the decision, and the military authorities would act accordingly. But for no evident reason, Flanders was judged to be different. The most the nation's civilian rulers might do regarding it was wring their hands and look about for additional military advisers to offer 'a second opinion'. No such opinion, clearly, would be forthcoming during what remained of 1917's campaigning season. So, as the rain fell in Flanders and thousands of Haig's soldiers prepared to struggle through mud to their doom, the Prime Minister who was proclaiming the futility of this undertaking failed to raise a finger to stop it.

Indeed there was a large positive consequence of Lloyd George's chillingly negative announcement that, in three weeks' time, the War Cabinet would assemble to record the lack of success of the operation. This forewarning of failure and futility constituted his authorization for the campaign to continue.

Part VI
The Lower Depths

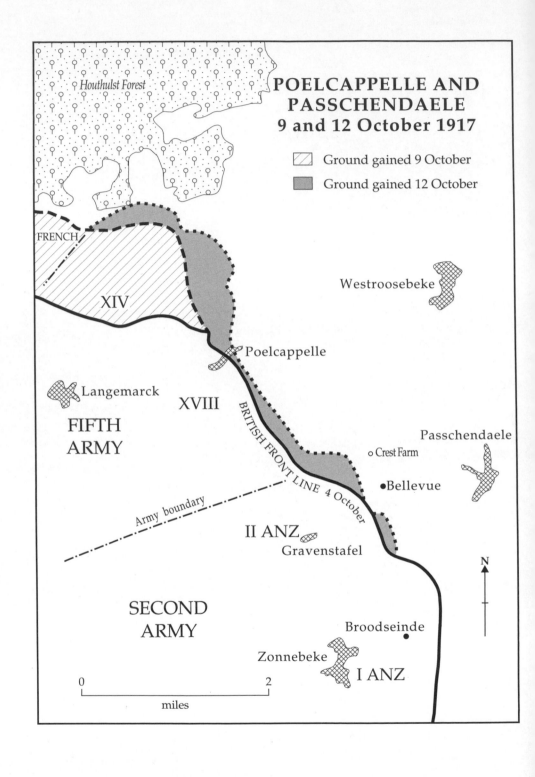

POELCAPPELLE AND PASSCHENDAELE
9 and 12 October 1917

Ground gained 9 October

Ground gained 12 October

Houthulst Forest

FRENCH

XIV

Westroosebeke

Poelcappelle

Langemarck

XVIII

FIFTH
ARMY

Passchendaele

o Crest Farm

BRITISH FRONT LINE 4 October

•Bellevue

Army boundary

II ANZ

Gravenstafel

SECOND
ARMY

N

Broodseinde

Zonnebeke

I ANZ

0   2

miles

15

Poelcappelle

I

In the aftermath of Broodseinde, optimism among the British command reached new heights. None of the shortcomings evident in that operation was identified. All agreed that the assault scheduled for the 10th should be brought forward one day so as to exploit the fact that the enemy 'has been very seriously demoralized by our attack'.[1]

The command was determined to make the most of the expected victory. The cavalry were brought up behind the Yser Canal; the reserve brigades of infantry with their mobile batteries and tanks were put into position.[2] Haig had laid down wide-ranging objectives for these units. First the Passchendaele Ridge was to be captured. Then a variety of further points, which included such distant towns as Roulers and Thourout, were to be swept up by the cavalry. The Canadian Corps would be held in readiness to assist with yet further exploitation.[3]

Yet all these preparations were proceeding in disregard of a major consideration. The rain had started to fall on the afternoon of the 4th. It did not cease thereafter, increasing in volume until the very eve of the new battle. By that time over 30 millimetres had fallen, more than enough to turn the devastated, drainage-deprived battlefield into a lake.[4]

The effect on the preparations was evident. Supplies could not reach the front in sufficient quantity because of the appalling state of the roads, men who strayed from the duckboard tracks drowned in the mud, rifles became clogged, and infantrymen struggling forward from rest billets to the front line collapsed with exhaustion.[5]

Yet more compelling was the effect on the artillery. In the words of one official historian:

Seldom has the supply of ammunition, food and water to guns in action presented greater difficulties. It could not be done to batteries more than

150 yards from the main roadways. The journey by pack animals, the only possible form of transport, from the wagon lines to the guns, instead of taking the normal hour, might require anything from six to sixteen hours. If animals slipped off the planks into the quagmires alongside, they often sank out of sight. On arrival, shells had to be cleaned of the slime coating before they could be used. The heavy wastage from sickness was not surprising, for the flooding both in the wagon lines and on gun positions forced men to sleep on wet blankets or sodden straw. . . . The effective strength fell rapidly, and lack of numbers made reliefs impossible, just when they were most needed. The heavy artillery suffered almost as much from the conditions as the field.[6]

In these circumstances, according to J.E. Edmonds, Haig called a conference with Plumer and Gough. Its purpose was to decide on future operations. In this account, 'though willing to continue', the two army commanders told Haig that 'they would welcome a closing down of the campaign'.[7] Haig nevertheless decided to persist, at least until the Passchendaele Ridge had been secured.[8] His only concession was to cancel the attempt to exploit the expected victory. The cavalry and tanks and reserve infantry brigades were stood down.

If this account is accurate, then Haig, in deciding to continue the campaign, was acting on his own and contrary to the inclinations of his army commanders. Yet there are difficulties in accepting Edmonds's tale. In the first place, no contemporary record of the conference can be found, despite the existence of files which contain every other conference between Haig, Gough, and Plumer mentioned in the official history.[9] Nor does Haig refer to the alleged conference in his seemingly comprehensive diary entry for 7 October. This is at odds with his apparent custom of recording all such events. Secondly, the one participant at that conference to write his memoirs (Gough) makes no mention of the meeting, even though it would clearly have been to his advantage to dissociate himself from the continuation of the campaign.[10]

Further, there is contemporary evidence pointing the other way; that the two army commanders endorsed Haig's inclination to press ahead despite the adverse conditions. So on the day before the supposed conference, Gough wrote to H.A. Gwynne, editor of the *Morning Post*:

The weather has turned very wintry & rather wet, but I hope it will hold a bit longer. We have a lot to do yet![11]

As for Plumer, just before the battle his trusted chief of staff, Tim Harington, gave a lecture to the war correspondents. He told the assembled journalists that he was strongly in favour of continuing the battle, and that after one or two more 'bangs' [!] the cavalry would be ready to go through.[12] It is difficult to believe that Harington would have spoken thus without authorization from Plumer. Moreover, a few days later, even though conditions had deteriorated further, Plumer indicated to Repington, who was visiting the front, that he was 'heart and soul' for the Flanders offensive.[13]

II

The weather, meanwhile, continued to play havoc with battle preparations. Worst affected was the artillery. The bombardment plan was the same as that for 4 October. The heavy guns were supposed to commence counter-battery activity and pillbox destruction on the 5th; the creeping barrage, 1,000 yards in depth, would open at zero hour.[14]

Weather conditions negated this programme. No aerial spotting was possible between the 5th and the 9th, so the counter-battery and destruction shoots had to be fired blind. Moreover, conditions on the ground, where soil was turning into ooze, denied stable platforms for the heavy guns. Between them, these factors nullified the crucial contribution of Haig's largest weapons. Much the same was true of the field artillery, whose platforms sank in the mud after only a few rounds. And for the majority of these pieces it proved well nigh impossible to get them within effective range. Most had to remain west of the Steenbeek, some 6,000 yards from the first objective of the infantry and with little chance of laying down an accurate barrage. When attempts were made to advance these weapons, usually they simply wrecked the flimsy plank roads upon which they were supposed to proceed.[15]

One statistic is sufficient to indicate the consequence of all this. In support of 66 Division, only 25 guns were able to participate in the attack, and some of these only came into action after the battle had commenced.[16] This may be contrasted with the 90 guns which had supported the successful attack by 41 Division on 20 September.[17]

As if this paucity of artillery support were not problem enough, the foot soldiers who were supposed to carry out the advance were encountering difficulties of their own. Some of the divisions making their first appearance in the battle had to traverse the bog for 3.5 miles in order to reach their start line, and for the last 2.5 miles of these the only way forward was by a narrow and unstable duckboard track. To step or fall from this track carried the risk of drowning in the slime, and such a mishap to one man impeded the progress of a whole unit. As a result of the perils of the approach march, 197 Brigade of 66 Division had only one battalion on the start line at zero hour. A further battalion was 400 yards back and two more were 1,000 yards behind them.[18] Even among formations which had managed to assemble in time for the attack, exhaustion was usually acute and there had been no opportunity to reconnoitre the ground thoroughly.[19]

Those troops that had remained in the line since Broodseinde, though spared this dismal journey, were hardly in a better state. The Australians were exhausted, wet, and under strength, as were the 5 and 7 Divisions of X Corps.[20]

III

On the other side the Germans seemed to be faring much better. After Broodseinde, new divisions had been brought forward into the line or placed behind the Passchendaele Ridge in readiness to counter-attack. By the eve of battle the eleven British and French assaulting divisions faced seven German divisions in the line and a further six counter-attack divisions. Of these no less than six were fresh.[21]

The German artillery had also been reinforced. Allied intelligence summaries noted an increasing volume of shells directed against their front line, assembly positions, and rearward battery concentrations. On the 8th, just twelve hours before the troops went over the top, 1 Anzac Corps intelligence recorded:

> In retaliation to our practice barrages enemy shelled [our forward areas with the heaviest calibre guns]. At 5.30 p.m. a very heavy barrage was placed on and in front of our front line; from there it jumped back to our support line, and then took another jump further back again. There appeared to be a considerable increase in number of batteries taking part . . . and the main volume of fire was from S.E. [behind the yet uncaptured section of the Gheluvelt Plateau]. The impression conveyed was that it was a more methodical barrage than those he has been recently placing.[22]

In short, the attacking infantry would be advancing against fresh German forces supported by an invigorated artillery in conditions where the British guns would be hard put to it even to locate the exact whereabouts of their own troops.

IV

For the attack on Poelcappelle the Second Army had undergone some minor reorganization. The main attack was to be made by II Anzac

Corps – consisting of 2 Australian Division and two British divisions (49 and 66). Their objective, requiring an advance of 800–1,000 yards, was the slope just below Passchendaele village. Other units were to make small advances or diversionary attacks, usually with the purpose of providing II Anzac Corps with flank protection.[23]

As against all the difficulties which the infantry were encountering, two factors did tend to favour the three principal divisions (at least in relation to other units involved in the attack). The ground on this southerly section of the Passchendaele Ridge was slightly elevated and therefore not quite so affected by the rain, and its sandy soil provided some good going.[24] And the Germans here chanced to be rather in disarray when the British attacked. Ludendorff, after the disastrous experience on the 4th, had rightly given up the attempt to hold the front line in strength, and was reverting to a system of lightly held outpost zones. As it happened, his forces were in the process of changing back to the old system when II Anzac attacked on the 9th.[25]

But such slender advantages could not much offset the difficulties under which the principal British divisions were labouring. Initially, it is true, 2 Australian Division, and later 66 Division, did make progress. But support could not get through to them, and ferocious flanking fire drove them back.[26]

Hardly anywhere else among the forces operating towards Passchendaele village was even this fleeting success equalled. The 6 Australian Brigade was under strength and exhausted before the battle began. In the attack it received little support from its own barrage (described as 'ragged and thin'), and it encountered machine-gun and rifle fire from shell holes directly ahead and from a succession of unsubdued strongpoints. By evening the condition of this brigade had become so parlous that reinforcements had to be sent forward to aid it even in holding its original line.[27]

Elsewhere on the front facing Passchendaele it was much the same story: the state of the ground, the nebulous nature of the artillery support, and unsubdued opposition from pillboxes and shell-hole defences halted all attempts to advance. The 49 Division had the melancholy distinction of failing on account of a further factor not much remarked upon since the start of the Third Ypres campaign: barbed-wire entanglements which (owing to the weather) had escaped aerial observation and destruction by bombardment.[28]

If we are to look for action that day that both overran enemy territory and managed to retain it, this can only be found on the extreme flanks of the operation, where the British advance was not directed towards the Passchendaele Ridge. On the far right, X Corps made minor advances which improved observation across small sections of the Gheluvelt Plateau. On the extreme left, XIV Corps, along with the French, progressed about 800 yards, bringing them up against the southern fringe of the Houthulst Forest.[29] Neither action contributed to Haig's main purpose.

V

There seems an obvious reason why, in unhappy contrast with Plumer's three 'successes', the attack on 9 October proved so barren. The deterioration in the weather had been disastrous in its effect: on the terrain upon which the artillery was supposed to operate, on the conditions required for aerial observation, and on the circumstances under which foot soldiers – denied adequate artillery support – were required to claw their way forward.

Yet this is not the whole explanation. What has been noticed about Plumer's succession of operations – even while the weather held – is their steadily diminishing yield. To that decline Poelcappelle provided an exaggerated climax rather than an abrupt reversal.

In good part, the reason lay in a factor to which reference has already been made: the progressive diminution in the time-gap between operations. This was the consequence of Haig's conviction that the enemy were teetering on the brink of collapse and must be given no pause, combined with his determination to accomplish a swift advance towards the coast to link up with the amphibious operation before the campaigning season ran out.

Poelcappelle, then, was unlikely in the kindest of circumstances to have produced a noteworthy success. There had not been time since Broodseinde to get forward a sufficiency of guns, let alone to range them upon key targets. And the troops designated for the attack, in the absence of time for a substantial turnaround, had either been in the front line too long or were reaching it depleted and exhausted. As the commanding officer of 5 Australian Brigade compellingly put it, his forces were 'so fatigued and worn out through exposure and exhaustion' that he doubted their fitness for battle.[30] Bad weather made all this worse. But rather than denying Plumer a crowning success, the weather converted what might have been an insignificant advance at disproportionately heavy cost into a predictable and quite unwarranted calamity.

16

Neverending Story

I

The Battle of Poelcappelle had not advanced the British line a yard towards Passchendaele Ridge. At the end of the day the troops of I Anzac and II Anzac and XVIII Corps were, with trivial exceptions, occupying their original front line.

This, however, was not the view held by the high command. Perhaps grasping at the fleeting appearance of small groups from 66 and 2 Australian Divisions at their final objectives, Plumer expressed himself satisfied with the day's result. He told Haig that a good line had been seized from which to capture Passchendaele village and that operations should continue on the 12th.[1] Haig hardly needed urging. He ordered the attack to go forward and even instructed Rawlinson (languishing but not forgotten on the coast) 'to make all arrangements to carry out your full plan of operations'.[2] So favourably did Haig regard events that he told Rawlinson he would be quite justified in employing for the purpose two divisions just dispatched to him despite their inadequate training.[3]

During the next 24 hours it became clear that progress on the 9th had not been 'so great as at first stated'.[4] Plumer declared the situation on his battle front to be obscure.[5] Maxse and Gough were openly sceptical as to whether the Second Army had advanced at all.[6] Australian patrols found their men and the British in occupation of their original line.[7]

Yet this intelligence made little impact on the high command. Haig and Plumer, along with the corps commanders who were to conduct the next battle (Godley and Birdwood), persisted in the view that some gains had been made. Contact with junior officers at the front would certainly have revealed a different situation, but none of these commanders nor most of the divisional generals sought out information at first hand. Monash (commander of 3 Australian Division) seems to have received at least some negative reports, but he took no decisive action.[8]

In any case Haig was certain that the Germans were at the end of their tether. He told the French President, Poincaré, of his determination to push on, as 'the enemy is now much weakened in moral[e] and lacks the desire to fight'.[9] When the chief of intelligence at the War Office, General Macdonagh, had the temerity to suggest that the recent battles should give the German command 'no cause for anxiety' in the area of morale, Haig launched into the following remarkable outburst:

> I cannot think why the War Office Intelligence Dept. gives such a wrong picture of the situation except that Gen. Macdonagh (DMI) is a Roman Catholic and is (perhaps unconsciously) influenced by information which doubtless reaches him from tainted (i.e. catholic) sources.[10]

Self-deception could go no further.

II

Meanwhile, the men who would pay the price for the misjudgements of the high command were being prepared for battle. The task they were asked to perform was formidable. II Anzac Corps (now consisting of 3 Australian and the New Zealand Division) and the right of XVIII Corps (9 Division) were set a distance of 2,000–2,500 yards for their final objective: Passchendaele village and a considerable section of the ridge to its north. This represented a depth of advance of approximately 1,000 yards more than had been achieved in any of Plumer's first three steps – all of which had been carried out after an extended period of fine weather and a preparation time of between six and twenty-one days. Now the weather was continuing abysmal, so that preparation was confined effectively to just 10 and 11 October.

The artillery could fulfil none of its roles adequately. Rain denied the preliminary bombardment the assistance of aerial and even ground observation. So the destruction of strongpoints and wire, which needed to be a matter of certainty, became a matter of chance. The counter-batteries, operating under the same conditions (and denied the assistance of the sound-rangers, who were languishing well behind the battle front), quite failed to subdue the German guns. As zero hour approached, the enemy artillery intensified its efforts, inflicting high casualties on Haig's forces.[11] In the Fifth Army area, as Maxse sourly recorded, 'the enemy was considered to be in a sufficient state of demoralisation, as the result of previous attacks, to dispense with the necessity of a preparatory bombardment. This fact was not borne out by events.'[12]

Then there were the inadequacies in the creeping barrage. Many of the guns which were supposed to provide it never even got forward through the mire. One New Zealand battery, by making the most strenuous efforts, did bring four of its six 18-pounder guns into position, only to find that their intended locale lay in the middle of a shell hole. They improvised as best they could, but 'every time we fired a shot the trail [of the gun] would dig deep into the mud, so with every shot we had to try to lift it back and re-lay the gun before we could fire again. It was a nightmare.'[13] Given these conditions, the chief gunner of the New Zealand Division stated that he could not guarantee effective artillery support for the troops. His opinion went unheeded.[14]

The infantry were soon to experience the consequences of inadequate artillery support. Even before the troops had reached the front many had been drenched in mustard gas and had suffered casualties from conventional shelling.[15] When zero hour arrived (5.25 a.m. on 12 October), so feeble was the creeping barrage that troops attempting to form up behind it could not distinguish it from the enemy shells.[16] As one battalion commander commented, 'We made no attempt to conform with it. . . . There was really nothing to conform to'.[17]

In the circumstances the pace of the barrage (eight minutes per 100 yards) proved much too fast. Yet the alternative of a slower barrage did not exist. A reduction in the rate of advance would have meant a longer barrage requiring more shells. There had been no opportunity to bring to the front such a quantity of shells as would have been needed to fire a barrage that crept, say, at the more realistic rate of 100 yards in 10 or 12 minutes.[18] This was but part of the burden inflicted on the infantry by the obsession of the high command with rapid operations.

So, without artillery protection the troops set off for the Passchendaele Ridge. Most did not get far. Massed machine-guns on the Bellevue Spur, Crest Farm, and a host of pillboxes cut them down in swaths. In XVIII Corps men from 27 Brigade (9 Division), on the left of II Anzac Corps, advanced into such a swamp that they became literally stuck in the mud. Reinforcing battalions sent forward to rescue them also became bogged down. In the end elements from all battalions in the brigade were trapped by the morass. Unable to move, they became victims of the heavy machine-gun fire.[19]

The 18th Division, attacking on the left of the 9th, went down in large numbers to massed machine-gun fire from the ruins of Poelcappelle. The divisional report drives home the reasons for failure:

The fact of there being no preparatory bombardment undoubtedly enabled the enemy to employ more machine guns in the front line than would have been the case had they been subjected to a bombardment. Some of these machine guns pushed close up to our front line and [were] miss[ed] [by] our barrage. . . . All reports received agree that the volume and intensity of machine gun fire encountered by our troops yesterday were far heavier than on any recent battle day.[20]

Some troops on slightly higher ground towards Bellevue Spur did manage to advance a few hundred yards. This availed them nothing. Before the New Zealand infantry attacked they could see a great bank of wire glinting on the Bellevue Spur. In the last moments before the battle, in the words of the New Zealand Official History, 'there were few whose thoughts . . . did not revert to the barbed wire . . . and whose prayers were not fervent for an overwhelming barrage, sufficient of itself to blast a passage through the thicket of wire, or to spread such an efficient shield before them that they could cut their way through by hand'.[21] It was not to be. The bombardment was 'weak and patchy' and in any case left the troops far behind as they clambered through the ooze.[22] Those few troops who had not been swept away by the unsubdued machine-guns were forced to fall back in the face of uncut wire.

On their right, 3 Australian Division was also retiring. The Australians had taken their first objective and were moving towards the second when they were enfiladed from Bellevue on the left and by unsubdued machine-guns on their right.[23]

All attempts by divisional commanders to ascertain the situation at the front proved futile. The 9 Division's description of the communications hiatus – not without its farcical elements – reveals the impotence of commanders to influence events:

> Communications were worse than I have ever known them; wires were all out and visual [signalling] was difficult owing to gun flashes. Pigeons could not fly against the wind, and the men with the [messenger] dogs became casualties. The dogs themselves got loose and started a battle of their own. . . . Runners took hours to get through the awful going.[24]

Not even local fire support could be offered. Machine-guns and rifles became clogged with mud; trench mortars could not fire because their ammunition was too wet and dirty.[25]

The flanking attacks, likewise, achieved nothing of significance. On the right of II Anzac Corps, 4 Australian Division failed to gain any ground. On the far left, the French and XIV Corps penetrated a hundred yards or so into the Houthulst Forest.[26]

In these appalling conditions even the much sought after 'Blighty' wound[27] could prove a calamity. The commander of the 7 Seaforth Highlanders reported:

One man left the front line wounded slightly at dusk on the 12th and on the morning of the 13th was discovered stuck fast in a shell hole a few yards from where he started. Repeated efforts were made to get him out with spades, ropes etc. At one time 16 men were working at once under enemy view. But he had to be left there when the Battalion was relieved on the night 13th/14th.[28]

His fate can only be surmised.

III

The First Battle of Passchendaele, the name by which the fiasco just described has since been dignified, is surely one of the lowest points in the British exercise of command during the Third Ypres campaign. The equivalent of a division of infantry (13,000 men) had become casualties for no appreciable gain. Given the conditions of the ground and the haste which had marked the preparations for battle, such a result was unavoidable. A beggarly two days was quite inadequate to prepare for the new action, or even to ascertain the results of the old one. The effects of deteriorating weather were either ignored or minimized by commanders who possessed the clear and recent guide of Poelcappelle to indicate what might transpire from a hastily prepared attack in these conditions.

Haig, of course, maintained his faith in the dogma of collapsing German morale (undeterred by the attempts of the Catholic disinformation machine to enlighten him). Yet the responsibility was not his alone. There is no evidence of any highly placed individual – Plumer or Harington or Gough or Birdwood or Godley – pleading with him to halt the battle. The Belgian coast was Haig's obsession. Perhaps the Passchendaele Ridge fulfilled that function for the lower orders of command. As for the troops whose gains could only be measured in yards, it mattered little to them whether the objectives set by the command were two or twenty miles distant.

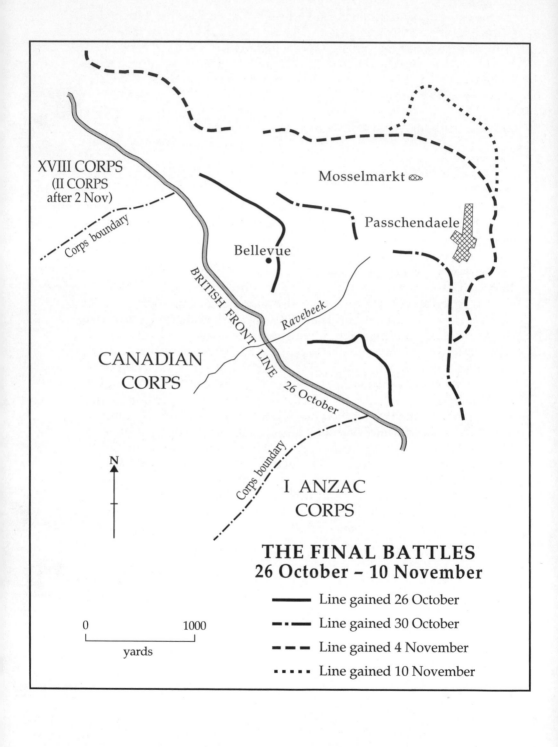

XVIII CORPS
(II CORPS
after 2 Nov)

Corps boundary

Mosselmarkt ⊗

Passchendaele

BRITISH FRONT LINE

Bellevue

Ravebeek

CANADIAN
CORPS

26 October

N

Corps boundary

I ANZAC
CORPS

THE FINAL BATTLES
26 October – 10 November

0   1000
yards

——— Line gained 26 October

—·—·— Line gained 30 October

– – – Line gained 4 November

········· Line gained 10 November

17

Final Folly

I

The failure before Passchendaele on 12 October, unlike that on the 9th, was immediately evident to the command. Haig noted that, prior to the next operation, communications would have to be improved so as to bring up the guns, and that a long bombardment must be fired in order to reduce the German defences and subdue their artillery. These two factors would mean a delay of about ten days.[1]

This was a welcome breath of realism. But Haig had little option. The Second Army divisions confronting the Passchendaele Ridge were worn out. Birdwood announced that the Australians could do no more; after 12 October the New Zealand Division was in desperate need of relief; and the British divisions of II Anzac Corps were hardly in better shape. Replacements for these depleted forces were not wanting – the Canadian Corps had been alerted for battle early in the month. But to take over the front from I and II Anzac Corps would – especially in the prevailing conditions of weather and terrain – require time.

Moreover General Currie, the Canadian Corps commander, insisted that he ought not to launch his divisions into the attack until as much artillery as possible had been brought into play. The next operation, therefore, could not take place before 26 October.[2] This would give the Canadians the two weeks for preparation which had been denied to the British and Anzac divisions on 9 and 12 October.

Currie insisted on even greater realism. He would not attempt to overrun the Passchendaele Ridge in one operation. That ridge still lay about 1,500 yards from the British front line – too distant, in prevailing circumstances, to be taken at a single bound. Instead he planned to capture it in three steps, each of 500 yards. The steps would be separated by five or six days, or longer if the state of the ground so dictated.[3] 'Bite and hold' as a *modus operandi* was being restored.

II

If all this seems familiar, we need only cast our minds back to the end of August. Then, consequent upon Gough's increasingly futile operations in the mud, a new army commander had been called in. Plumer was able to make certain demands that were accepted with alacrity by Haig. There would be careful preparation before his first attack. Artillery must be present in sufficient quantity to overwhelm the German defences, at least for the duration of the attack; the 'hurroosh' would be replaced by deliberate steps of a modest nature across the plateau; attacks would be renewed only when the troops and the guns were ready.

By early October Plumer appeared to have forgotten most of this wisdom. Operations were being rushed, there was a lack of protecting artillery, and atrocious conditions at the front line were simply passing unnoticed. In short, Plumer's operations in the second week of October had come to resemble those of Gough in August.

This might have continued had not the necessity to reorganize the front intervened. With the appearance of Currie at the head of the Canadian Corps, Haig slipped into the same reasonableness that he had shown to Plumer when the latter had been the new man in September. Delays not to be countenanced on the 9th were accepted on the 13th. A decent bombardment before the next attack was once more deemed essential. Conditions of ground were now held to be of some importance. The change is sometimes attributed to the fact that Currie, being a commander of colonial forces, was in a position to impose upon Haig conditions that would not have been accepted from a British commander. But there is no certainty of this. Haig had already shown similar consideration to Plumer – no favourite of his – in September, whereas he had revealed no particular delicacy towards other colonial forces (Australians and New Zealanders) during the most recent operations. Rather it was that Currie in October (like Plumer in September) was entering the scene just after a succession of failures that was bound to give Haig pause. The commander-in-chief was becoming aware once more that willing a victory, like imagining that the enemy is on his last legs, was not enough. Method was being restored as a necessary substitute.

Currie's situation in late October, nevertheless, was not entirely analogous to that of Plumer a month and a half earlier. In September a new army commander had been introduced to conduct wide-front operations on an Army scale at a time when the larger objectives of the campaign still seemed (at least to the British command) feasible. Now in mid-October no more than a corps commander was being called in to conduct small-scale operations on a narrow front. No more would be heard from the commander-in-chief about the Belgian coast – or even of the almost mythical Roulers and Thourout. If Haig was still yearning for a strategic victory in 1917, it was ceasing to be in Belgium. Haig's attention, even while still mounting one Flanders attack after another, was turning south – to a sector of the Western Front situated between Arras and the Somme and not hitherto the scene of much fighting. Haig may never, in so many words, have announced the abandonment of the hopes he had once placed in the Third Ypres operation. But the fact that the troops needed to pursue those hopes were now being diverted to an offensive at Cambrai spoke plainly enough.

Meanwhile, the great campaign in the north had become a matter of three or four Canadian divisions crawling up a promontory of no evident importance. Should they ever secure Passchendaele village, they would not be achieving any tactical objective. The ridge on which the village rested stretched on for miles to the north and there were only two ways to capture all of it. The first was for the Canadians to attack along it towards Westroosebeke. Such an operation was almost certain to fail: the narrow front of attack (the ridge was less than 500 yards wide in this area) would allow the Germans, employing their artillery concentrations behind the ridge on the right and in the Houthulst Forest on the left, to pour heavy enfilade fire into both flanks of the attackers.

The second method was for the Fifth Army on the left of the Canadians to advance on the northern section of the ridge at the same time as Currie's forces were attacking Passchendaele village. This method was unlikely to fare any better. At least the Canadians had the advantage of the slightly better going which prevailed on the lower slopes of the ridge. The Fifth Army lay in the swamps and morasses and lakes beneath the ridge, and so were unlikely to get forward. Moreover, the British line curved back sharply to the west in the Fifth Army's area. Westroosebeke was still 4,000 yards distant from Gough's front at Poelcappelle – a similar distance to that covered by Gough (in dry weather) during all of September.

In sum, the most that could have been hoped for from the forth-coming operations by the Canadians was the capture of some of the ridge around Passchendaele village, an achievement whose end result would be the placing of Haig's forces in a most pronounced salient. So although the operations proposed by Currie made more sense than those which had just preceded them, their overall purpose was not sensible at all.

III

From the middle of the month preparations proceeded for the attack on 26 October. The first thing necessary was to boost artillery support. To this end roads were repaired and extended, as many batteries as possible were rested, reinforcements in the form of the Canadian batteries were brought up, and many guns were recalibrated to improve the accuracy of their fire.[4]

The effectiveness of these measures should not be exaggerated. The Canadians never managed to have more than 60 per cent of their heavy artillery in action at any one time.[5] The conditions for firing remained atrocious (it rained on nine of the fourteen days before the battle),[6] so counter-battery was still a matter of chance.

Nevertheless some important tasks, impossible in the haste of 9 and 12 October, were accomplished by the artillery in the two weeks leading up to the 26th. Passages through the wire at Bellevue were cut for the infantry;[7] and, on those days when it was possible for the Royal Flying Corps to operate, many hostile batteries were located.[8]

Currie's plan for the attack was quite straightforward. The Canadians were to attempt an advance of 500 yards. The 4 Canadian Division would move on Passchendaele village from the south. On its left, though separated from 4 Division by the impenetrable bog of the Ravebeek, 3 Canadian Division would capture Bellevue and entrench to the southeast of Passchendaele village. The whole attack would be covered by a barrage 700 yards in depth which would creep at a rate of 100 yards in eight minutes.[9]

On the left of the Canadians, the Fifth Army would endeavour to close on the north of the Passchendaele Ridge. Two divisions would be involved, the 58th and (appropriately, given the state of the battlefield) the 63rd or Royal Naval Division. On the right, the Australians would provide flank protection.[10]

In the event, neither flanking operation succeeded on 26 October. The Australians were not able to make sufficient progress even to protect the Canadians' right from enfilading machine-gun fire. Even more noteworthy was the failure of 58 and 63 Divisions on the left. In a preliminary operation four days earlier they had made good progress, gaining 300–400 yards around Poelcappelle, but that was because the Germans had already evacuated most of the area.[11] On the 26th the attacking divisions here were not so lucky. Even before the battle started 63 Division had been deluged with gas and high explosive from the German batteries. In one brigade,

> Almost all the senior officers of the four attacking battalions had become casualties. Some were blinded by mustard-gas, while others were hit and rolled into shell holes where they were drowned.[12]

Then at zero hour 58 and 63 Divisions advanced into a series of machine-gun nests. The terrain was so bad that many of the leading waves sank up to their shoulders. Rifles and Lewis guns became clogged and the barrage was lost. Only a derisory amount of ground was gained for a cost of 2,000 casualties.[13]

By contrast with what was happening on the flanks, the Canadians overall achieved their objectives. Many things went wrong in the course of the operation. Stokes mortars could not be fired because of the state of the ammunition,[14] the bad going caused the infantry eventually to lose the barrage, and (as mentioned earlier) failure on the flanks rendered the Canadians subject to enfilade machine-gun fire. Nevertheless the supporting barrage was substantial and although the pillbox defences were formidable, they did have one weakness, as a Canadian soldier explains:

> their range of fire was limited and unless covered by other pill-boxes on the flanks the blind points in the range of fire made it possible for individual attackers to crawl up under cover and bomb the garrison behind.[15]

To a large extent this is what happened on the 26th. The pillboxes were not so frequent as to offer a coherent defence and they were eliminated one by one. And this time lanes had been cut by the artillery through the notorious Bellevue wire, enabling the infantry to get close enough to employ their well-rehearsed small-group tactics against them, as another Canadian describes:

> We had to take them by stealth – get our men together, work our way in sections behind the pillboxes, and start bombing. Of course, by doing it this way, in sections and not altogether, we blinded the enemy. He had no real target to destroy. There was terrible fighting, and we had many, many casualties, but we did achieve something.[16]

IV

The 'something' that was achieved on 26 October, let it be stressed, was only the advancement of the Canadian line the planned 500 yards – a modest enough accomplishment given that it cost the Canadians 3,400 casualties.[17] But it was enough to reinforce Haig's determination to launch his next attack four days later. Such a course did not recommend itself to the Fifth Army, which had fared so badly on 26 October. Cavan and Maxse concluded that progress was impossible in their low-lying area until frost had hardened the ground,[18] and Gough passed on the judgement to Haig. But the commander-in-chief declared himself 'entirely opposed to any idea of abandoning the operations',[19] and the Canadians were deemed to require action on their flanks by the Fifth Army. Currie agreed that the offensive should go on. After all, for step two the Canadians would not require the lengthy preparatory stage which had preceded step one. For so restricted had been the advance on 26 October that the artillery was already in place to support a second, equally modest, forward move.

Once again the Canadian plan was to advance on Passchendaele village from the south and south-east, the attacks still separated by the Ravebeek. Once again the hapless XVIII Corps of the Fifth Army was expected to provide some support on their left. This time weather conditions on the ridge at least were slightly more favourable.

> The two preceding days had been fine and the shell-torn ground dried somewhat, enabling the men to pick their way over fairly solid ground around the lips of the shell craters.[20]

Even so, the attack on the 30th was made under most difficult conditions.

> The bombardment was murderous – ours and the Germans' – and they weren't only flinging over shells, they were simply belting machine-gun fire for all they were worth. . . . The shells were falling thick and fast and by some sort of capillary action the holes they made filled up with water as you looked at them.[21]

In many areas men could only get forward by pulling each other through the mire.[22] On the other hand the barrage was good and the Canadians faced no obstacles as formidable as Bellevue. Hence, despite heavy enfilade fire from the right and left, the required 500 yards was gained. Currie's offensive had now reached the very outskirts of Passchendaele village.[23]

Once again the main misery was concentrated on the left. Here two days of fine weather were woefully inadequate for drying the ground. The same divisions of the Fifth Army which had tried and failed on 26 October – 58 and 63 – attacked again on the 30th with identical results: barely a yard of ground was gained for about 2,000 casualties.[24] The abysmal quality of this sector of the operation is graphically revealed in the following excerpts from the report of the officer commanding 58 Division. He lists a comprehensive number of reasons for failure:

> – more difficulty was experienced in maintaining communication on this occasion than I have hitherto experienced during the war. . . . Many

messages [were] sent back by runners who got bogged and were shot down. The majority of the company signallers were hit. . . . Pigeons were saturated in mud and water and couldn't fly. No contact aeroplane went out.

– the ground was impassable and so powerless were the troops to manoeuvre that they were shot down whilst stuck in the mud.

– the Barrage was ineffective and troops were unable to keep up with it.

– oblique hostile M.G. fire was very effective.

– the only Lewis Gun which succeeded in getting into action was useless in three minutes [because of the mud].

– all uncovered rifles were useless, all covered rifles ditto within ten minutes.

– power of manoeuvre was nil.

– to sum up the situation, neither FIRE NOR MOVEMENT was possible, and any prospects of success under these conditions was nil.[25]

One passage from the report of 174 Brigade of 58 Division, from which this officer drew many of the above judgements, apparently seemed to him so damning that he chose not to include it. It stated that if the infantry advanced upright, 'they were an easy target', whereas if they advanced 'on all fours the men were exhausted in a few minutes'.[26] Even today the vision of sections of Haig's army crawling into battle in an attempt to stay alive induces a sense of inexpressible melancholy.

V

The experience of XVIII Corps on 30 October convinced Haig that operations from that sector should be closed down. The Fifth Army had fought its last battle of the campaign. It was withdrawn. As a substitute, II Corps – last heard of struggling across the Gheluvelt Plateau in August – was returned to the front to provide flank protection for the left of the Canadians. The culminating attack on Passchendaele village scheduled for 6 November would, however, be confined to the Canadians.

The battlefield over which they were to advance has been graphically described by a British gunner:

The conditions are awful, beyond description, nothing we've had yet has come up to it, the whole trouble is the weather which daily gets worse. One's admiration goes out to the infantry who attack and gain ground under these conditions. Had I a descriptive pen I could picture to you the squalor and wretchedness of it all and through it the wonder of the men who carry on. Figure to yourself a desolate wilderness of water-filled shell craters, and crater after crater whose lips form narrow peninsulars [*sic*] along which one can at best pick but a slow and precarious way. Here a shattered tree trunk, there a wrecked 'pill box' sole remaining evidence that this was once a human and inhabited land. Dante would never have condemned lost souls to wander in so terrible a purgatory. Here a shattered wagon, there a gun mired to the muzzle in mud which grips like glue, even the birds and rats have forsaken so unnatural a spot. Mile after mile of the same unending dreariness, landmarks are gone, of whole villages hardly a pile of bricks amongst the mud marks the site. You see it best under a leaden sky with a chill drizzle falling, each hour an eternity, each dragging step a nightmare. How weirdly it recalls some half formed horror of childish nightmare.[27]

The Canadians did have the advantage of five days virtually free of rain in which to prepare their attack. And the troops who were to undertake it actually experienced the luxury of practising their manoeuvres behind the lines.[28] Again the assault was to be carried out by two divisions: 1 Canadian Division attacking from the south-east; 2 Canadian Division from the south.[29] The battle was rather formulaic. The barrage was good and the German troops holding the shell-hole defences were overrun by the first waves of Canadians. The experience of one battalion sums up the battle:

Tense and expectant for hours, the men now rose from their cramped positions and, in perfect formation, ploughed heavily forward behind the barrage. They overran the trench which, earlier in the morning had caused them so much worry, only to find that . . . trench mortars had disposed of this enemy garrison effectively. An officer and about a dozen Germans, machine gun and all had been destroyed. No. 1 Company under [the CO's] . . . skilful direction headed for a cluster of 'pill-boxes' on the side of the ridge, near the Mosselmarkt Road. The lift of the barrage brought the shells smashing amongst them, sending the enemy to cower for protection within the thick concrete walls. Before they could emerge, No. 1 Company was on top of them. Several brisk fights were engaged in; but the enemy had already been subjected to some tremendous punishment and they required little persuasion to surrender.[30]

Then casualties began to mount as machine-guns opened up on the right and left of the attack, but at last the assaulting forces in the south penetrated into Passchendaele village itself. A Canadian soldier describes the scene:

The buildings had been pounded and mixed with the earth, and the shell exploded bodies were so thickly strewn that a fellow couldn't step without stepping on corruption. Our opponents were fighting a rearguard action which resulted in a massacre for both sides. Our boys were falling like ninepins, but it was even worse for them. If they stood up to surrender they were mown down by their own machine gun fire aimed from their rear at us; if they leapfrogged back they were caught in our barrage.[31]

Further north, while 2 Canadian Division was entering Passchendaele, the First Canadian Division overran Mosselmarkt. The lower section of the ridge now lay in British hands.[32]

For Haig it was still not enough. On 10 November the Canadians were ordered to capture a further section of the ridge by attacking along it from Passchendaele village. II Corps were ordered to support the attack by advancing across the low ground to the left of the Canadians. The latter attack, predictably, gained nothing. The Canadians did advance 100 to 200 yards but were then halted by withering flanking fire.[33] Meanwhile the rain began to fall in torrents. This time Haig had no choice. The Canadians had suffered 12,000 casualties since zero hour on 26 October and there were no immediate reserves to hand, for Haig's new operation at Cambrai was about to start. In the absence of fresh forces, tolerable weather, and any prospect of meaningful resolution, the Battle of Passchendaele stumbled to a close. The Third Ypres campaign had run its course.

VI

As he reflected on the final assaults at Passchendaele, Sir Douglas Haig initially declared himself well satisfied. The British were securely on the ridge; the enemy was unlikely to be able to 'maintain his present unfavourable position'.[34] But a few days' reflection obliged even the commander-in-chief to recognize the negative aspects of the situation. So he wrote to Robertson on 15 November: 'The positions already gained [in Flanders] fell short of what I had wanted to secure before the winter.' He concluded that the present position 'may be difficult and costly to hold if seriously attacked . . . I think this latter contingency must be expected as soon as the enemy realizes that he has regained the initiative.'

Two other British observers expressed an even more disenchanted view of the position in which Haig's forces found themselves at the end of the campaign.

Lt-Col. Lyne was a gunner with a British field artillery regiment which had supported the last attacks. After the conclusion of the battle on the 10th he wrote:

> It has rained in torrents all day, we were fighting at 3.30 this morning in a perfect deluge, until I was soaked and coated in mud. The mud which was horrible before became absolutely impassable. I had to get 2 guns into new places, one stuck muzzle deep in mud, and for hours defeated our most frenzied efforts. Finally the Hun strafed blue hell out of us unceasingly throughout the day . . . just as it got dark, and I was changing my sodden garments, one of the dugouts got blown in with a direct hit, and out we went in mud and dark to excavate the survivors! The place was absolutely wrecked, the wonder was that a single occupant was left alive. Horrible groans from inside and with great difficulty we at last extracted some battered looking figures and hurried them off on stretchers to the dressing station during which process, we all, including the wounded men, fell repeatedly into shell holes full of water, cost me 5 casualties which makes a great difference as I am only keeping two or three men per gun up in the unsavoury spot. We returned to our shelter and found it, alas, submerged, torrents of rain – awful life –.[35]

The second observer was an army commander. He arrived in the salient soon after 10 November to inspect the British positions. It was many moons since he had first carried out such an inspection, then in anticipation of an offensive which he had believed he was going to direct. His appearance was occasioned by the fact that General Plumer had been dispatched to Italy, at the head of four British divisions intended to stabilize the front after the disaster at Caporetto on 26 October. So General Rawlinson, who had watched the course of the Flanders campaign from the disappointing obscurity of the Belgian coast, at last moved to centre stage, if only in time to put on paper some reflections about what had been accomplished.

It so happened that as Rawlinson took over, the strategic situation was manifestly changing. Britain's manpower position, he learned at an army commanders' conference on 7 December, was 'really very serious', whereas the Germans were now free of combat commitments in Russia and were transferring huge numbers of troops to the Western Front. In consequence, Rawlinson noted in his diary: 'by the end of Feby we are likely to have quite a lively time'. He went on: 'Any how we shall be thrown on the defensive and shall have to fight for our lives as we did at first Ypres. Not a pleasant prospect. D.H. quite realises this and gave us a dissertation on the defensive' – something, one may speculate, concerning which he would have needed to brush up his knowledge.

Rawlinson discussed this 'change of policy' with his chief of staff,

Archibald Montgomery. In doing so he offered some pungent comments on what had been achieved by the Third Ypres campaign. He deemed Passchendaele 'at present a really untenable position against a properly organised attack', and he summoned a conference of corps commanders to discuss falling back on a 'straight and more defensible' line. Later he noted:

> Nothing we can hope to do can make the line now held a really satisfactory defensive position. We must therefore be prepared to withdraw from it, if the Germans show signs of a serious and sustained offensive on this front, or if an attack elsewhere necessitates the withdrawal of more troops from the front of Second Army.[36]

This was a solemn summing up of the outcome of the endeavours of Haig's forces over a period of three and a half months. At a cost to Britain of a sizeable proportion of its alarmingly dwindling reserves of manpower, a succession of attacks often delivered in abysmal conditions had advanced the British army only to positions it could not hope to retain if confronted by an enemy riposte.

Part VII
Political Interlude (ii)

18

The Last Inaction: The War Cabinet, October–November 1917

I

In those desperate last weeks of the Third Ypres operation, the British government had both cause and opportunity to halt the campaign. It gave clear indications of disbelief in its efficacy. It did nothing to stop it.

Various grounds for calling off the campaign presented themselves. Throughout October and November, the French authorities were demanding that the BEF take over from them more of the Western Front. In justification, they put forward their own projected operations in Syria, and their need to employ French combat forces to bring in the harvest. Members of Lloyd George's cabinet suspected that a desire to grant leave to French troops at the expense of British troops also played a part. The response of Haig and Robertson to this proposal was forthright: if the British army took over more of the front, it would have to call off the Passchendaele offensive.

Here, although the high command apparently did not realize it, was an ideal opportunity for Britain's civilian rulers to terminate the Third Ypres campaign without reference to its heavy cost and meagre results. Lloyd George could simply offer the requirements of Britain's principal ally as compelling him to take an unwelcome decision.

The War Cabinet declined this escape route. On 24 October its members concluded that they could not agree to extend the British sector of the Western Front while the present offensive was continuing and while the issue of resuming it – or not resuming it – in the spring of 1918 remained unresolved.

A more direct reason for terminating the campaign came before the War Cabinet, at its behest, in October and early November. This was the effect of Third Ypres on Britain's resources of manpower, and hence on its ability to remain in the war. On 11 October, possibly for the first time since the offensive began, the War Cabinet turned its attention to the matter of casualties.[1] It might have been expected that the casualty question would be coupled with the equally germane issue of objectives: how far, for the losses sustained, Haig had fulfilled his promise of a breakthrough to the Belgian coast. But no inquiry on this matter was raised. Indeed, on 16 October the War Cabinet sent Haig a message of congratulation 'on his continuous, persistent, and dogged advance of $4\frac{1}{2}$ miles in conditions of great difficulty'.

Only regarding the human cost of making such unremarkable progress did the War Cabinet seem about to stir. Smuts on 11 October urged the necessity to establish the relative attrition of German and British forces as a result of the Flanders campaign, and to learn what had happened to the 42 divisions with which Haig had started out on 31 July. This led Curzon to say that they also needed to know the effect of the offensive on Britain's reserves of manpower: a matter, whether or not he realized it, quite distinct from the issue of *relative* attrition. Strong words were then uttered by Lloyd George and others concerning the inadequate information the War Cabinet had been receiving about losses resulting from wastage and sickness – seemingly without noticing that they had always been in a position to demand such information.

In response, on 17 October the director of military operations, Sir Frederick Maurice, produced estimates of the comparative losses by Germans and Britons in the Flanders offensive. From 31 July to 5 October, casualties for the British had been slightly less than 150,000; for the Germans, rather more than 250,000. Derby, the War Minister, added that British losses in the fortnight since 1 October amounted to 41,000.

The War Cabinet had further discussions concerning casualties during October, and on 1 November received an update on the October statistics. These revealed that losses for that month alone amounted to 110,000. In extenuation it was pointed out that, in a quiet month, the Ypres salient would have exacted 35,000 casualties. So the offensive could only be held responsible for the additional 75,000.

What was plain from these figures was that, by the start of October, the Ypres offensive had already caused a fearful drain on Britain's manpower. Certainly, the figures of German losses suggested that the enemy was suffering even more heavily. (In the event, these figures would prove to have been greatly exaggerated.) But that had supposedly been the case with the Somme campaign of 1916, the costly and largely immobile operation to which – the War Cabinet had once proclaimed – this offensive must bear no resemblance. (Since 31 July, comparisons with the Somme appear to have vanished from consideration.) Further, matters were not improving as Third Ypres continued. Losses during the barren operations of October were on the increase over August and September.

Yet having (somewhat crossly) demanded these statistics, the War Cabinet seemed not altogether distressed by them. For example, what exercised it at a meeting on 17 October was not the – reasonably accurate – figures of British casualties which it received from the military authorities, or the consequential question, which Curzon had raised, of how long Britain's manpower resources could withstand such a drain. Instead it worried about the exaggerated casualty reports which were circulating in the country, and especially the rumours then current that a large proportion of these losses were being sustained by colonial forces: by the Australians, Canadians, and New Zealanders. The War Cabinet concluded that 'an occasional statement by the Prime Minister' would set these falsehoods at rest.

A comment seems called for on the bizarre nature of this transaction. Since the First World War, much ink has been spilt concerning the terrible British losses at Third Ypres. And much wrath has been expended against the cruel process of deception, whereby first the nation's (gullible) civilian leaders and after them the general public were denied knowledge of the true figures. If the government and the nation had had any inkling, it is generally believed, of what Third Ypres was costing them, then the operation could never have proceeded. Yet the record tells another story. The War Cabinet received accurate figures, as far as British losses were concerned, the moment it troubled to ask for them. Its initial – if not necessarily its long-term – response was to conclude that publication of these figures would scotch unwelcome rumours of heavy losses, and so would put the public's mind at rest.

II

All this may suggest that the War Cabinet was entirely changing the stance it had adopted early on, and was determined – in face of all the evidence – to appear well disposed to the Flanders campaign. Yet this was not so. Indeed, one aspect of its deliberations in October and November points in just the contrary direction. This was the matter of calling forth Sir John French and Sir Henry Wilson from apparently deserved obscurity to offer a considered judgement on Western Front operations.

It was no secret that neither French nor Wilson felt any affection for Haig and Robertson. As the latter two had moved into the chief military positions, so the careers of French and Wilson had waned. Hence it could hardly have come as a surprise that French's report contained observations so critical of Haig and Robertson that it had to be toned down before being made available to them, or that the recommendations proposed by French and Wilson constituted an attempt to diminish the role in decision-making of the commander-in-chief and the CIGS.

What is noteworthy in the present context is how welcome Lloyd George found reports so condemnatory of the actions of Haig and Robertson. Yet, sadly, what French and Wilson proposed had no practical bearing on the issue that mattered most in these weeks: calling off the Passchendaele offensive. (Their recommendations would have little or no bearing on anything that happened in 1918 either.) Their reports advocated the establishment of an Inter-Allied General Staff – to consist, as far as the British contingent was concerned, of people like Wilson and not at all of people like Robertson. Its role would be to view the war 'as a whole' and to make recommendations. But it would have no executive authority; and although its British representatives would be independent of the War Office, they would send their recommendations to cabinet through that body. Nothing of immediate relevance to the Flanders offensive would result from this proceeding.[2]

All told, therefore, the obvious stratagems which the War Cabinet might employ to halt the Ypres campaign – invoking the needs of the French, or expressing outrage at massive casualties incurred for minuscule advances, or resurrecting military figures known to be hostile to Haig – were never applied to that purpose. Two other events, over which the War Cabinet had no control, had more effect in turning the thrust of military operations somewhat away from Belgium. One was the quite unexpected reverses suffered by the Italian army as a result of the appearance of German forces in that theatre: the battle of Caporetto. The other was Haig's own spectacular, if short-lived, success on another part of the Western Front: the battle of Cambrai.

The temporary collapse of Italian resistance late in October left Britain's civilian and military directors little alternative, whatever their strategic inclinations, but to rush aid to Italy in the form of both men and weapons. (Haig did think it rather bizarre that the War Cabinet should insist on appointing as commander of the British forces in Italy the fully occupied Plumer, rather than the under-employed Rawlinson.) This turn of events gave Lloyd George the opportunity to vent all his resentment against the decision-making process in the first half of the year. He claimed, rather questionably, that back in January, if his proposals concerning operations in Italy had been acted upon, the present setback there could not have occurred. But the obvious inference – that it would be better late than never to switch all endeavour from Flanders to Italy (if hardly for offensive purposes) – was not drawn.

On 2 November, on learning that recent actions in Belgium had brought near the capture of Passchendaele, the War Cabinet pondered the alternatives. Haig was still conducting an important offensive in Flanders which needed to be brought to completion before winter set in. But was this as important as saving Italy? No resolution emerged. Haig was called on to send more divisions from France to Italy, and to hold others in readiness. But nothing about his Flanders plans was consequently amended. On 7 November the War Cabinet noted further progress on the Passchendaele Ridge. It also received an account from the Prime Minister about the situation in Italy (whence he had repaired). Apart from the fact that Lloyd George had resolved to move Plumer from the one front to the other, these two aspects of the war seemed to be proceeding without regard to each other.

Late in November, events in Italy were overshadowed by Haig's belated triumph at Cambrai. Briefly, this success gave Robertson an opportunity to bring the discussion back to the merits of Western Front offensives in general, and to argue that the situation in Italy (which anyway was improving) did not warrant further diversions there of British resources. Success at Cambrai, he claimed, vindicated not just the concentration of British endeavours on the Western Front but the actual campaign in Flanders. Haig's attacks in the latter region had forced the Germans to concentrate their reserves there, and so to thin severely their forces on other parts of the Western Front. That had rendered them vulnerable at Cambrai.

Momentarily, these events even lured Robertson into a display of wide-ranging optimism, of a sort usual for Haig but not for the CIGS. He argued that 'the position of the Germans [might be] worse than we were sometimes inclined to think'. They had sent only six or seven divisions to Italy, and these possibly on account of calls for aid from the Austrians. 'The failure to exploit the Italian *débâcle* was significant.' Warming to his subject, Robertson continued:

On the whole, it was difficult to explain the cessation of the offensive against Roumania and the failure to exploit the Italian *débâcle* except on the ground of inactivity, and the Chief of the Imperial General Staff thought that Germany's military power was probably a good deal less and the condition of the Austrian armies a good deal worse than we had thought to be the case.

Such sentiments seemed pretty odd, given that, only a week before, the War Cabinet had been presented with mounting evidence of the appearance of German divisions – transferred from the Eastern Front – opposite Passchendaele, possibly as a prelude to a counter-attack.

Assurances had then been offered that Haig's forces were still superior in the region and had the advantage of position, but this had not prevented the view being strongly expressed that nothing could be worse for the country than the loss of Passchendaele Ridge.

If Robertson's burst of optimism seemed unwarranted even when it was made (despite the glow of success occasioned by the first thrust at Cambrai), it soon became a millstone round his neck. The Germans counter-attacked at Cambrai on 30 November. Their action, as the War Cabinet sourly noted, was a complete surprise. In a matter of days, the British gains had vanished and the sense of a modest but satisfying success was entirely eliminated. The War Cabinet promptly indulged in some well-merited recrimination. The enemy, it was pointed out, had secured a success inconsistent with information supplied by Haig concerning the strength and condition of the German army. This lapse suggested severe shortcomings in his intelligence staff. There were also indications that the nature of the setback had not been frankly conveyed to the War Cabinet, 'which body was responsible to Parliament and the public'. And finally there was the matter of Robertson's surge of optimism not two weeks before:

> Attention was also called to the discrepancy between the nature of the German success and the reports which had been consistently received from official sources in regard to their [the Germans'] weakness and the deterioration of their *moral[e]*.

By the time of this breast-beating early in December, the Passchendaele offensive was at an end. It was followed in a matter of days by an entirely new scenario. The CIGS, along with the Minister of War, began raising the alarm on account of the run-down condition of Haig's army and the massive build-up of German forces confronting it. There was no point, Lord Derby told the War Cabinet on 6 December, in trying to decide military policy in France for the coming year. That policy would be decided by the Germans. Far from Haig – whose shortage of men Derby estimated at 100,000 – breaking through the German line, the question was whether a German breakthrough of his line could be prevented.

By 19 December Robertson (undeflected by enquiries a few days earlier about what had become of his cheerful prognosis of 23 November) was waxing yet more alarmist. In the course of a positive litany of dismay, he spoke of an imminent German attack, of the inadequacy of British defences (compared with those captured from the Germans), of difficulties of supply created by the devastation of regions behind the British front, of the feebleness of those Portuguese and Belgian forces to which the BEF were supposed to look for aid, of the inadequacy of the junior officer class now available to Haig's army for preparing a defensive battle, and of the limited opportunities open to the Flanders forces for making a strategic retreat owing to the proximity of the Channel ports. Haig, in Robertson's view, fully recognized that there could be no more offensives at present. For some time, his army must stand on the defensive.

This was an extraordinary finale to the Third Ypres campaign. Certainly the situation had been transformed by the collapse of Russia, enabling the Germans to transfer great numbers of men and weapons to the west. But the threat of Russia's disintegration had been evident before Third Ypres was even launched, and the event itself had been proceeding during each stage of the Flanders campaign. Robertson had never been entitled to advise the continuation of attacks in Flanders – with consequent British losses – in disregard of what was happening on the Eastern Front. Anyway the CIGS, whether or not he chose to recognize it, was saying momentous things not just about the aftermath of events in Russia but about the outcome of Third Ypres. According to his summation, Britain's forces in Flanders were desperately drained of manpower, were surrounded by painfully unreliable allies, had placed themselves in vulnerable positions from which to conduct a defence, could be supplied only with difficulty, and were most disadvantageously situated strategically. As the outcome of an operation which had been intended to clear the Germans out of Belgium and turn the enemy flank on the coast, this amounted to a terrible self-indictment.

III

Clearly, quite apart from events on the Eastern Front and the setbacks sustained in Italy and at Cambrai, the sorry denouement of Third Ypres seemed to require the meting out of punishment. And this must involve individuals more highly placed than Haig's intelligence staff. (The purge of this body, for all it mattered, would soon get under way.) Presumably the Prime Minister and War Cabinet were not prepared to shoulder their own considerable share of the responsibility, or to apply suitable chastisement to themselves. Nor, given the absence of acceptable political alternatives, would it have been wise of them to do so. But that made it all the more appropriate to inflict punishment one level down: on the military authorities about whom, in any case, they took so dim a view, and who had helped to bring Britain's military forces to so unhappy a pass. Haig and Robertson seemed to be doomed.

One prerequisite only was necessary to their banishment. Robertson –

of all people – was providing a calamitous assessment of the outcome of Third Ypres. That assessment, preparatory to his and Haig's supersession, must be endorsed by their civilian masters. Lloyd George, in particular, must go all the way in confirming this assessment of the peril of Britain's forces in the west. It might be supposed that this would not be a difficulty. Yet, astonishingly, the Prime Minister refused his endorsement. He may have predicted all along, and most recently in early October, that nothing but sorrow would flow from a great endeavour in Flanders. But, in the strangest about-turn in this campaign of irony, now that the cup of sorrow was indeed running over Lloyd George refused to notice. To him Robertson's desperately realistic warning about the peril of the British army on the Western Front was just another trick by the military to fasten attention on that theatre. Thereby they would forestall, yet again, the application of an imaginative strategy elsewhere.

On 10 December, in the aftermath of Robertson and Haig's first cries of impending disaster, Lloyd George made clear his unwillingness to respond. Even should the Germans move all their serviceable divisions from the east, he said, they would still be in a minority on the Western Front. He complained that he could not understand the rather alarmist tone that was being exhibited. The public was considerably disturbed, he said, and quite unnecessarily so having regard to the actual facts. It was highly desirable that it receive official assurance. The person Lloyd George had in mind to render this assurance, evidently, was himself. Two days later Derby wrote to him expressing 'dismay' at Lloyd George's expressed intention to announce that the Allies were 'in a large majority' on the Western Front. They might, according to Derby, still have a nominal superiority in men. But the British forces were weary whereas the German divisions (from a front that had seen little real fighting in 1917) were fresh.

When, on 19 December, Robertson resumed his unaccustomed role as prophet of impending danger, this time with his detailed enumeration of the unsatisfactory aspects evident on the Western Front, Lloyd George was no more convinced. The enemy, he responded to Robertson, had been talking a great deal about their intention soon to launch an attack on Britain's forces in the west. In his mind, this raised doubts about whether they meant to attack anywhere at all. Alternatively, they might be preparing to launch an offensive somewhere else.

Here in truth was a strange coda to a sorry military endeavour. Haig would remain, but not because he had accomplished anything that justified retention of his command. Rather, his survival – at the moment when the military chiefs were themselves proclaiming failure – depended on the response of his most severe critic in Britain's governing circles.

Having predicted the barrenness of Third Ypres, Lloyd George simply refused to acknowledge the fearful danger to which these operations had helped expose Haig's army. Finding himself ideally placed to cast into limbo the military authors and advocates of the Flanders campaign, the Prime Minister denied that any such opportunity was now present.

19

Conclusion

I

The termination of the Third Ypres campaign constituted no sort of a climax. The undertaking did not cease because it had reached some meaningful culmination. It simply came to a halt.

This raised an obvious question. What was going to happen next? Haig's view was straightforward. Although concerned about the appearance of reinforcements on the German side of the front, he took the view that the British offensive in Flanders should be resumed as soon as the campaigning season returned. At a meeting with Robertson on 10 November, during which the CIGS stressed the government's concern regarding the precarious situation in Italy, Haig responded as follows:

> I pointed out the importance of the Belgian coast to Great Britain, and urged that nothing should be done to stop our offensive next spring.[1]

The government's view was less clear-cut. It needs to be recalled that, even while pondering a winter operation designed to remove Turkey from the war, Lloyd George had alluded to the prospect of resuming the Flanders campaign in the spring of 1918. But by early November he appeared to be talking otherwise, and not just in private. On the 12th, returning from Italy, the Prime Minister stopped off in Paris to deliver a public utterance which implied deep dissatisfaction with the Flanders operation. He called for the establishment of an Allied body which might propose alternative strategic undertakings. And he offered a scarcely veiled repudiation of Haig's – and, it might be noted, the War Cabinet's – manner of proceeding. Lloyd George proclaimed:

> We have won great victories. When I look at the appalling casualty lists I sometimes wish it had not been necessary to win so many.[2]

This was combative talk, but it hardly indicated what strategy might be pursued hereafter. All that emerged of substance from Lloyd George's fulminations was the establishment of a body misleadingly called the Supreme War Council, possessing advisory functions but no executive authority. There could be no way of knowing whether this body would recommend a radical departure in strategy or, alternatively, would go along with Haig – if not quite certainly with the War Cabinet – in proposing the resumption of the Flanders offensive. (The fact that Henry Wilson, not Robertson, was to be the British representative on this body hardly pointed either way, given the variableness of Wilson's judgements up to this point.) Further, there could be no certainty how Britain's decision-makers would respond to whatever advice the Supreme War Council managed to give them.

In the event, the course of strategy was left neither to the discretion of this new body nor to the varying wisdom of the British War Cabinet and the commander-in-chief. With the dawning of 1918, the threatened German offensive in the west, about which Robertson and Haig had begun to speak with alarm, and which Lloyd George had chosen to regard as an invention of the high command, rapidly became the all-encompassing fact of the war. Plumer would soon be returned to his accustomed position in the Ypres salient, this time to preside over the hurried evacuation of everything that had been captured – and more – in the Third Ypres campaign. So the Flanders offensive of 1917, far from leading anywhere or having any sort of sequel, appeared at the last to be just one more sorry episode in a war of anguished incidents, unrelated to each other and lacking discernible consequences or achievements.

II

The Third Battle of Ypres, including its overture at Messines, cost the British army approximately 275,000 casualties. Of these, 70,000 were killed and an unknown number wounded so badly that they could not return to the front. In all, the campaign probably reduced the strength of the BEF by the equivalent of 10 to 12 divisions out of a total strength of 60. No significant accessions of territory were made as a result. The only reward for these endeavours was a great diminution in the fighting strength of the enemy, although to a lesser extent than the reduction of Britain's forces. (Germany probably suffered just under 200,000 casualties during the Third Ypres campaign.) In the perilous months that lay ahead, consequent upon the collapse of the Eastern Front against Germany and the failure of the Americans to put in an appearance on the Western Front, this balance sheet was plainly to Britain's disadvantage.

The Third Ypres campaign imposed a further cost on Britain's army, but one less quantifiable than numbers of men killed and wounded. Several witnesses relate the harm dealt to the morale of Britain's fighting men by their involvement in such barren operations. In December 1917 the minister for national service, in a cabinet document endorsed by the adjutant-general to the forces, recounted increases among the fighting forces of drunkenness, desertion, and psychological disorders. Men home from the front, he reported, frequently spoke with great bitterness about 'the waste of life during the continued hammerings against the Ypres Ridge'.[3] And a gunner who participated in the fighting of 11 October relates how a 'month of incessant attacks', with little progress, appalling casualties and severe fighting, was having 'a bad effect on the morale of everybody concerned'. He continued:

> Reinforcements of the new armies shambled up past the guns with drag-
> ging steps and the expressions of men who knew they were going to
> certain death. No words of greeting passed as they slouched along; in
> sullen silence they filed past one by one to the sacrifice.[4]

In the year when the command structure of the Russian army disintegrated utterly and large numbers of French soldiers mutinied, the question poses itself: how close did Haig's forces come to acts of 'collective indiscipline'? The remarkable fact is that, however resentful and disillusioned rank-and-file soldiers became, no significant instances of their refusing to obey orders attended the progress of the campaign. We have no convincing explanation as to why; historians have difficulty enough accounting for why things do happen, without trying to explain why they do not. But some points may be noted. First, Britain's social and political structure, in marked contrast to that of Tsarist and post-Tsarist Russia, remained strong and resilient. Second, commitment to the purposes – if not necessarily to the manner of conduct – of the war continued firm, despite a marginal increase in manifestations of dissent during 1917. Finally, the wearing down of the British army, both absolutely and as a percentage of population, was still nowhere approaching the terrible blood-sacrifice of France.

Nevertheless, the clear weakening of resolve of the French army in the first half of 1917, and the utter collapse of the Russian army in the second half, renders it bewildering that the British military command should have risked their own troops' fighting spirit by persisting in the Third Ypres battle. As for the political command's preparedness to let them do so, that beggars comprehension.

It was in no sense inevitable or inescapable that Britain should subject itself to this ordeal. Certainly, the British army in the second half of

1917 was under considerable pressure to engage in offensive action somewhere. And, after the whole range of extraneous operations had been explored, this could only mean action on the major front and against the major enemy. Given both the parlous state of its principal allies, Russia and France, and the precarious position of the Italians, Britain had to go on the offensive. And this meant taking the war, not to lesser adversaries, who anyway were at best only partly accessible, but to the Germans. That required action in the one sector where the Germans could be obliged to fight, and where the British could effectively concentrate soldiers and weapons: the Western Front.

Moreover, to do so was not self-evidently hopeless. It had already become clear, and was being further demonstrated, that by mid-1917 the British army was capable of mounting effective operations against the Germans in the west. Certain episodes of the Somme campaign in the second half of 1916, along with British endeavours at Vimy and Arras in early April 1917 and the devastating attack at Messines in June, placed the matter beyond doubt. The British munitions industry was at last pouring forth the quantities of high-class weaponry necessary to mount attacks with some prospect of success. The British army, and above all its artillery officers, were acquiring the necessary expertise to employ their weapons in a manner to maximize the discomfort of the enemy. And the British infantry were being trained in more effective ways to take advantage of the artillery support now being provided and to make better use of the greater variety of their own weapons. There was every prospect, therefore, of the British army on the Western Front in the second half of 1917, if allowed to operate in appropriate weather and provided with suitably limited objectives, delivering a series of hammer blows to the enemy. These might not accomplish the destruction of whole enemy armies or a sweeping advance. But they did hold out the prospect both of capturing some worthwhile ground and of inflicting severe loss on the enemy, without involving the martyrdom of Britain's own troops.

That Haig's forces did not engage in this sort of operation plainly owed nothing to inevitability. The opportunity, the weaponry, the expertise, and the experience for such undertakings were all present. Influential voices in the British military hierarchy, such as the CIGS, were prepared (if they could find an appropriate politico-military context) to recommend such a manner of proceeding. Third Ypres, that is, was in no sense a tragedy, if that expression is taken to mean an unrewarded undertaking that its initiators had no choice but to embark on. Sensible choices were on offer. They were not taken, and far more questionable choices were made instead. That was the result of decisions taken jointly by the nation's political leaders and their military advisers.

The reasons why Haig failed to propose a series of 'bite and hold' operations, posited on good weather, feasible targets, and the accumulation of troops and weapons for short-term undertakings, are only too clear. He envisaged large campaigns for great objectives producing decisive outcomes: the rupturing of the enemy line, the destruction of the enemy's will to resist, and the overrunning of vast tracts of territory. He managed to convince himself that the highly developed state of the British army, and the fundamentally impaired state of the German army, enabled him to embark on such an undertaking in July 1917. There was never serious justification for this belief. The British army had certainly reached a high state of development, especially in the field of weaponry, but only for operations of a limited sort. As for the German army, it was providing no evidence of the degree of decrepitude which might allow a powerful blow by Haig's army to transform itself into unlimited forward movement.

Haig's recommendation, therefore, laid itself open – simply on its merits – to rejection by his political masters. They confronted no insuperable difficulty in taking this course. Their political position was secure: never was an alternative government so conspicuous by its absence. Their role in military decision-making was also secure. No major operation had been undertaken by British forces in the war without the necessary political endorsement. Indeed, some earlier undertakings had been initiated by the civilian authorities without unqualified military approval. And in the first half of 1917 these civilian authorities had not hesitated to embark on the most drastic rearrangement of the command structure of the British army in the teeth of opposition from its highest military advisers. All that was required now of the civilians was, not the displacement of the British commander-in-chief, but an exhortation to him to produce a modest plan that lay within his army's capabilities.

The political rulers of Britain failed to act in this way, not because they feared for their jobs or were in awe of their military advisers, but because they also were not prepared to take on board the realities of the battlefield. They might, like Haig, notice the existence of what became called the Pétain method (although it could equally have been dubbed the Vimy method or the Messines method). And they might also acknowledge the possibility of Britain's forces remaining on the defensive until – some day – the Americans arrived. Neither course would long hold their attention. They, along with Haig, yearned for a large undertaking accomplishing dramatic results. Some of them, and particularly Lloyd George, chose to believe that this large undertaking could be carried out by one of Britain's allies, or by a British army operating away from the Western Front against one of Germany's associates.

The first of these ways of proceeding failed for the want of any ally of Britain's that proved both willing and able to bear the brunt of a major campaign. The second was simply a notion so insubstantial that the nation's civilian rulers could never bring themselves to embrace it. Thereby they painted themselves into the corner of endorsing Haig's campaign.

In a widely held view, once this endorsement was given the terrible course of the Third Ypres offensive, with its long months of ill-rewarded struggle in frequently dire weather, was inescapable. A great military campaign, supposedly, takes on a life of its own.

Two things may be said about this. First, the War Cabinet only endorsed the first stage of the campaign, with the proviso that they would then review it and, unless it was shaping up appropriately, call it off. The reason that this did not happen was not that, having looked at the campaign and found it wanting, they then discovered that they had no power to call a halt. They did not look, and did not choose to call a halt.

Secondly, the Third Ypres campaign was eminently haltable. This is demonstrated by the number of occasions on which, at least temporarily, fighting actually ceased. On none of these occasions was there a clear imperative to resume it: except the imperative felt by political and military leaders alike to avoid admitting that something they had embarked upon could not be carried to its full conclusion.

The Third Ypres campaign was prefigured by the Messines operation. This, certainly, had been planned as a first step. But it was followed by a seven-week gap and need never have been succeeded by a second stage. (Standing alone it constituted a considerable success.) And once Third Ypres proper had commenced, it was brought to a stop on 28 August, when Gough's control was abruptly halted. The operation was only resumed on 20 September, when it appeared (the appearance proved deceptive) to be taking the form of a quite different undertaking – one which, had wisdom prevailed, it might well have become. Finally, the campaign ceased on 10 November, not because it had by then reached some sort of a conclusion, or achieved any satisfactory results, but because weather conditions rendered further action all but intolerable and the high command had chosen to launch an offensive elsewhere. In short, what we are witnessing during the course of Third Ypres is the ability of the command to control events at every stage. There was no question of the logic of events controlling the high command.

What, nevertheless, is noteworthy about these stop–start aspects of Third Ypres is that they did not constitute, on the part of the high command or even of the commanders of the Fifth and Second Armies, a reorientation of the campaign to a bite-and-hold operation. Haig's overarching determination to exploit the supposed crack in German morale and accomplish a great sweep to the coast distorted the course of action at every stage. On the first day of the undertaking proper, Gough attacked on too wide a front towards too distant objectives on account of Haig's large scheme. And he continued to attack during a month of adverse weather because of Haig's determination to get within sight of the coast at a date amenable to an amphibious operation. Plumer's first assaults, although made in an area that accorded with Haig's larger objectives, could have been the prelude to a more modest approach. They proved not to be. Plumer, despite what looked at first like some bite-and-hold successes, soon revealed that he too was pursuing larger purposes. From early October to mid-November he attacked without regard to the obstacles presented by weather and the condition of the ground. And he oriented his attacks in an inappropriate direction – funnelling his forces into a salient which restricted his ability to employ his own artillery, and laying his infantry open to undue flanking fire from the unattacked guns of the enemy.

The delusions of the military command, and the waywardness of the political leadership, brought dire consequences upon Haig's army in the Flanders campaign of 1917. Further dire consequences lay ahead. When the massive German offensive opened in March 1918, two results of the Third Ypres campaign became apparent. The first was that the ground so desperately fought for between July and November of the preceding year was impossible to hold. What had taken four months to win was evacuated in three days. The second was that the ten or more British divisions consumed in the campaign formed the missing reserve that might have halted the German advance a great deal sooner and at less cost. Thereby the Allies would have been spared the gravest crisis of the war.

Certainly, in the German spring offensive of 1918, Lloyd George and Haig responded with calm resolve. That was a welcome change from their respective performances in 1917. It was also their last significant contribution to the course of the conflict on the battlefield. When in July and August of 1918 the British army recovered the initiative and commenced its advance to victory, it would be employing just those methods of battle which neither Haig nor Lloyd George had cared to entertain in the arguments over strategy which accompanied Third Ypres. Consequently, the path to victory saw the Prime Minister and the commander-in-chief moving steadily to the sidelines of the First World War. But that course of events, although profoundly important, is a different story.

Notes

1 The Conundrum

1. Arthur Bryant, *English Saga (1840–1940)* (London: 1942, The Reprint Society), p. 293.

4 Decisions: May–July 1917

1. A. J. P. Taylor (ed.), *Lloyd George: A Diary by Frances Stevenson* (London: Hutchinson, 1971), p. 157.
2. The idea of inevitability is often hinted at, but rarely explored, in discussions of the Flanders campaign. For example, John Terraine's valuable *The Road to Passchendaele* (London: Leo Cooper, 1977) carries the challenging subtitle 'A Study in Inevitability'. Anti-climactically, the issue of inevitability is nowhere addressed in the course of the book.
3. Hankey diary, 30 June 1917 (recounting events of the previous ten days), Hankey Papers, Churchill College, Cambridge.
4. War Policy Committee Minutes, 21 June 1917, CAB27.
5. Hankey diary, 30 June 1917.
6. War Policy Committee Minutes (Attachments), 23 June 1917.
7. An interpretation that, over the years, has gone in and out of fashion ties the initiation of Third Ypres to the German submarine campaign against merchant shipping unleashed in 1917. According to this argument, alarmist views held in the British Admiralty, to the effect that Britain would be unable to carry on the war unless the army captured enemy submarine bases on the Flanders coast, drove both political and military leaders into endorsing the Third Ypres offensive.

It is the case that Sir John Jellicoe raised the matter in most anxious terms at a meeting of the War Policy Committee on 20 June. There is no evidence that his views carried conviction either with the civilians or with the military. Indeed it is noteworthy that Haig, who might – without necessarily believing a word Jellicoe said – have endorsed Jellicoe's claims in order to further his own cause, did nothing of the sort. He wrote in his diary for 20 June: 'No one present shared Jellicoe's view, and all seemed satisfied that the food reserves in Great Britain are adequate.' The records of subsequent meetings of the War Policy Committee provide no confirmation for the view that either the political or the military leaders came down for Third Ypres on account of Jellicoe's fears.

5   Making Plans

1. 'Army Instructions for Main Offensive on Second Army Front', War Office (WO) Papers, Public Record Office, Kew, 12/12/16, WO 158/214.
2. Kiggell to Second Army 6/1/17, WO 158/38.
3. Kiggell to Plumer 27/1/17, Kiggell Papers V78, Liddell Hart Centre, King's College, London.
4. Sir James E. Edmonds, *Military Operations: France and Belgium 1917* (London: HMSO, 1948), vol. 2, p. 14.
5. Second Army to GHQ 30/1/17, WO 158/38.
6. 'Distribution of Artillery – 4th March, 1917', Australian War Memorial (AWM) file 45/29/1.
7. Lt-Col. Macmullen, Note 15/1/17, AWM 45/33/1.
8. Haig Diary, National Library of Scotland, Edinburgh, 10/2/17.
9. Haig's marginalia on Macmullen's note of 15/1/17, AWM 45/33/1.
10. Edmonds, *Military Operations*, vol. 2, p. 17.
11. Haig Diary 14/3/17; Haig to Nivelle 21/3/17, quoted in John Terraine, *The Road to Passchendaele: the Flanders Offensive of 1917: a Study in Inevitability* (London: Leo Cooper, 1977), p. 57.
12. Plumer to GHQ 20/4/17, AWM 45/39/4.
13. 'Record of Instructions issued verbally by the Field Marshal Commanding-in-Chief at the Army Commanders Conference held at Doullens, at 11 a.m. on Monday 7th May, 1917', AWM 45/32/23.
14. See Second Army intelligence files for May 1917 in AWM 26/7/187/14.
15. 'Résumé of Interview between General Debeney and Haig held at Bavincourt on 2 June 1917', Benson Papers, Liddell Hart Centre for Military Archives, King's College, London.
16. Ibid.
17. Cyril Falls, *Military Operations: France and Belgium, 1917*, vol. 1 (London: Macmillan, 1940), pp. 509–12.
18. Haig Diary 18/5/17.

6   False Dawn: Messines

1. G. C. Wynne, *If Germany Attacks: The Battle in Depth in the West* (London: Faber & Faber, 1940), p. 262.
2. Lt-Col. A. F. Brooke, 'The Evolution of Artillery in the Great War', *Journal of the Royal Artillery*, vol. 53, 1926–7, p. 242.
3. Ibid., p. 243.
4. Brig. E. C. Anstey, 'History of the Royal Artillery 1914–18', Anstey Papers, Royal Artillery Institution, Woolwich, p. 141.
5. Ibid., p. 142.
6. Ibid., p. 143.
7. Brooke, 'Evolution of Artillery', p. 242.
8. Cyril Falls, *Military Operations: France and Belgium 1917*, vol. 1 (London: Macmillan, 1940), p. 497.
9. Plumer to Haig 18/3/17, Operational Records, Australian War Memorial (AWM) Canberra, AWM 45/32/6.
10. Haig to Second Army (OAD 349) 3/4/17, AWM 51.
11. Lt-Col. Macmullen interview with Plumer 5/4/17, AWM 45/33/1; Plumer to Haig 9/4/17, AWM 45/32/6.
12. 'Note on the Messines–Wytschaete attack' (OAD 432) 5/5/17, AWM 51.
13. Second Army Operation Order

No. 1, 10/5/17, AWM 26/6/187/9.

14. Sir James E. Edmonds, *Military Operations: France and Belgium 1917*, vol. 2 (London: HMSO, 1948), p. 42.

15. Anstey, 'History of the Royal Artillery', p. 160.

16. Ibid., p. 161.

17. Ibid.

18. Ibid., p. 165.

19. Edmonds, *Military Operations*, vol. 2, p. 44.

20. Second Army Intelligence Report 29/5/17, AWM 26/6/187/14.

21. Anstey, 'History of the Royal Artillery', p. 164.

22. See Second Army Intelligence Reports for the first week of June 1917, AWM 26/6/187/14.

23. Kiggell to Plumer 29/5/17, AWM 51.

24. 'Summary of Proceedings of a Conference held at Pernes at 11 a.m., 30th May, 1917' (OAD 464), AWM 51.

25. Translation of the history of the 204 (German) Division in AWM 26/6/188/30.

26. 23 Division, 'Narrative of Events in connection with Second Army Attack on 7th June, 1917', AWM 26/6/190/1.

27. Ibid.

28. 37 Australian Battalion Narrative, AWM 26/6/194/1.

29. C. E. W. Bean, *Official History of Australia in the War of 1914–18, vol. 4: The Australian Imperial Force in France: 1917* (Sydney: Angus & Robertson, 1938), p. 594.

30. Col. H. Stewart, *The New Zealand Division 1916–1919: A Popular History based on Official Records* (Auckland: Whitcombe & Tombs, 1921), p. 194.

31. 'Report on Operations for the Capture of Messines–Wytschaete Ridge by IX Corps', AWM 26/6/189/10.

32. Edmonds, *Military Operations*, vol. 2, p. 72.

33. Ibid., pp. 73–4.

34. See accounts in 3 Australian Division file in AWM 26/6/194/1 and in 25 Division Report AWM 26/6/190/5.

35. Anstey, 'History of the Royal Artillery', p. 167.

36. 25 Division Report.

37. See Edmonds, *Military Operations*, vol. 2, pp. 85–7.

38. Diary of Private W. D. Galway, AWM Ms 1355.

39. Harington to Advanced GHQ 3/6/17, AWM 51.

40. Edmonds, *Military Operations*, vol. 2, p. 89.

41. Ibid.

42. Ibid., p. 87, n. 2.

7 The New Commander

1. Grand Quartier Général GQG, 'Etude d'une opération de débarquement dans la région d'Ostende', 7/12/16, Operational Records, Australian War Memorial (AWM) Canberra, AWM 45/35/20.

2. War Office Conference 12/12/16, AWM 45/35/28.

3. Sir James E. Edmonds, *Military Operations: France and Belgium 1917*, vol. 2 (London: HMSO, 1948), pp. 109–10.

4. Col. W. G. S. Dobbie, 'The Operations of the 1st Division on the Belgian Coast in 1917', *Royal Engineers Journal*, June 1924, p. 191.

5. Edmonds, *Military Operations*, vol. 2, pp. 120–22.

6. Dobbie, 'Operations of the 1st Division, pp. 190–3.

7. Ibid., p. 186.

8. Cyril Falls, *Military Operations: France and Belgium 1917*, vol. 1 (London: Macmillan, 1940), Chapter XVIII.

9. General Sir Hubert Gough, *The Fifth Army* (London: Hodder & Stoughton, 1931), p. 193.
10. A. H. Farrar-Hockley, *Goughie: the Life of Sir General Hubert Gough* (London: Hart-Davis/ MacGibbon, 1975), p. 227.
11. For details of the German defensive system at Ypres see G. C. Wynne, *If Germany Attacks* (London: Faber & Faber, 1940), Chapter XII, and by the same author, 'The Development of the German Defensive Battle in 1917, and its Influence on British Defensive Tactics', *Army Quarterly*, vol. 34, April 1937, pp. 15–34.
12. Annex to Fifth Army Intelligence Report 27/7/17, AWM 26/7/189/3.
13. Translation of the German Official Account of the Third Ypres Campaign held in the Royal Artillery Institution Library, Woolwich, p. 37.
14. General Sir Martin Farndale, *History of the Royal Regiment of Artillery: Western Front 1914–18* (Woolwich: Royal Artillery Institution, 1986), p. 199.
15. Haig to Gough 13/5/17 (OAD 443), War Office Papers (WO), Public Record Office, Kew, WO 158/249.
16. Edmonds, *Military Operations*, vol. 2, p. 108.
17. 'Notes on Conference held at Lovie Château, June 6th', Fifth Army War Diary June 1917, WO 95/519.
18. John Terraine, *Douglas Haig: The Educated Soldier* (London: Hutchinson, 1963), p. 289; Haig Diary, National Library of Scotland, Edinburgh, 10/4/17.
19. See the Fifth Army Intelligence Reports in AWM 26/6/189/2-3. Rather confusingly, these reports are filed with the Messines operations files. They seem to have survived in the Australian War Memorial and nowhere else.

20. Major-General Sir John Davidson, *Haig: Master of the Field* (London: Peter Nevill, 1953), pp. 26–9.
21. All quotations from this memorandum dated 25/6/17 have been taken from a copy in the Maxse Papers, 69/53/8 in the Imperial War Museum (IWM). The memorandum is reproduced in Edmonds, *Military Operations*, vol. 2, Appendix XV.
22. 'Memorandum by Army Commander, Sir H. Gough 26/6/17', Maxse Papers 69/53/8, IWM.
23. See Maxse's annotations on the copy in the IWM.
24. Davidson, *Haig*, p. 31.
25. Haig Diary 27/6/17.

8   31 July: The Implements

1. Sir James E. Edmonds, *Military Operations: France and Belgium 1917*, vol. 2 (London: HMSO, 1948), p. 148.
2. 'Note on possible employment of the Cavalry Corps during the coming operations' (OAD 563/1), 22/7/17, Operational Records, Australian War Memorial (AWM), Canberra, AWM 51.
3. 'Third Battle of Ypres: Operations of XVIII Corps on 31st July, 1917', Maxse Papers 69/53/8/33, Imperial War Museum (IWM).
4. Ibid.
5. Diary of Captain W. A. C. Wilkinson (Guards Division) 5/8/ 17, IWM.
6. 'Third Battle of Ypres: Operations of XVIII Corps on 31 July, 1917'.
7. 'Report on the Operations of the 51st (Highland) Division N.E. of Ypres July 31st–Aug 1st, 1917', Maxse Papers 69/53/8/34, IWM.
8. Ibid.
9. The best source to demonstrate the great variety of attack formations adopted by units on 31 July is an appendix to the proceedings of a

court of inquiry set up to examine the actions of 30 Division on that day. See 30 Division War Diary May–Aug. 1917, War Office Papers, Public Record Office, Kew WO 95/2312.

10. '72nd Infantry Brigade Instructions No. 4', 72 Infantry Brigade War Diary 1917, WO 95/2211; Guards Division Answers to Questions, Guards Division War Diary 1917, WO 95/1193.
11. Guards Division Answers to Questions.
12. 'Report on action of Tanks on 31st July, 1917', Tank Corps War Diary, AWM 45/24/6.
13. 'Report on the Operations of the 51st (Highland) Division'.
14. Edmonds, *Military Operations*, vol. 2, p. 108.
15. Ibid., pp. 108–9.
16. Cyril Falls, *Military Operations: France and Belgium 1917*, vol. 1 (London: Macmillan, 1940), p. 182.
17. Edmonds, *Military Operations*, vol. 2, p. 41.
18. 'Operations of the XVIII Corps on 31st July, 1917'. The rate was the same for all corps.
19. General Sir Martin Farndale, *History of the Royal Regiment of Artillery* (Woolwich: Royal Artillery Institution, 1986), p. 166.
20. Major-General Williams to II Corps 3/7/17, 30 Division War Diary May–Aug. 1917, WO 95/2312.
21. Major-General Williams to II Corps 30/7/17, ibid.
22. 'XIV Corps Operations Instructions', XIV Corps War Diary Jan.–July 1917, WO 95/912.
23. Ibid.
24. The insufficiency of guns possessed by XIV Corps would have been greater if Gough had gone along with Haig's urging to concentrate more of his artillery against the Gheluvelt Plateau.
25. Edmonds, *Military Operations*, vol. 2, p. 108.
26. Fifth Army Intelligence Summary 28/7/17, AWM 26/6/189/3.
27. German Official Account of the Third Ypres Campaign held in the library of the Royal Artillery Institution, Woolwich, p. 54.

9 First Strike

1. Note by Kiggell 28/7/17, Operational Records, Australian War Memorial (AWM), Canberra, AWM 33/1.
2. Haig Diary, National Library of Scotland, Edinburgh, 25/7/17.
3. General Sir Hubert Gough, *The Fifth Army* (London: Hodder & Stoughton, 1931), p. 196.
4. Haig Diary 27/7/17.
5. Ibid.
6. Sir James E. Edmonds, *Military Operations: France and Belgium 1917* vol. 2 (London: HMSO, 1948), p. 138, n. 2.
7. Fifth Army Intelligence Summaries 16 to 30 July, 1917, AWM 26/6/189/3.
8. This statistic comes from II Corps Heavy Artillery War Diary August, 1917, War Office Papers, Public Record Office, Kew, WO 95/655. There is no reason to believe that the artillery of the northern corps were having any more success with this method.
9. This figure has been compiled from an exhaustive survey of those operational reports which have survived from the various units attacking on 31 July. The figure can only be regarded as approximate.
10. See previous note for the method of calculation.
11. See Fifth Army Intelligence Reports in AWM 26/6/189/3.
12. Haig Diary 28/7/17.
13. Ibid., 30/5/17.

14. *Les Armées françaises dans la grande guerre*, 103 vols (Paris: Imprimerie nationale 1922–38), Tome V, vol. 2, p. 664.
15. Ibid., pp. 671–2.
16. Ibid., p. 675.
17. Ibid.
18. C. Headlam, *History of the Guards Division in the Great War* (London: John Murray, 1924), p. 225.
19. Ibid., pp. 228–9.
20. 'Narrative of operations of 3rd Guards Brigade in the attack from Boesinghe on 31st July, 1917', Guards Division War Diary Jan.–Dec. 1917, WO 95/1193.
21. 'Narrative of Operations by Guards Division. 31st July 1917', ibid.
22. 2 Guards Brigade Narrative, ibid.
23. 'Narrative of Operations by Lt.-Col. C. R. de Crespigny DSO, Commanding 2nd Battalion Grenadier Guards', ibid.
24. 'Narrative of the attack of the Pilckem Ridge by the 38th (Welsh) Division', 38 Division War Diary Aug. 1916–Feb. 1919, WO 95/2540.
25. Edmonds, *Military Operations*, vol. 2, p. 178, n. 1.
26. Details taken from 'The First World War Diaries of Lt. W. B. St Leger MC', entry for 31 July 1917, Imperial War Museum (IWM), IWM 62.1.
27. 'Third Battle of Ypres. Operations of XVIII Corps on 31st July, 1917', Maxse Papers, 69/53/8, IWM.
28. 'Report on the operations of the 51st (Highland) Division N.E. of Ypres July 31st–Aug. 1 1917', Maxse Papers, 69/53/8; 'Operations of 31st July 1917: 39th Division', 39 Division War Diary Jan.–Sept. 1917, WO 95/2566.
29. Operations of 39 Division.
30. See 51 Division Report for good descriptions of tank–infantry co-operation.
31. See the respective divisional reports for these details.
32. 51st Division Situation Map at Dawn on 1 August 1917, Maxse Papers, 69/53/8.
33. Operations of 39 Division.
34. Edmonds, *Military Operations*, vol. 2, p. 178, n. 1.
35. 45 Brigade, 'Report on Operations Ypres – 29/7/17 to 3/8/17', 15 Division War Diary Aug. 1917–Apr. 1919, WO 95/1915; '55th (West Lancashire) Division, Report on Operations, Ypres, July 29th to August 4th, 1917', 55 Division War Diary Jun.–Sept. 1917, WO 95/2903.
36. 55 Division Report on Operations.
37. 164 Brigade, 'Operations – 31st July 1917', 164 Brigade War Diary Aug. 1917–Apr. 1919, WO 95/2921; 45 Brigade Report on Operations.
38. 55 Division Report on Operations.
39. 45 Brigade Report on Operations.
40. 'Report on Operations by the 24th Inf. Brigade. 31st July–1st August, 1917', 24 Brigade War Diary July 1917–Mar. 1919, WO 95/1718.
41. 30 Division Narrative (untitled), 30 Division War Diary May.–Aug. 1917, WO 95/2312; 24 Division, 'Account of Operations 24th Divisional Front 31st July 1917', 24 Division War Diary July.–Dec. 1917, WO 95/2191.
42. Ibid.
43. Untitled 30 Division document in 30 Division War Diary May–Aug. 1917, WO 95/2312.
44. 30 Division Court of Enquiry – Evidence of General Williams, ibid.
45. 73 Brigade Narrative 31/7/17, 73 Brigade War Diary Jan. 1917–Mar. 1919, WO 95/2217; 30 Division Narrative.
46. See 24 and 30 Division Narratives.
47. 73 Brigade Narrative.
48. Edmonds, *Military Operations*, vol. 2, pp. 149–50.

49. German Official Account of the Third Ypres Campaign held in the Library of the Royal Artillery Institution, Woolwich.
50. Edmonds, *Military Operations*, vol. 2, p. 171, n. 2.
51. 45 Brigade Report.
52. See, for example, the Reports of 45 Brigade, 164 Brigade, and 39 Division.
53. 55 Division Report on Operations.
54. See 164 Brigade Report on Operations.
55. See, for example, 46 Brigade, 'Operations – Ypres 1917', 15 Division War Diary Aug. 1917–Jun. 1918, WO 95/1915.

10 Rain

1. 17/Kings Liverpool Battalion, 'Precis of Operations – 30th July to 3rd August 1917', 30 Division War Diary May–Aug. 1917, War Office Papers (WO), Public Record Office, Kew, WO 95/2312.
2. All rainfall statistics subsequently quoted are taken from GHQ War Diary August 1917, WO 95/14.
3. Diary of Sergeant R. McKay, 109th Field Ambulance (36th Ulster Division), 5/XIX/36, Imperial War Museum (IWM).
4. Captain G. H. F. Nichols, *The 18th Division in the Great War* (London: Blackwood, 1922), p. 214.
5. Edwin Campion Vaughan, *Some Desperate Glory: The Diary of a Young Officer, 1917*, ed. John Terraine (London: Warne, 1981), pp. 228–9.
6. Fifth Army Operation Order No. 11, 31 July 1917, quoted in Sir James E. Edmonds, *Military Operations: France and Belgium 1917*, vol. 2 (London: HMSO, 1948), Appendix XVII, pp. 445–6.
7. Haig Diary National Library of Scotland, Edinburgh, 31/7/17.
8. 'Memorandum on the Situation on the II Corps front by GHQ (Operations), 1 August 1917', quoted in Edmonds, *Military Operations*, vol. 2, Appendix XIX, pp. 447–8.
9. Haig Diary 1/8/17.
10. For the various changes made to Gough's tactical planning in the early days of August see Fifth Army Operational Orders Nos 12 and 13 issued on 3 August and 'Note on Conference held at Lovie Château on the 7th August'. All are to be found in Fifth Army War Diary August 1917, WO 95/520.
11. See 55 Brigade, 'Attack on Inverness Copse. August 10th 1917', 55 Brigade War Diary Jan.–Dec. 1917, WO 95/2047; 74th Infantry Brigade, 'Operations 10th, 11th August, 1917', 74 Brigade War Diary Jan. 1917–July 1919, WO 95/2245.
12. 'Note of a conference held at the C-in-C's House at Cassel on the 15th August, 1917, at 10.30 a.m.', in 'Fifth Army Operations' File, WO 158/249.
13. *Les Armées françaises dans la grande guerre*, 103 vols (Paris: Imprimerie nationale, 1922–38) Tome V, vol. 2, pp. 681–3.
14. For these operations see 'Report of Operations by 29th Division on 16th August, 1917', 29 Division War Diary May–Aug. 1917, WO 95/2282; 'Summary of Operations Carried Out by 20th (Light) Division between 6th to 19th August 1917', XIV Corps War Diary Aug.–Oct. 1917, WO 95/913.
15. 'Summary of Operations Carried out by 20th Division'.
16. See information on the German Order of Battle opposite Fifth Army in maps file WO 153/601.
17. Edmonds, *Military Operations*, vol. 2, p. 200.
18. W. Seymour, *The History of the Rifle Brigade in the War of 1914–*

1918 (London: Rifle Brigade Club, 1936), vol. 2, p. 124.

19. 11 Division, 'Narrative of Operations 8th to 30th August, 1917', Maxse Papers 69/53/8, IWM.

20. Ibid.

21. 145 Brigade, 'Report on Attack by 145th Infantry Brigade near St Julien on 16th August, 1917', 145 Brigade War Diary, Nov. 1916–Oct. 1917, WO 95/2761.

22. 'Operations of the 1/7th Battalion The Worcestershire Regiment 16th–17th August 1917', 144 Brigade War Diary Sept. 1914–Oct. 1917, WO 95/2757.

23. 16 Division 'Extracts from Narrative of Events from 30th July to 18th August, 1917', Operational Records, Australian War Memorial (AWM), Canberra, AWM 26/7/217/1.

24. 48 Brigade, 'Operations East of Ypres – August 16th 1917', 48 Brigade War Diary Jun. 1917–Apr. 1919, WO 95/1973.; Cyril Falls, *History of the Thirty-Sixth (Ulster) Division* (London: McCaw Stevenson & Orr, 1922) p. 116.

25. See narratives of the 16 and 36 Divisions in WO 95/2492 and AWM 26/7/217/1 respectively.

26. Falls, *36th Division*, pp. 121–2.

27. Edmonds, *Military Operations*, vol. 2, pp. 197–8, n. 1.

28. Haig Diary 17/8/17.

29. II Corps 'Review of the Enemy's Operations and Changes in Dispositions Opposite II Corps Front during August, 1917', WO 106/407.

30. 8 Division 'Account of Operations 16th August, 1917', 8 Division War Diary WO 95/1677.

31. 'Operations Carried out by 56th Division from 5th to 17th August, 1917', AWM 26/7/218/23.

32. Brig. E. C. Anstey, 'History of the Royal Artillery' 1914–1918, Anstey Papers, Royal Artillery Institution, Woolwich, p. 179.

33. '53rd Infantry Brigade Narrative of Operations 9th to 18th August 1917', WO 95/2035.

34. Ibid.

35. Haig Diary 16/8/17.

36. Ibid. 17/8/17.

37. 'Notes on Army Commanders' Conference Held at Lovie Château on 17th August, 1917', Fifth Army War Diary June–Aug. 1917, WO 95/520.

38. Ibid.

39. Ibid.

40. For this operation see 'Preliminary Report on Operations on 19th Aug. 1917', Maxse Papers 69/53/8, IWM; Tank Operation Reports Jul.–Sept. 1917, WO 158/839.

41. See 11 Division Narrative and XVIII Corps report in Maxse Papers 69/53/8, IWM.

42. Edmonds, *Military Operations*, vol. 2, p. 203.

43. Report of 8/Seaforth Highlanders in 44 Brigade War Diary Jun.–Dec. 1917, WO 95/1935.

44. 14th (Light) Division. 'Report on Operations, 18th–28th August 1917', 14 Division War Diary Aug. 1917, WO 95/1871. For German defensive tactics see G.C. Wynne, 'The Other Side of the Hill no. XIV: the Fight for Inverness Copse 22nd–24th of August, 1917', *Army Quarterly*, vol. 29, no. 2, Jan. 1935, pp. 297–303.

45. Haig Diary 19/7/17.

46. Ibid. 25/7/17.

47. Ibid.

48. See Gough's marginalia on draft Chapter XVII of the official history, Cabinet Papers, Public Record Office, Kew, CAB 45/140.

49. Haig to Gough 28/7/17 (OAD 609), Fifth Army Operations File Aug.–Oct. 1917, WO 158/250.

50. 'Notes of a Conference held at Cassel at 11.30 a.m. on Thursday, 30th August, 1917', ibid.

51. Plumer to Kiggell 31/8/17, AWM 51.

52. 'Summary of Operations of Fifth Army for Week ending 7 and 14 September, 1917', Fifth Army War Diary Jun.–Aug. 1917, WO 95/520.
53. Haig Diary 9/9/17.
54. Ibid.
55. '184th Infantry Brigade Attack on the Battery Position on Hill 35, 10th September, 1917', 184 Brigade War Diary Sept. 1915–Sept. 1917, WO 95/3063.
56. Haig Diary 11/9/17.
57. Ibid.

11 Menin Road

1. Plumer to GHQ 29/7/17, Operational Records, Australian War Memorial (AWM), Canberra, AWM 45/33/1.
2. Haig Diary, National Library of Scotland, Edinburgh, 30/7/17.
3. The number of German divisions facing the British and the number of counter-attack formations supporting them had been accurately estimated by Second Army intelligence. See the German order of battle maps in War Office Papers (WO) Public Record Office, Kew, WO 153/506.
4. Translation of German Official Account of the Third Ypres Campaign held in the library of the Royal Artillery Institution, Woolwich, p. 46.
5. Estimates derived from Second and Fifth Army intelligence maps in WO 153/1118 and WO 153/1128 respectively.
6. See Plumer to GHQ 26/8/17, AWM 45/33/1 and Second Army Corps Commanders Conference 27/8/17, AWM 45/39/4.
7. Estimate derived from the number of batteries in V Corps given in Sir James E. Edmonds, *Military Operations: France and Belgium 1917*, vol. 2 (London: HMSO, 1948), p. 264, n. 3.
8. Ibid., p. 238 and p. 292, n. 1.
9. Ibid.
10. In previous battles cutting belts of wire in front of trenches and strongpoints would have been an added task. By September no such continuous belts of wire existed in the salient. From this point on the British artillerymen discounted barbed wire as an obstacle to be dealt with. It will be seen that this over-optimism led to difficulties in later battles.
11. Ibid.
12. See, for example, X Corps Artillery Instructions No. 39, 2/9/17, X Corps Artillery War Diary WO 95/865.
13. X Corps: 'Brief Plan of Operations', n.d., X Corps War Diary Jul.–Dec. 1917, WO 95/853.
14. Corps Artillery Instructions No. 48, 11/9/17, X Corps Artillery War Diary.
15. X Corps, Brief Plan of Operations.
16. See Lt-Col. H. R. Sandilands, *The 23rd Division 1914–1919* (Edinburgh: Blackwood, 1925), p. 171; 2nd Australian Division, 'Operation of 20th September, 1917', AWM 26/7/242/6.
17. First World War Diaries of Captain A. M. McGrigor, entry for 14/9/17, Imperial War Museum (IWM), London, IWM 73.
18. J. Macartney-Filgate, *History of the 33rd Division Artillery in the War 1914–18* (London: Vacher, 1921), p. 116.
19. Diary of Captain H. W. Yoxall 18/9/17, IWM 68.
20. J. Ewing, *History of the 9th (Scottish) Division 1914–1919* (London: John Murray, 1921), p. 230.
21. Diary of Captain W. B. Mackie 17/9/17, Royal Artillery Institution, Woolwich, MD 233.
22. See Second Army Daily Intelligence Reports 13–20 Sept. 1917, AWM 26/7/209/4 and Fifth Army

Intelligence Reports 13–20 Sept. 1917, AWM 26/7/274/13 and 33.

23. Ibid.
24. For these artillery deficiencies see Brig. E. C. Anstey, 'History of the Royal Artillery 1914–1918', Anstey Papers, Royal Artillery Institution, Woolwich, p. 184; Haig Diary 18/9/17; V Corps Artillery Instructions No. 72, 16/9/17, AWM 26/7/212/9.
25. These German tactics can be noted on the maps of hostile battery positions kept by Second and Fifth Army intelligence. The positions marked on these maps as 'battery active' are twice as numerous as the actual number of German guns gathered around the salient. We must thank Elizabeth Greenhalgh for her painstaking efforts to identify the active battery positions on these maps. The maps themselves can be found in WO 153/934.
26. Edmonds, *Military Operations*, vol. 2, pp. 250–51.
27. Ibid., p. 251.
28. 1 Australian Division, 'Report on Operations near Polygon Wood 20/21 September 1917', AWM 26/7/239/2.
29. For these operations see Captain V.E. Inglefield, *History of the Twentieth (Light) Division* (London: Nisbet, 1921), p. 169 and 'Summary of Operations carried out by the 20th (Light) Division between 11th and 29th September, 1917', 20 Division War Diary Aug. 1917–Jan. 1919, WO 95/2097.
30. For these operations see 39 Division, 'Report on Operations of 20th September 1917', X Corps War Diary July–Dec. 1917, WO 95/853; 'Supplementary Narrative on Operations (2nd Stage) by the IX Corps on 20th–23rd Sept. 1917', IX Corps War Diary Jun. 1916–Nov. 1917, WO 95/835; Edmonds, *Military Operations*, vol. 2, p. 279.

31. C. E. W. Bean, *Australian Imperial Force in France: 1917* (Sydney: Angus & Robertson, 1938), p. 756.
32. For statements of this kind see XVIII Corps, 'Third Battle of Ypres: Second Phase', Maxse Papers 69/53/8, IWM; Ewing, *History of the 9th (Scottish) Division*, p. 232; 'Report on Operations by 2nd Aust. Inf. Brigade Sept. 20th–21st', AWM 26/7/237/2; 'Second Army Offensive: 20th September, 1917', 23 Division War Diary Jul.–Oct. 1917, WO 95/2169.
33. Edmonds, *Military Operations*, vol. 2, p. 279; Bean, *Australian Imperial Force*, p. 789, n. 169.
34. Information compiled from reports by 1 Anzac Corps, 1 Australian Division, 2 Australian Division, and brigade and battalion reports in AWM 26/7/220/13, 232/1, 237/2, 239/2, 242/6 and 245/6.
35. Compiled from XVIII Corps and 51 Division Reports in Maxse Papers 69/53/8, IWM and 58 Division Report in WO 95/2987.
36. 55th (West Lancashire) Division, 'Report on Operations East of Ypres Sept. 19th–Sept. 24th 1917', 55 Division War Diary WO 95/2903.
37. Ewing, *History of the 9th (Scottish) Division*, p. 230.
38. V Corps, 'Operations of 20th & 21st September 1917', V Corps War Diary WO 95/748.
39. Captain H. W. Yoxall, Diary, IWM, 24/9/17.
40. Ibid.
41. Ibid.; Edmonds, *Military Operations*, vol. 2, pp. 261, 279.
42. See Second and Fifth Army Enemy Order of Battle Maps WO 153/506 and WO 153/601 respectively. Also Edmonds, *Military Operations*, vol. 2, p. 273, n. 3.
43. Information on German counterattacks has been taken from a document, 'Report on the Enemy's

Counter-attacks against the Fifth and Second Armies on the 20th September 1917' compiled by GHQ and in Maxse Papers 68/53/8, IWM.

44. 20th Battalion AIF, 'Second Phase of the Battle of Flanders', 25/9/17, AWM 26/7/245/6.

12   Polygon Wood

1. Haig to Plumer and Gough 21/9/17 (OAD 628), Operational Records, Australian War Memorial (AWM), Canberra, AWM 45/39/4.
2. Haig to Plumer and Gough 22/9/17 (OAD 629), AWM 45/39/4.
3. Haig Diary, National Library of Scotland, Edinburgh, 23/9/17.
4. Ibid.
5. Rainfall figures taken from charts in GHQ War Diary Sept. and Oct. 1917, War Office (WO) Papers, Public Record Office, Kew, WO 95/15.
6. Brig. E. C. Anstey, 'History of the Royal Artillery 1914–1918', Anstey Papers, Royal Artillery Institution, Woolwich, p. 186.
7. Ibid.
8. See Second Army Intelligence Reports for 21–25 Sep. in AWM 26/7/209/5–6.
9. J. McCartney-Filgate, *History of the 33rd Division Artillery in the War, 1914–1918* (London: Vacher, 1921), pp. 120–1.
10. Ibid., p. 121. Emphasis added.
11. See Fifth Army Intelligence Reports for 21–25 Sept. in AWM 26/7/275/14.
12. Anstey, 'History of the Royal Artillery 1914–18', p. 187.
13. 50th (German) Reserve Division orders 23/9/17 translated in 100 Brigade War Diary July 1917–Sept. 1919, WO 95/2429. See also Edmonds, *Military Operations* Sir James E.: *France and Belgium*

1917, vol. 2 (London: HMSO, 1948), p. 283, no. 1.

14. 98 Brigade, 'Narrative of Operations of 25th–27th September 1917', 98 Brigade War Diary WO 95/2427.
15. Extracts from 33 Division War Diary 25/9/17 in AWM 26/7/218/3.
16. See 50th (German) Reserve Division orders 23/9/17.
17. Anstey, 'History of the Royal Artillery 1914–18', p. 186.
18. 100 Brigade, 'Report on Operations, September 25th, 26th, 27th, 1917', 100 Brigade War Diary July 1917–Sept. 1919, WO 95/2429.
19. See C. E. W. Bean, *Australian Imperial Force in France 1917* (Sydney: Angus & Robertson, 1938), pp. 798–813 for a highly detailed account of this operation. For a more jaundiced view of 33 Division's response to the German attack see the accounts compiled by 15 Australian Brigade in the Elliot Papers AWM, 1DRL/264. Elliot and most of the Australians wrote in ignorance of the terrible artillery storm which had descended on 33 Division.
20. 98 Brigade Report.
21. Edmonds, *Military Operations*, vol. 2, p. 292 and sketches 23 and 24.
22. Ibid., p. 292, n. 2.
23. Ibid., pp. 280–81.
24. XVIII Corps, 'Report on Operations of September 26th 1917', Maxse Papers 13, Imperial War Museum (IWM) London.
25. 39 Division 'Report on Operations of Sept. 29th 1917', X Corps War Diary WO 95/853.
26. 33 Division War Diary 26/9/17, AWM 26/7/218/3.
27. 15th Australian Brigade, 'Report on Operations South of Zonnebecke for Period 22nd September to 27th September 1917', AWM 26/7/261/7.

28. 3 Division, 'Report on Operations Carried out by 3rd Division during the Period 19th September to 1st October, 1917', 3 Division War Diary WO 95/1379.

29. Extracts from *59 Division War Diary*, AWM 26/7/218/27.

30. This account is taken from 'Report on the Attack on Polygon Wood by the 14th Aust. Inf. Brigade on the 26th Sept. 1917', AWM 26/7/268/7.

31. T.P. Chataway, *History of the 15th Battalion, Australian Imperial Force: War of 1914–1918* (Brisbane: William Brooks, 1948), pp. 190–1.

32. Information on the German counter-attacks has been taken from a document written by GHQ, 'Report on the Enemy's Counter-Attacks against the Fifth and Second Armies on the 26th September, 1917', Maxse Papers 15.2, IWM.

33. Edmonds, *Military Operations*, vol. 2, p. 293, n. 3.

13 Broodseinde

1. Haig Diary, National Library of Scotland, Edinburgh, 28/9/17.

2. Conference at Second Army HQ 26/9/17, Operational Records, Australian War Memorial (AWM), Canberra, AWM 45/33/1.

3. Ibid.

4. Haig to Jellicoe 29/9/17; Rawlinson to Haig 4/10/17, ibid.

5. Plumer to Haig 30/9/17, ibid.

6. Gough to Haig 1/10/17, ibid.

7. Conference at Second Army HQ 2/10/17, ibid.

8. Plumer to corps commanders 2/10/17, AWM 45/39/4.

9. Translation of the German Official Account of the Third Ypres Campaign held in the library of the Royal Artillery Institution, Woolwich, pp. 50–51; W. Beumelberg, *Flandern 1917* (Oldenburg: Stallung, 1928), pp. 120–21.

10. Conference at Second Army HQ 29/9/17.

11. Sir James E. Edmonds, *Military Operations: France and Belgium 1917*, vol. 2 (London: HMSO, 1948), p. 311.

12. See 'Summary of Operations of 5th Division October 4th–October 11th, 1917', Fifth Division War Diary War Office Papers (WO), Public Record Office, Kew, WO 95/1515; 21 Division, 'Account of Operations September 29th to October 8th, 1917', 21 Division War Diary WO 95/2132.

13. Edmunds, *Military Operations*, vol. 2, p. 304.

14. These reports can be found in AWM 26/7/236/1.

15. 'Report on Operation by 2nd Aust. Inf. Brigade on 4th October 1917', AWM 26/7/237/5.

16. Col. H. Stewart, *The New Zealand Division 1916–1919* (Auckland: Whitcombe & Tombs, 1921), pp. 261–70.

17. P. A. Pedersen, *Monash as Military Commander* (Melbourne: Melbourne University Press, 1985), pp. 192–7.

18. XVIII Corps, 'Third Battle of Ypres – Third Phase', Maxse Papers, Imperial War Museum (IWM), London, IWM 20.

19. Ibid., Appendix III, Tank Operations.

20. C. E. W. Bean, *The Australian Imperial Force in France 1917* (Sydney: Angus & Robertson, 1938), p. 875.

21. Edmonds, *Military Operations*, vol. 2, p. 315.

22. John Terraine, *Douglas Haig: The Educated Soldier* (London: Hutchinson, 1963), p. 366; Geoffrey Powell, *Plumer: The Soldiers' General* (London: Leo Cooper, 1990), p. 220.

23. See 'Report of the Operations carried out by 13th Infantry Brigade on the morning of October 4th 1917', 13 Brigade War Diary Apr.–Nov. 1917, WO 95/1550; 'Narrative of Operations of the 62nd Infantry Brigade from October 2nd to October 7th, 1917', 21 Division War Diary Apr.–Dec. 1917, WO 95/2132; 'Extracts from War Diary of HQ 4th New Zealand Infantry Brigade', AWM 26/7/215/15; 'Account of Operations by the 4th Division N.E. of Ypres between the 4th and 12th October 1917', 4 Division War Diary Aug.–Dec. 1917, WO 95/1477.

24. Rainfall statistics taken from GHQ War Diary Sept. and Oct. 1917, WO 95/15.

14 Deciding and Not Deciding: The War Cabinet and the War Policy Committee, August–November 1917

1. Hankey Diary, 11 Aug. 1917, Churchill College, Cambridge.
2. Unless otherwise indicated, the account in this and subsequent chapters of events in the War Policy Committee and the War Cabinet (including direct quotations) is derived from the minutes of those bodies compiled by Sir Maurice Hankey and the cabinet secretariat.
3. Henry Wilson Diary, Imperial War Museum (IWM), London, 7 Aug. 1917.
4. Hankey Diary, 15 Aug. 1917.
5. For this episode see Hankey Diary, 27 Aug. 1917 ff.; *Lord Riddell's War Diary 1914–1918* (London: Ivor Nicholson & Watson, 1933), pp. 266–70; Lord Hankey, *The Supreme Command 1914–1918*, vol. 2 (London: Allen & Unwin,

1961), pp. 693–5; Stephen Roskill, *Hankey: Man of Secrets*, vol. 1 (London: Collins, 1970), pp. 428–9.

6. It is not clear from Wilson's diary whether the adverse judgement on the proposed coastal operation was his alone or was shared by Rawlinson. But Rawlinson was certainly commenting very gloomily on the campaign as a whole. He doubted if Haig's forces would get to Roulers or even take the Staden Ridge, and he said that Haig was transferring a section of the front from Gough to Plumer 'because even he (Haig) began to see that Goughie was quite unable to do the job' (Wilson Diary, 29 Aug. and 5 Sept. 1917).

7. Lloyd George would not have been mollified by a subsequent message from Cadorna, relayed to the War Cabinet three days later, stressing that the Italian commander alone was in a position to decide upon offensive or defensive operations on his front. This put paid to delusions among Britain's rulers that they had the power to decree the Italian option.

8. It is difficult to identify the German campaigns in winter months to which Lloyd George is alluding: operations against the Russians, Serbians, and Romanians in 1915 and 1916 were not primarily in these months.

9. Lloyd George seemed to be ignoring the fact that the military commanders named were ultimately dependent for their positions on the approval of the War Cabinet, as the dismissal of Murray in mid-1917 might have reminded him.

15 Poelcappelle

1. Haig Diary, National Library of Scotland, Edinburgh, 4/10/17; Sec-

ond Army Intelligence Report 4–5
Oct. 1917, Operational Records,
Australian War Memorial
(AWM), Canberra, AWM 26/7/
209/7.
2. Second Army Order No. 7, 5/10/
17, AWM 45/39/4.
3. Haig Diary 5/10/17.
4. GHQ Rainfall Statistics, GHQ
War Diary Oct. 1917, War Office
Papers (WO) Public Record Office,
Kew, WO 95/15.
5. Lyn Macdonald, *They Called it
Passchendaele* (London: Michael
Joseph, 1978), pp. 195–9.
6. Brig. E. C. Anstey, 'History of
the Royal Artillery 1914–1918',
Anstey Papers, Royal Artillery
Institution, Woolwich, p. 189.
7. Sir James E. Edmonds, *Military
Operations: France and Belgium
1917*, vol. 2 (London: HMSO,
1948), p. 325.
8. Ibid.
9. Records of these conferences can
be found in AWM 45 and AWM
51. Some conference proceedings
are located in the Haig Papers in
Edinburgh and in the Second and
Fifth Army Records in the PRO.
10. General Sir Hubert Gough, *The
Fifth Army* (London: Hodder &
Stoughton, 1931), p. 213.
11. Gough to Gwynne 6/10/17,
Gwynne Papers, HAG24, Imperial
War Museum (IWM) London.
12. Bean Diary, 'Notes on Gen.
Harington's lecture to War Correspondents', AWM 3DRL606, item
89. Bean was mightily unim-
pressed with Harington's reason-
ing.
13. Lt-Col. C. à Court Repington, *The
First World War* (London: Constable, 1920), vol. 2, p. 99.
14. Second Army Order No. 7, 4/10/
17, AWM 45/39/4.
15. For these artillery matters see
Anstey, 'History of the Royal Artillery 1914–18', pp. 188–9.
16. Ibid.

17. Edmonds, *Military Operations*,
vol. 2, p. 253, n. 2.
18. 197 Brigade, 'Report on Operations on 8th October and subsequent days', 66 Division War
Diary Feb.–Dec. 1917, WO 95/
3120.
19. See, for example, 11 Division,
'Narrative of Operations 24 Sept.
to 11th Oct. 1917', Maxse Papers,
12, IWM.
20. 5 Australian Brigade, 'Report on
Operations from 8th/9th October
to 9th/10th October', AWM 26/7/
245/7; 'Report on Operations of
the 15th Infantry Brigade North of
Ypres–Menin Road, 9th/10th
October, 1917', 15th Brigade War
Diary Jan.–Nov. 1917, WO 95/
1568.
21. German Official Account of the
Third Ypres Campaign held in the
library of the Royal Artillery
Institution, Woolwich, p. 54.
22. Second Australian Division Intelligence Summary 8/10/17, AWM
26/7/239/2.
23. Second Army Order No. 7, 4/10/
17.
24. Edmonds, *Military Operations*,
vol. 2, p. 332.
25. German Official Account, p. 52.
26. See 5 Australian Brigade, 'Report
on Operations' and 197 Brigade
'Report on Operations'.
27. 6 Australian Brigade, 'Report on
Operations 6th to 10th Oct. 1917',
AWM 26/7/245/7.
28. 49 Division, 'General Narrative',
49 Division War Diary Oct. 1917–
Feb. 1919, WO 95/2768.
29. Edmonds, *Military Operations*,
vol. 2, pp. 334–7.
30. Australian Brigade, 'Report on
Operations'.

16   *Neverending Story*

1. Plumer to Haig 9/10/17, Operational Records, Australian War

Memorial (AWM), Canberra, AWM 45/33/1.
2. Haig to Rawlinson 9/10/17, ibid.
3. Ibid.
4. Haig Diary, National Library of Scotland, Edinburgh, 10/10/17.
5. Second Army Intelligence Report 10/10/17, AWM 26/7/209/7.
6. Fifth Army Conference 9/10/17, Fifth Army War Diary Jun.–Aug. 1917, War Office Papers, Public Record Office, Kew, WO 95/520.
7. P. A. Pedersen, *Monash as Military Commander* (Melbourne: Melbourne University Press, 1985), p. 200.
8. Ibid.
9. Haig Diary 10 and 11/10/17.
10. Ibid. 15/10/17. Some historians have sought to portray Haig's diary as a sanitized version of events largely compiled after the war. The passage quoted above is strong evidence that this is not remotely the case.
11. Brig. E. C. Anstey 'History of the Royal Artillery, 1914–18', Anstey Papers, Royal Artillery Institution, Woolwich, p. 189.
12. 'Extracts from War Diary of XVIII Corps 12/10/17', AWM 26/7/214/15.
13. Gunner B. O. Stokes, quoted in Lyn Macdonald, *They Called it Passchendaele* (London: Michael Joseph, 1978), p. 206.
14. Anstey, 'History of the Royal Artillery 1914–18', p. 189.
15. Ibid.
16. C. E. W. Bean, *The Australian Imperial Force in France 1917* (Sydney: Angus & Robertson, 1938), p. 911.
17. Ibid., p. 912.
18. Diary of the War 1914–1918 by Major-General Sir Hugh Tudor, Royal Artillery Institution, Woolwich, MD 1167.
19. 'Report on Operations of 27th Infantry Brigade on 12th Oct.

1917', 9 Division War Diary Jun.–Dec. 1917, WO 95/1740.
20. XVIII Corps, 'Report on Operations of 12th October 1917', Maxse Papers, Imperial War Museum (IWM), London, IWM 24.
21. Col. H. Stewart, *The New Zealand Division 1916–19* (Auckland: Whitcombe & Tombs, 1921), p. 282.
22. Ibid.
23. 2 NZ Infantry Brigade, 'Report on Operations on 12th October, 1917', AWM 26/7/251/16; 3 Australian Division Narrative 12/10/17, AWM 26/7/251/3.
24. 9 Scottish Division, 'Comments', 9 Division War Diary Jun.–Dec. 1917, WO 95/1740.
25. Captain G. H. F. Nichols, *The 18th Division in the Great War* (Edinburgh: Black, 1922), p. 237.
26. Sir James E. Edmonds, *Military Operations: France and Belgium 1917*, vol. 2 (London: HMSO, 1948), p. 324.
27. A wound that did not kill its recipient but was sufficiently serious to qualify him for a journey back to Britain (nicknamed 'Blighty' as in the popular song, 'Take me back to dear old Blighty').
28. 7 Seaforth Highlanders, 'Narrative: 10 to 14th October 1917', AWM 26/7/16/8.

17 Final Folly

1. Haig Diary, National Library of Scotland, Edinburgh, 13/10/17.
2. Second Army Note 16/10/17, Operational Records, Australian War Memorial (AWM), Canberra, AWM 51.
3. Second Army Conference held at Canadian Corps HQ 16/10/17, AWM 49/39/4.
4. 'Artillery Appreciation of the Situation on Assumption of Command

by Canadian Corps', Canadian Corps CRA War Diary Apr. 1919, War Office Papers (WO), Public Record Office, Kew, WO 95/1059.

5. Ibid.

6. GHQ Rainfall Statistics, GHQ War Diary Oct. 1917, WO 95/15.

7. Canadian Corps Intelligence Summary 24/10/17, Canadian Corps War Diary Sept.–Dec. 1917, WO 95/1051.

8. Canadian Artillery Appreciation.

9. Ibid.

10. Extracts from XVIII Corps War Diary, AWM 26/7/214/5.

11. XVIII Corps, 'Report on Operations of 22nd October', Maxse Papers 25, Imperial War Museum (IWM), London.

12. Papers of Thomas Macmillan 189 Brigade RND, 70, IWM.

13. Extracts from XVIII Corps War Diary.

14. Testimony of Private Willans, 5 Canadian Division, quoted in Lyn Macdonald, *They Called It Passchendaele* (London: Michael Joseph, 1978), p. 223.

15. S. G. Bennett, *The 4th Canadian Mounted Rifles 1914–1919* (Toronto: Murray Printing, 1926), p. 80.

16. Sergeant McLellan, 5th Canadian Mounted Rifles, quoted in Macdonald, *Passchendaele*, p. 220.

17. Sir Janes E. Edmonds, *Military Operations: France and Belgium 1917*, vol. 2 (London: HMSO, 1948), p. 351.

18. Extracts from XVIII Corps War Diary.

19. Haig Diary 26/10/17.

20. 5th Canadian Mounted Rifles, 'Summary of Operations Oct. 30th–31st 1917', 8th Canadian Brigade War Diary Jan.–Dec. 1917, WO 95/3868.

21. Private J. Pickard, 7th Winnipeg Grenadiers, quoted in Macdonald, *Passchendaele*, p. 224.

22. 5th Canadian Mounted Rifles, 'Summary of Operations'.

23. 4th Canadian Division, 'Passchendaele Attack – Phase 2', Canadian Division War Diary July 1917–Mar. 1918, WO 95/3881.

24. Edmonds, *Military Operations*, vol. 2, p. 355. Casualties are not listed separately for this battle, but as one brigade of 63 Division suffered 900 the total cannot have been much less than 2,000.

25. 58 (London) Division, 'Report on Operations 26th & 30th October 1917', Maxse Papers 27, IWM.

26. 174 Brigade (58 Division), 'Preliminary Report on Operations of 30th October 1917', 58 Division War Diary Aug.–Dec. 1917, WO 95/2987.

27. Papers of Lt-Col. C. E. L. Lyne, entry for 4 Nov. 1917, 78, IWM.

28. 6 Canadian Brigade, 'Narrative Report of Operations for Capture of Passchendaele', 6 Canadian Brigade War Diary July–Dec. 1917, WO 95/3828.

29. Canadian Corps, 'Summary of Operations Nov 2nd to Nov 9th, 1917', Canadian Corps War Diary Sept.–Dec. 1917, WO 95/1051.

30. W. W. Murray, *The History of the 2nd Canadian Battalion (East Ontario Regiment) Canadian Expeditionary Force in the Great War, 1914–1919* (Ottawa: Mortimer/Historical Committee, 2nd Battalion, CEF, 1947), p. 219.

31. Corporal H. C. Baker, 28th North-West Battalion, quoted in Macdonald, *Passchendaele*, p. 226.

32. Canadian Corps, 'Summary of Operations Nov. 2nd–Nov 9th'.

33. Edmonds, *Military Operations*, vol. 2, p. 358.

34. See Haig Diary entries for 6 to 10 Nov. 1917.
35. Letters of Lt-Col. C. E. L. Lyne, IWM 78.
36. For Rawlinson's opinions on Passchendaele see Robin Prior and Trevor Wilson, *Command on the Western Front; the Military Career of Sir Henry Rawlinson, 1914–18* (Oxford/Cambridge, Mass.: Blackwell, 1992), pp. 273–4.

18   The Last Inaction: The War Cabinet, October–November 1917

1. The matter may have come up six days earlier, at a stormy meeting of the War Policy Committee where Lloyd George and Robertson fell out over the transfer of two divisions to Egypt (and thence to Palestine). Hankey was ill on that day and so no minutes were kept, but Sir John French picked up a story that the casualty issue had also been raised (Henry Wilson Diary, Imperial War Museum [IWM], London, 6 Oct. 1917).
2. It might be concluded from Lloyd George's eagerness to transfer a measure of influence over strategy from Robertson to Henry Wilson that the latter had proved steadily opposed to the Flanders offensive. This was not the case. In so far as Wilson revealed any consistent position, it was a querulous but recurring endorsement of Haig's operations. So, at the outset, he backed the Flanders campaign as a means of reinforcing France's commitment to the war. Haig expressed warm gratitude. When early in July Bonar Law raised the spectre of large British casualties as grounds for resisting a Flanders campaign, Wilson replied that this was a good reason for staying out of a war, but a bad reason for not fighting when in it. Thereafter he supported the devotion of men and weapons to Haig's campaign, as late as 5 October telling Lloyd George that only with the onset of the mud months (from mid-November) should resources be directed to the Middle East, with the Flanders operation being resumed in the spring.

   None of this prevented Wilson from delivering most adverse judgements on the progress of the Flanders operations. So on 4 September he deplored Haig's resistance to sending guns to the Italians, 'especially as Haig is not going to do anything really serious at Ypres this year'. Perhaps it was his willingness to disparage Haig, but not actually to want to halt his operations, that made Wilson agreeable to Lloyd George.

Conclusion

1. Haig Diary, National Library of Scotland, Edinburgh, 10/11/17.
2. Quoted in Trevor Wilson, *The Myriad Faces of War* (Cambridge: Polity, 1986), p. 547.
3. David R. Woodward, *Lloyd George and the Generals* (East Brunswick, NJ: Associated University Presses, 1983), p. 230.
4. Aubrey Wade, *The War of the Guns* (London: Batsford, 1936), pp. 57–8.

Note on Sources

This book is largely based on documentary collections in the Public Record Office (Kew) and the Australian War Memorial (Canberra).

As far as military operations are concerned, the single most important collection consists of the Unit War Diaries in PRO Series WO 95 and AWM Series 26. 'War Diaries' were compiled by each unit involved in the conflict, from GHQ down through Army and Corps to Division, Brigade, and Battalion. It is not the diaries themselves that are of great use. Most provide the barest summary of the daily action undertaken by a unit ('attacked', 'quiet day', etc.). What are of value are the appendices attached to the war diaries, and in particular the operations orders and battle narratives.

The operations orders set out what it was expected would be accomplished in an action and the methods and resources deemed necessary to accomplish it. They thus provide, on the very eve of battle, an insight into the strategic and tactical thinking (or the lack of it) of the various levels of command. They are thus to be preferred to the often post-facto expositions put forward by commanders in diaries, letters, and similar sources.

The battle narratives are the most immediate accounts of military operations available. They still require careful use, in that they were often written with a view to impress the next highest level of command. Nevertheless their authors (especially at the lower levels) had powerful imperatives to place before their seniors a responsible account of events – if only in order to influence subsequent actions by identifying causes of failure and spelling out reasons for success. Comparison and analysis of battle narratives in relation to those of neighbouring units, and of higher and lower formations in the same unit, facilitate reconstruction of the course of a battle in an all but complete form. Certainly, allowance must be made for diaries that are missing and narratives that reveal little. Yet it is unlikely that more complete documentation would, in the light of what is already available, substantially change the broad outline of any of the actions related in this volume.

The military chapters have been supported by other primary series. The most important are WO 158 (files removed from WO 95 by the War Office for instructional purposes); WO 157 (intelligence files which indicate what the British knew of enemy intentions and dispositions); and AWM 45 and 51 (correspondence and orders from the higher levels of command). Concerning the last of these, it may be noted that many documents preserved in the AWM do not seem to have survived in any form in the PRO.

To incorporate the personal element into the battle scenes, and to illustrate the response of individuals to military actions, the participant collections of the Imperial War Museum have been culled under the expert guidance of the staff of that body.

Secondary sources include the various official histories (notwithstanding the reservations concerning the British volume expressed in the Introduction), unit histories (an often neglected but generally useful source), published accounts of the campaign – in which Lyn Macdonald's *They Called it Passchendaele* stands out –, and articles in professional military journals.

The political chapters are based largely on the records of the War Cabinet (CAB 23) and of the War Policy Committee (CAB 27) – sources which have been employed in other works but not often analysed in conjunction with the actual course of the military events. These series have been supplemented by private diaries, correspondence, memoirs, and an array of secondary literature.

If the sources available to reconstruct the British side of the campaign are indeed copious, the same cannot be said for the German side. Most German war diaries were destroyed during the Second World War. As for the German official history, *Der Weltkrieg*, it was written entirely during the Nazi period, and is the work of groups of ex-soldiers who were trying to explain away their own responsibility for Germany's eventual defeat. Hence it is of little value on matters of high policy, but is more reliable on tactical matters. The works of G. C. Wynne, as a member of the British official history team who was an expert on German defensive tactics, provide a useful supplement. A German monograph, *Ypres 1917*, written soon after the event, reveals something of the feelings of the participants but contains little specific military detail. Individual German documents are often to be found in translation in the British war diaries and these can be revealing of German responses to British actions. Much about German tactics is also found in British battle narratives.

There is no doubt, nevertheless, that the German sources are thin compared to the British. But it is our conviction that this has not proved a bar to a comprehensive account of the Third Ypres campaign.

Bibliography

1. Official Manuscript Collections

Cabinet Papers, Public Record Office, Kew

CAB 23	War Cabinet Minutes
CAB 27	War Policy Committee Minutes
CAB 45	Postwar Official History Correspondence
CAB 103	Postwar Official History Correspondence – Passchendaele

War Office Papers, Public Record Office, Kew

WO 95	Operational War Diaries
WO 106	Directorate of Military Operations Files
WO 153	Operational Artillery Maps
WO 157	Directorate of Military Intelligence Files
WO 158	Miscellaneous Operations Files

Operational Records, Australian War Memorial, Canberra

AWM 26	Operations Files, 1914–18 War
AWM 45	Copies of British war diaries and other records
AWM 51	AWM security classified records (a series of operational documents and high-level correspondence between GHQ and army commanders)

2. Private Papers

Australian War Memorial, Canberra

C. E. W. Bean
Brigadier-General H. E. Elliot
Private W. D. Gallwey
General Sir John Monash

Imperial War Museum, London

Colonel J. H. Boraston
H. A. Gwynne

Lieutenant-Colonel C. E. L. Lyne
Captain A. M. McGrigor
Sergeant R. McKay
Colonel R. Macleod
Brigadier-General G. Macleod Ross
Leading Seaman Thomas Macmillan (Royal Naval Division)
General Sir Ivor Maxse
Major-General Lothian Nicholson
Captain H. B. Owens
General Sir R. Stephens
Lieutenant W. B. St Leger
Colonel W. A. C. Wilkinson
Field Marshal Sir Henry Wilson
Colonel H. E. Yeo
Captain H. W. Yoxall

Liddell Hart Centre for Military Archives, King's College, London

Reverend John Bloxam
Lieutenant-General Sir Sidney Clive
Brigadier-General Sir James E. Edmonds
Lieutenant-General Sir L. Kiggell
Field Marshal Sir A. A. Montgomery-Massingberd
Field Marshal Sir William Robertson

Royal Artillery Institution, Woolwich

Colonel E. G. Angus
Brigadier E. C. Anstey
Captain A. F. Becke
Lieutenant-Colonel A. H. Burne
Major T. H. Davidson
Lieutenant J. Hussey
Captain W. B. Mackie
Brigadier E. E. Mockler-Ferryman
Major S. W. H. Rawlins
Major-General Sir H. H. Tudor

Others

Field Marshal Earl Cavan, Public Record Office, Kew
Field Marshal Sir Douglas Haig, National Library of Scotland, Edinburgh
Lord Hankey, Churchill College, Cambridge
General Sir Henry Rawlinson, Churchill College, Cambridge; National Army
  Museum, London
Major Clive Wigram, Royal Archives, Windsor

3. British Army Official Publications

Great Britain: B. E. F. General Staff, *Co-operation of Aircraft with Artillery* (various
  editions 1916–18)

——*Notes on the Interpretation of Aeroplane Photographs* (various editions 1916–18)
——*Notes on the Use of Smoke* (SS175) [1917]
——*Range Table for 60 Pounder Gun* [1916]
——*Range Table for 4.5″ Howitzer* [1916]
Great Britain: War Office: General Staff, *Instructions for the Training of the British Armies in France* (SS152) (January 1918)
——*Notes on Recent Operations on the Front of First, Third, Fourth and Fifth Armies* (SS158) (London: War Office, May 1917)
——Geographical Section, *Report on Survey on the Western Front 1914–18* (London: War Office, 1920)

4. Books and Articles

Les Armées françaises dans la grande guerre, 103 vols (Paris: Imprimerie Nationale 1922–38), Tome V, vol. 2
C. T. Atkinson, *The History of the South Wales Borderers, 1914–18* (London: Medici Society, 1931)
——*The Queen's Own Royal West Kent Regiment, 1914–1919* (London: Simpkin Marshall, 1924)
——*The Seventh Division, 1914–1918* (London: John Murray, 1927)
A. H. Atteridge, *History of the 17th Northern Division* (Glasgow: Maclehose, 1929)
Lt-Col. W. S. Austin, *The Official History of the New Zealand Rifle Brigade* (Wellington: Watkins, 1924)
T. M. Banks and R. A. Chell, *With the 10th Essex in France* (London: Gay & Hancock, 1924)
C. E. W. Bean, *Official History of Australia in the War of 1914–18*, vol. 4: *The Australian Imperial Force in France: 1917* (Sydney: Angus & Robertson, 1938)
Major A. F. Becke, 'The Coming of the Creeping Barrage', *Journal of the Royal Artillery*, vol. 58, 1931–2, pp. 19–42
W. C. Belford, *Legs-Eleven: Being the Story of the 11th Battalion AIF in the Great War of 1914–1918* (Perth: Imperial Printing Co., 1940)
S. G. Bennett, *The 4th Canadian Mounted Rifles 1914–1919* (Toronto: Murray Printing, 1926)
R. Berkeley, *The History of the Rifle Brigade in the War of 1914–1918* (London: Rifle Brigade Club, 1927)
Brevet-Col. B. A. Bethell, *Modern Guns and Gunnery* (Woolwich: Cattermole, 1910)
W. Beumelberg, *Flandern 1917* (Oldenburg: Stallung, 1928)
F. W. Bewsher, *History of the 51st (Highland) Division, 1914–1918* (Edinburgh: Blackwood, 1921)
Shelford Bidwell, 'An Approach to Military History', *Army Quarterly*, Jan. 1949, pp. 243–6
——*Gunners at War* (London: Arrow Books, 1972)
——and Dominick Graham, *Coalitions, Politicians & Generals: Some Aspects of Command in Two World Wars* (London/New York: Brassey's, 1993)
——and Dominick Graham, *Fire-Power: British Army Weapons and Theories of War, 1904–45* (London: Allen & Unwin, 1982)
Lt-Gen. Sir Noel Birch, 'Artillery Development in the Great War', *Army Quarterly*, vol. 1, 1920–21, pp. 79–89

Robert Blake (ed.), *The Private Papers of Douglas Haig, 1914–1919* (London: Eyre & Spottiswoode, 1952)

Capt. O. G. Body, 'Lessons of the Great War: The Barrage versus Concentration on Selected Targets', *Journal of the Royal Artillery*, vol. 53, 1926, pp. 59–67

Lt-Col. J. H. Boraston, *Sir Douglas Haig's Despatches* (London: Dent, 1919)

Lt-Col. S. H. Boraston, and Cptn Cyril E. O. Bax, *The Eighth Division in War, 1914–1918* (London: Medici Society, 1926)

Lawrence Bragg and Others, *Artillery Survey in the First World War* (London: Field Survey Association, 1971)

V. Brahms, *The Spirit of the 42nd: Narrative of the 42nd Battalion, 11th Infantry Brigade, 3rd Division, Australian Imperial Forces, during the Great War* (Brisbane: 42nd Battalion AIF Association, 1938)

Lt-Col. C. N. F. Broad, 'Army Intelligence and Counter-battery Work', *Journal of the Royal Artillery*, vol. 49, 1922–3, pp. 187–98, 221–42

——'The Development of Artillery Tactics 1914–1918', *Journal of the Royal Artillery*, vol. 49, 1922–3, pp. 62–81, 127–48

Lt-Col. A. F. Brooke, 'The Evolution of Artillery in the Great War', *Journal of the Royal Artillery*, vol. 51, 1924–5, pp. 359–72; vol. 52, 1925–6, pp. 37–51, 369–87; vol. 53, pp. 233–49

John Buchan, *The History of the South African Forces in France* (London: Nelson, 1920)

Bryant, Sir Arthur, *English Saga (1840–1940)* (London: Reprint Society, 1942).

Lt J. R. Byrne, *New Zealand Artillery in the Field 1914–1918* (Auckland: Whitcombe & Tombs, 1922)

W. A. Carne, *In Good Company – An Account of the 5th Machine Gun Company AIF in Search of Peace 1915–19* (Melbourne: 5th Machine Gun Company, 1937)

Brigadier-General John Charteris, *At G.H.Q.* (London: Cassell, 1931)

——*Field Marshal Earl Haig* (London: Cassell, 1929)

T. P. Chataway, *History of the 15th Battalion, Australian Imperial Force: War of 1914–1918* (Brisbane: William Brooks, 1948)

Captain E. J. Colliver and Lieutenant B. H. Richardson, *The Forty-Third: The Story and Official History of the 43rd Battalion, A.I.F.* (Adelaide: Rigby, 1920)

J. O. Coop, *The Story of the 55th Division* (Liverpool: Daily Post, 1919)

Duff Cooper, *Haig* (2 vols) (London: Faber & Faber 1935)

D. J. Corrigall, *The History of the Twentieth Canadian Battalion (Central Ontario Regiment) Canadian Expeditionary Force in the Great War* (Toronto: Stony & Cox, 1935)

Lt-Col. W. D. Croft, 'The Influence of Tanks upon Tactics', *Journal of the Royal United Services Institute*, Feb. 1922, pp. 39–53

——*Three Years with the 9th (Scottish) Division* (London: Murray, 1919)

A. Crookenden, *The History of the Cheshire Regiment in the Great War* (Chester: Crookenden, 1939)

Major-General Sir John Davidson, *Haig: Master of the Field* (London: Peter Nevill, 1953)

A. Dean and E. W. Gutteridge, *The Seventh Battalion AIF: A Résumé of the Activities of the Seventh Battalion in the Great War, 1914–1918* (Melbourne: Dean & Gutteridge, 1933)

George A. B. Dewar and Lt-Col. J. H. Boraston, *Sir Douglas Haig's Command: December 19, 1915 to November 11, 1918* (2 vols) (London: Constable, 1922)

Col. W. G. S. Dobbie, 'The Operations of the 1st Division on the Belgian Coast in 1917', *Royal Engineers Journal*, June 1924, pp. 185–204

Sir James E. Edmonds, *Military Operations: France and Belgium 1917*, vol. 2 (London: HMSO, 1948)

Captain A. D. Ellis, *The Story of the Fifth Australian Division* (London: Hodder & Stoughton, n. d.)

J. Ewing, *History of the 9th (Scottish) Division, 1914–1919* (London: John Murray, 1921)

—— *The Royal Scots 1914–1919* (Edinburgh: Oliver & Boyd, 1925)

E. Fairey, *The 38th Battalion A.I.F.* (Bendigo: Bendigo Advertiser, 1920)

Cyril Falls, *History of the Thirty-Sixth (Ulster) Division* (London: McCaw Stevenson & Orr, 1922)

—— *Life of a Regiment*, vol. 4: *The Gordon Highlanders in the First World War, 1914–1919* (Aberdeen: Aberdeen University Press, 1958)

—— *Military Operations: France and Belgium 1917*, vol. 1 (London: Macmillan, 1940)

General Sir Martin Farndale, *History of the Royal Regiment of Artillery: Western Front 1914–18* (Woolwich: Royal Artillery Institution, 1986)

A. H. Farrar-Hockley, *Goughie: The Life of General Sir Hubert Gough* (London: Hart-Davis/MacGibbon, 1975)

R. R. Freeman, *Hurcombe's Hungry Half Hundred: A Memorial History of the 50th Battalion A.I.F., 1916–1919* (Adelaide: Peacock Publications, 1991)

J. F. C. Fuller, *Tanks in the Great War* (London: John Murray, 1920)

John Giles, *Flanders Then and Now: The Ypres Salient and Passchendaele* (London: Leo Cooper, 1970)

S. Gillon, *Story of the 29th Division* (London: Nelson, 1925)

E. G. Godfrey, *The Cast-Iron Sixth: A History of the Sixth Battalion London Regiment* (London: Old Comrades Association, 1938)

Huntley Gordon, *The Unreturning Army: A Field-Gunner in Flanders 1917–18* (London: Dent, 1967)

E. Gorman, *'With the Twenty-Second': A History of the Twenty-Second Battalion, A.I.F. 1914–1919* (Melbourne: H. H. Champion, 1919)

Lieut.-Colonel A. A. Goschen, 'Artillery Tactics', *Journal of the Royal Artillery*, vol. 52, 1924, pp. 254–60

General Sir Hubert Gough, *The Fifth Army* (London: Hodder & Stoughton, 1931)

W. E. Grey, *The 2nd City of London Regiment (Royal Fusiliers) in the Great War* (London: Regimental HQ, 1922)

Paddy Griffith, *Battle Tactics of the Western Front: The British Army's Art of Attack 1916–18* (New Haven/London: Yale University Press, 1994)

—— *Forward into Battle: Infantry Tactics from Waterloo to Vietnam* (London: Antony Bird, 1982)

F. C. Grimwade, *The War History of the 4th Battalion, the London Regiment (Royal Fusiliers), 1914–1919* (London: Regimental HQ, 1922)

Lt.-Col. R. G. A. Hamilton (Master of Belhaven), *The War Diary of the Master of Belhaven 1914–1918* (London: John Murray, 1924)

Lord Hankey, *The Supreme Command, 1914–1918*, 2 vols (London: Allen & Unwin, 1961)

S. Hare, *The Annals of the King's Royal Rifle Corps* (London: John Murray, 1932)

Major H. C. Harrison, 'Calibration and Ranging', *Journal of the Royal Artillery*, vol. 47, 1920, pp. 265–8

B. H. Liddell Hart, 'The Basic Truths of Passchendaele', *Journal of the Royal United Service Institution*, vol. 104, 1959, pp. 433–9

—— 'How Myths Grow – Passchendaele', *Military Affairs*, vol. 28, no. 4., 1961, pp. 184–6

——*The Tanks*, vol. 1: *1914–1939* (London: Cassell, 1959)

J. Hayes, *The Eighty Fifth in France and Flanders* (Halifax: Royal Print, 1920)

C. Headlam, *History of the Guards Division in the Great War* (London: John Murray, 1924)

J. Q. Henriques, *War History of the 1st Battalion, Queen's Westminster Rifles, 1914–1918* (London: Medici Society, 1923)

Historical Records of the Queen's Own Cameron Highlanders (London: Blackwood, 1909–31)

Ian V. Hogg, *The Guns 1914–18* (London: Pan, 1973)

——and L. F. Thurston, *British Artillery Weapons and Ammunition 1914–1918* (London: Ian Allen, 1973)

Major N. Hudson, 'Trench-Mortars in the Great War', *Journal of the Royal Artillery*, vol. 42, 1920, pp. 17–31

Jackson Hughes, 'The Monstrous Anger of the Guns: British Artillery Tactics on the Western Front in the First World War' (Ph.D. thesis, University of Adelaide, 1994).

A. H. Hussey and D. S. Inman, *The Fifth Division in the Great War* (London: Nisbet, 1921)

G. S. Hutchison, *The Thirty-Third Division in France and Flanders, 1915–1919* (London: Waterloo, 1921)

Capt. V. E. Inglefield, *History of the Twentieth (Light) Division* (London: Nisbet, 1921)

John A. Innes, *Flash Spotters and Sound Rangers: How they Lived, Worked and Fought in the Great War* (London: Allen & Unwin, 1935)

H. S. Jervis, *The 2nd Munsters in France* (Aldershot: Gale & Polden, 1922)

H. A. Jones, *The War in the Air*, vol. 2 (London: Hamish Hamilton, 1969) (reprint of 1928 edn)

——*The War in the Air*, vol. 6 and one vol. of appendices (Oxford: Clarendon Press, 1937)

H. K. Kahan, *The 28th Battalion, Australian Imperial Force: A Record of War Service* (n.p., H. K. Kahan, 1968)

E. J. Kennedy, *With the Immortal Seventh Division* (London: Hodder & Stoughton, 1916)

H. B. Kennedy, *War Record of the 21st London Regiment, First Surrey Rifles 1914–1919* (London: Skinner, 1928)

A. W. Keown, *Forward with the 5th: The Story of Five Years' War Service Fifth Infantry Battalion A.I.F.* (Melbourne: Specialty, 1921)

C. L. Kingsford, *The Story of the Royal Warwickshire Regiment* (London: Newnes, 1921)

Col. R. M. St G. Kirke, 'Some Aspects of Artillery Development during the First World War on the Western Front', *Journal of the Royal Artillery*, vol. 101, Sept. 1974, pp. 130–40

J. C. Latter, *The History of the Lancashire Fusiliers, 1914–1918*, 2 vols (Aldershot: Gale & Polden, 1949)

C. B. L. Lock, *The Fighting 10th – A South Australian Centenary Souvenir of the 10th Battalion, A.I.F. 1914–19* (Adelaide: Webb & Son, 1936)

C. Longmore, *The Old Sixteenth: Being a Record of the 16th Battalion A.I.F., during the Great War, 1914–1918* (Perth: History Committee 16th Battalion, 1929)

C. E. B. Lowe, *Siege Battery 94 during the World War* (London: Werner Laurie, 1919)

General E. Ludendorff, *My War Memories 1914–1918* (London: Hutchinson, 1919)

Captain Timothy L. Lupfer, *The Dynamics of Doctrine: the Changes in German Tactical Doctrine during the First World War* (Leavenworth Papers no. 4) (Leavenworth, Kansas: Combat Studies Institute, 1981)

J. McCartney-Filgate, *History of the 33rd Division Artillery in the War, 1914–1918* (London: Vacher, 1921)

Lyn Macdonald, *They Called it Passchendaele* (London: Michael Joseph, 1978)

K. W. Mackenzie, *The Story of the Seventeenth Battalion A.I.F. in the Great War 1914–1918* (Sydney: Shipping Newspapers, 1946)

Major-General M. N. Macleod, 'A Sapper Secret Weapon of World War I', *Royal Engineers Journal*, vol. 68, 1954, pp. 275–81

Laurie Magnus, *The West Riding Territorials in the Great War* (London: Kegan Paul, 1920)

General Sir James Marshall-Cornwall, *Haig as Military Commander* (London: Batsford, 1973)

A. H. Maude, *The 47th London Division, 1914–1919* (London: Amalgamated Press, 1922)

Peter Mead, *The Eye in the Air: History of Air Observation and Reconnaissance for the Army 1785–1945* (London: HMSO, 1983)

Charles Messenger, *Trench Fighting 1914–18* (London: Pan/Ballantine, 1973)

J. E. Munby, *A History of the 38th Division* (London: Rees, 1920)

C. C. R. Murphy, *The History of the Suffolk Regiment, 1914–1927* (London: Hutchinson, 1928)

W. W. Murray, *The History of the 2nd Canadian Battalion (East Ontario Regiment) Canadian Expeditionary Force in the Great War, 1914–1919* (Ottawa: Mortimer/ Historical Committee, 2nd Battalion, CEF, 1947)

Captain G. H. F. Nichols, *The 18th Division in the Great War* (Edinburgh: Blackwood, 1922)

Col. G. W. L. Nicholson, *Canadian Expeditionary Force 1914–1919* (Ottawa: Queen's Printer, 1962)

——*The Gunners of Canada: the History of the Royal Regiment of Canadian Artillery* (Beauceville, Quebec: Imprimerie L'Eclaireur, 1976)

H. C. O'Neill, *The Royal Fusiliers in the Great War* (London: Heinemann, 1922)

Douglas Orgill, *The Tank: Studies in the Development and Use of a Weapon* (London: Heinemann, 1970)

'Passchendaele', *Journal of the Royal United Service Institution*, vol. 80, 1935, pp. 21–32

P. A. Pedersen, *Monash as Military Commander* (Melbourne: Melbourne University Press, 1985)

Brigadier A. L. Pemberton, *The Development of Artillery Tactics and Equipment* (London: War Office, 1950)

Major John Penrose, 'Survey for Batteries', *Journal of the Royal Artillery*, vol. 49, 1922–3, pp. 253–70

Geoffrey Powell, *Plumer: The Soldier's General* (London: Leo Cooper, 1990)

Robin Prior, *Churchill's 'World Crisis' as History* (London: Croom Helm, 1983)

Robin Prior and Trevor Wilson, *Command on the Western Front: The Military Career of Sir Henry Rawlinson, 1914–18* (Oxford/Cambridge, Mass.: Blackwell, 1992)

Lt-Col. C. à Court Repington, *The First World War*, 2 vols (London: Constable, 1920)

Lord Riddell, *Lord Riddell's War Diary, 1914–1918* (London: Ivor Nicholson & Watson, 1933)

Stephen Roskill, *Hankey: Man of Secrets*, vol. 1 (London: Collins, 1970)
—— 'The U-Boat Campaign of 1917 and Third Ypres', *Journal of the Royal United Service Institution*, vol. 104, 1959, pp. 440–2
Captain R. B. Ross, *The Fifty-First in France* (London: Hodder & Stoughton, 1918)
Lt-Col. Sir John Ross-of-Bladensburg, *The Coldstream Guards 1914–1918*, vol. 2 (London: Oxford University Press, 1928)
Lt-Col. H. Rowan-Robinson, 'The Limited Objective', *Army Quarterly*, vol. 2, 1921, pp. 119–27
A. Russell, *The Machine Gunner* (Kineton, Warwickshire: Roundwood, 1977)
Lt-Col. H. R. Sandilands, *The 23rd Division, 1914–1919* (Edinburgh: Blackwood, 1925)
J. W. Sandilands and N. Macleod, *The History of the 7th Battalion Queen's Own Cameron Highlanders* (Stirling: Mackay, 1922)
Geoffrey Serle, *John Monash* (Melbourne: Melbourne University Press, 1982)
Mark Severn, *The Gambardier: Giving some Account of the Heavy and Siege Artillery in France, 1914–18* (London: Benn, 1930)
W. Seymour, *The History of the Rifle Brigade in the War of 1914–1918*, 2 vols (London: Rifle Brigade Club, 1936)
J. Shakespear, *The Thirty-Fourth Division 1915–1919* (London: Wetherby, 1921)
C. R. Simpson, *History of the Lincolnshire Regiment, 1914–1918* (London: Medici Society, 1931)
E. K. G. Sixsmith, *Douglas Haig* (London: Weidenfeld & Nicolson, 1976)
F. W. Speed, *Esprit de Corps: The History of the Victorian Scottish Regiment and the Fifth Infantry Battalion* (Sydney: Allen & Unwin, 1988)
F. H. Stevens, *The Story of the 5th Pioneer Battalion A.I.F.* (Adelaide, Callotype, 1937)
Col. H. Stewart, *The New Zealand Division 1916–1919: A Popular History based on Official Records* (Auckland: Whitcombe & Tombs, 1921)
J. Stewart and J. Buchan, *The Fifteenth (Scottish) Division, 1914–1919* (Edinburgh: Blackwood, 1926)
A. J. P. Taylor (ed.), *Lloyd George: A Diary by Frances Stevenson* (London: Hutchinson, 1971)
F. W. Taylor and T. A. Cusack, *Nulli Secundis: A History of the Second Battalion A.I.F. 1914–1919* (Sydney, New Century Press, 1942)
John Terraine, *Douglas Haig: The Educated Soldier* (London: Hutchinson, 1963)
—— 'Monash: Australian Commander', *History Today*, vol. 16, 1966, pp. 12–19
—— 'Mortality and Morale', *R.U.S.I. Journal*, vol. 112, Nov. 1967, pp. 364–9
—— 'Passchendaele and Amiens', *Journal of the Royal United Service Institution*, vol. 104, 1959, pp. 173–83 & pp. 331–40
—— *The Road to Passchendaele: The Flanders Offensive of 1917: a Study in Inevitability* (London: Leo Cooper, 1977)
—— *The Smoke and the Fire: Myths and Anti-Myths of War 1861–1945* (London: Sidgwick & Jackson, 1980)
—— *The Western Front 1914–18* (London: Arrow, 1970)
—— *White Heat: The New Warfare 1914–18* (London: Sidgwick & Jackson, 1982)
Tim Travers, *The Killing Ground: The British Army, the Western Front and the Emergence of Modern Warfare 1900–1918* (London: Allen & Unwin, 1987)
Edwin Campion Vaughan, *Some Desperate Glory: The Diary of a Young Officer, 1917*, ed. John Terraine (London: Warne, 1981)
A. Wade, *The War of the Guns* (London: Batsford, 1936)

N. Wanliss, *The History of the Fourteenth Battalion A.I.F. Being the Story of the Vicissitudes of an Australian Unit during the Great War* (Melbourne: Arrow Printery, 1929)

C. H. D. Ward, *The 56th Division – 1st London Territorial Division* (London: John Murray, 1921)

——*Regimental Records of the Royal Welch Fusiliers vol. III: 1914–1918 France and Flanders* (London: Forster Groom, 1928)

Major-General A. G. Wauchope, *A History of the Black Watch (Royal Highlanders) in the Great War, 1914–1918* (3 vols) (London: Medici Society, 1926)

Andrew A. Weist, *Passchendaele and the Royal Navy* (Greenwood Press: New York, 1995)

Der Weltkrieg (translation of Third Ypres section), Royal Artillery Institution Library, Woolwich

T. A. White, *The History of the Thirteenth Battalion A.I.F.* (Sydney: Tyrrells, 1924)

Trevor Wilson, *The Myriad Faces of War* (Cambridge: Polity, 1986)

——(ed.), *The Political Diaries of C. P. Scott 1911–1928* (London: Collins, 1970)

Denis Winter, *Death's Men: Soldiers of the Great War* (London: Allen Lane, 1978)

——*Haig's Command: A Reassessment* (Harmondsworth: Viking, 1991)

Lt-Col. H. St J. L. Winterbotham, 'Geographical and Survey Work in France, especially in connection with Artillery', *Journal of the Royal Artillery*, vol. 46, 1919, pp. 154–72

Leon Wolff, *In Flanders Fields* (London: Longmans, 1960)

David R. Woodward, *Lloyd George and the Generals* (East Brunswick, NJ: Associated University Presses, 1983)

E. Wren, *Randwick to Hargicourt: History of the 3rd Battalion A.I.F.* (Sydney: Ronald G. McDonald, 1935)

C. M. Wrench, *Campaigning with the Fighting 9th* (n.p.: Boolarong Publications, 1985)

H. C. Wylly, *The Border Regiment in the Great War* (Aldershot: Gale & Polden, 1924)

——*The First and Second Battalions, The Sherwood Foresters (Nottingham and Derbyshire Regiment) in the Great War* (Aldershot: Gale & Polden, 1926)

——*The Green Howards in the Great War* (privately printed, 1926)

——*History of the 1st and 2nd Battalions, the Leicestershire Regiment in the Great War* (Aldershot: Gale & Polden, 1928)

G. C. Wynne, 'The Development of the German Defensive Battle in 1917 and its Influence on British Defensive Tactics', *Army Quarterly*, vol. 34, April 1937, pp. 15–34

——*If Germany Attacks: The Battle in Depth in the West* (London: Faber & Faber, 1940)

——'The Other Side of the Hill, no. XIV: The Fight for Inverness Copse 22nd–24th of August, 1917', *Army Quarterly*, vol. 29, no. 2, Jan. 1935, pp. 297–303

E. Wyrall, *The Gloucestershire Regiment in the War, 1914–1918: the Records of the 1st (28th), 2nd (61st), 3rd (Special Reserve) and 4th, 5th and 6th (First Line T.A.) Battalions* (London: Methuen, 1931)

——*The History of the King's Regiment (Liverpool)* (London: Arnold, 1928–30)

——*The History of the 19th Division, 1914–1918* (London: Arnold, 1932)

——*The History of the Fiftieth Division, 1914–1919* (London: Lund Humphries, 1939)

Index